THE BRITISH
PAPER INDUSTRY
1495–1860

THE BRITISH PAPER INDUSTRY

1495–1860

A Study in Industrial Growth

BY

D. C. COLEMAN

Lecturer in Industrial History,
London School of Economics and Political Science,
University of London

GREENWOOD PRESS, PUBLISHERS
WESTPORT, CONNECTICUT

Library of Congress Cataloging in Publication Data

Coleman, Donald Cuthbert.
   The British paper industry, 1495-1860.

   Reprint of the ed. published by Clarendon Press, Oxford.
   Includes bibliographical references.
   1. Paper making and trade--Great Britain. I. Title.
HD9831.5.C6 1975   338.4'7'6760941   75-74
ISBN 0-8371-8015-5

Originally published in 1958 by the Clarendon Press, Oxford

This reprint has been authorized by the Clarendon Press Oxford

Reprinted in 1975 by Greenwood Press,
a division of Williamhouse-Regency Inc.

Library of Congress Catalog Card Number 75-74

ISBN 0-8371-8015-5

Printed in the United States of America

PREFACE

MUCH has been written about paper and little about the paper industry. In the substantial bibliography[1] of paper and paper-making, the history of the British paper industry has a comparatively meagre record. This is perhaps not surprising and certainly not exceptional. Industrial history is a *parvenu* in the distinguished and respectable world peopled by the traditional subjects of historical inquiry. Most British historians, with some admirable exceptions, have paid little heed to the growth of industry, just as most British industries and firms, again with some admirable exceptions, have remained indifferent to their past, if not indeed suspicious or even hostile towards its resurrection.

The present book is essentially not about paper or paper-making but about the paper industry. Its viewpoint is that of economics. It attempts to show the major economic and technical problems with which producers were periodically confronted and the way in which the answers found to those problems shaped the growth and organization of the industry. It deliberately makes use of a fairly large amount of statistical material. This does not make for that quality of compulsive readability which could with advantage enliven the heavy routine of figures. It may also have the effect of lulling first the writer and then the reader into believing that an industry is an abstraction related, if at all, only tenuously or fortuitously to the world of human beings. In the course of the three and a half centuries of growth covered by this book, the paper industry has had hundreds, indeed thousands, of *entrepreneurs*, many of whom were obscure men whose

[1] See, e.g., C. J. West, *Bibliography of Paper and Paper-Making* (1900–50, 4 vols., New York, 1929–51).

lives are inaccessibly buried in the past. So the biograph-
ical approach is hardly feasible, even were it desirable. I
have therefore tried to preserve for the individual his due
importance by referring wherever possible to the examples
of particular men and particular mills; in Chapters VI
and IX there will be found some very brief sketches of
such men and the enterprises with which they were
associated. The statistical material has been grouped, as
far as possible, into tables or Appendixes in order to try
to leave the ordinary flow of sentences reasonably free
from too many quantitative intrusions.

I have not attempted an exhaustive search for every
mill, its whereabouts, its work, its life history. Not only do
some mills thus go unrecorded in the pages which follow,
but it is quite likely that, had I looked farther afield, it
would have been possible to give earlier dates to the
beginning of the industry in England, Scotland, or
Ireland. I believe, however, that the sample examined is
reasonably typical and that such extensions would not
significantly alter the general picture of the industry's
growth. Similarly, the coverage given to the Scottish and
Irish industries is much less than that allotted to England,
but this again I hope reflects their comparative importance.

The dates which limit this work are not arbitrary. The
year 1495 is the earliest date yet known for a paper-mill
in this country; and 1860 has the twin significance of
marking, within a year or two, the repeal of the paper
Excise, after nearly a century and a half of existence, and
the introduction into British paper-making of the first
truly important substitute for rags, as the major raw
material of the industry. New raw materials, especially
wood-pulp, were soon to transform many of the economic
and technical relationships of the industry. The 1860's,

therefore, mark the end of an era. Within those 365 years the industry grew from nothing, spread and strengthened behind a protective wall, and duly underwent the experience of mechanization which the Industrial Revolution brought. In the course of that time its products came to play an important part in the distribution of goods and a vital part in the dissemination of ideas.

My first thanks are due to those who permitted me to consult records in their possession or custody: to Mr. Thomas Balston, not only for allowing me to work on his valuable collection of MSS but also for his unfailingly friendly co-operation on many matters pertaining to them; to Messrs. Lepard & Smith & Co., Longmans, Green & Co., Wiggins, Teape & Co., and the University Press, Oxford; and to the staffs of the several public archives and libraries to which reference is made in the text and footnotes. My particular thanks for helping me, in one way or another, in the search for material are due to Messrs. D. G. Allan, C. C. Blagden, H. G. Carter, P. Mathias, G. Pollard, E. W. Renwick, and Mrs. A. M. Millard; as well as to Messrs. G. S. Don and J. Eliot of *The Paper Maker* and F. H. Llewellyn Thomas of the British Paper & Board Makers' Association.

Mr. S. T. David gave me invaluable help on statistical matters; Dr. A. H. Shorter not only allowed me to quote extensively from his unpublished thesis but otherwise gave me the benefit of his wide knowledge of paper mills and their history.

At the London School of Economics, successive research assistants in the Economics Research Division have aided me in the collection of material. To all of them, but especially to Messrs. A. Templeton and K. G. Burley are due my thanks. Many of my colleagues at L.S.E.

particularly in the departments of Economic History and of Geography, have given help both useful and various. I thank them collectively. I owe especial debts to Professor T. S. Ashton and Mr. H. L. Beales, as well as to Professor R. S. Sayers whose helpful comments after reading the typescript led to some healthy slimming of its size. My greatest debt, however, is to Professor F. J. Fisher, both for particular critical comments and for a wider intellectual stimulus.

D. C. C.

London School of Economics
and Political Science
1958

CONTENTS

APPENDIXES

LIST OF TABLES

LIST OF FIGURES

LIST OF PLATES

ABBREVIATIONS

B.M.	British Museum.
C. & E.	Library of H.M. Customs and Excise.
P.R.O.	Public Record Office.
R.S.A.	Library of the Royal Society of Arts.

Private MSS.

Balston MSS.	MSS. in the possession of Thomas Balston, Esq.
Fourdrinier Papers	MSS. in the possession of the University Press, Oxford.
Lepard & Smith MSS.	MSS. in the possession of Messrs. Lepard & Smith & Co. Ltd.
Wiggins, Teape MSS.	MSS. in the possession of Messrs. Wiggins, Teape & Co. Ltd.

Official Records

B.P.P.	British Parliamentary Papers.
C.J.	Journals of the House of Commons.
C.J. (Ireland)	Journals of the House of Commons of Ireland.
Cal. S.P. Dom.	Calendar of State Papers, Domestic.
C. & E.: General Letter (1816)	Customs and Excise Library: General Letter Book No. 4, ff. 22–37 (being a list of paper-mills in England and Wales, 1816).
Children's Employment (1843)	Second Report of the Children's Employment Commission (and reports and evidence of Sub-Commissioners) (*B.P.P.* 1843, vols. xiii–xv).
Children's Employment (1865)	Fourth Report of the Commissioner on the Employment of Children and Young Persons in Trades and Manufactures not already regulated by the Law (*B.P.P.* 1865, vol. xx).
Eighth Report (1824)	Eighth Report of the Commissioners of Inquiry into Revenue arising in Ireland (*B.P.P.* 1824, vol. xi).
First Inland Revenue Report (1857)	First Report of the Commissioners of Inland Revenue (*B.P.P.* 1857, vol. iv).
Fourteenth Report (1835)	Fourteenth Report of the Commissioners of Excise Inquiry (Paper), 1835 (*B.P.P.* 1835, vol. xxxi).

Fourdrinier Committee (1807)	Minutes of Evidence taken before the Lords Committee to whom was referred the Bill for prolonging the term of certain Letters Patent assigned to Henry Fourdrinier and Sealy Fourdrinier for the Invention of making Paper by means of Machinery (*B.P.P.* 1807, vol. xiv).
Fourdrinier Committee (1837)	Report from the Select Committee on Fourdrinier's Patent (*B.P.P.* 1837, vol. xx).
H.M.C.	Historical Manuscripts Commission.
Select Committee (1861)	Report from the Select Committee on Paper (Export Duty on Rags), 1861 (*B.P.P.* 1861, vol. xi).
S.P. Dom.	State Papers, Domestic.

Other Sources

Arbitration on Wages (1874)	Arbitration on the Question of an Advance in Wages in the Paper Making Trade (1874)—Webb Trade Union Collection, British Library of Political and Economic Science.
Hunter	Dard Hunter, *Papermaking* (London, 1947).
Jenkins	Rhys Jenkins, 'Paper-Making in England, 1495–1788', *Collected Papers of Rhys Jenkins* (Cambridge, 1936).
Labarre	E. J. Labarre, *Dictionary and Encyclopaedia of Paper and Paper-Making* (Oxford, 1952).
New Statistical Account	*A New Statistical Account of Scotland* (by the ministers of the respective parishes under the superintendence of a Committee of the Society for the Benefit of the Sons and Daughters of the Clergy—15 vols., Edinburgh, 1845).
Old Statistical Account	Sir John Sinclair (ed.), *The Statistical Account of Scotland* (20 vols., Edinburgh, 1791–9).
Report of Meetings on Wages (1873)	Report of Meetings between Employers and Employees in the Paper Making Trade to consider the question of an Advance in Wages (1873).—Webb Trade Union Collection, British Library of Political and Economic Science.
Shorter, *Historical Geography*	A. H. Shorter, *The Historical Geography of the Paper-Making Industry in England*, unpublished Ph.D. thesis (London, 1954).
Spicer	A. Dykes Spicer, *The Paper Trade* (London, 1907).
Trans. Bib. Soc.	Transactions of the Bibliographical Society.
V.C.H.	Victoria History of the Counties of England.
William Balston—Paper Maker	T. Balston, *William Balston—Paper Maker* (London, 1954).

PART I

BEFORE THE
INDUSTRIAL REVOLUTION

I

Home Demand and Foreign Supply in the Sixteenth and Seventeenth Centuries

PAPER-MILLS were at work on the Continent long before they appeared in the British Isles. By the time the industry had obtained its first faltering and tentative footholds here, more than one continental country had a flourishing paper industry feeding an export trade. For a century or more after its successful establishment, the English industry had to face the power of its older and more experienced rivals in Italy, France, and Germany; to these were later added the rising and vigorous paper industry of Holland. The Scottish and Irish industries grew up still later, under the shadow of them all. In order, therefore, to see the early history of British paper-making in its true perspective, it must be viewed against the background of an early continental supremacy.

China is the traditional birthplace of paper-making and the Arabic countries of the eastern Mediterranean the gateway through which the art found its way to Europe. From the twelfth century there is evidence of the use of paper in Italy as well as in the Middle East and of its manufacture in Spain. During the succeeding centuries of the Middle Ages its use and manufacture slowly extended through the civilized centres of Europe. The famous mills at Fabriano were at work in the thirteenth century and by later medieval times both Venice and Genoa were concerned in the production and export of paper. The French industry grew from its early beginnings in the fourteenth century and its products, too, soon came to figure in international trade. From the last decade of the fourteenth century comes the first mention of the German industry with the setting up of a mill at Nuremberg.[1] In England, meanwhile, although the use of paper had spread to this country certainly by the fourteenth century, its manufacture remained foreign to us until, probably, the end of the fifteenth. As far as is at present known, the earliest paper-mill in England was at work in Hertfordshire in 1495.[2] But this did not mark the successful establishment of the English industry, for this mill apparently failed, and it seems probable that it was not until the later decades of the sixteenth century and the early years of the seventeenth that the foundations of a paper industry in this country were truly laid. Those of Scotland and Ireland followed still later. So the growing needs for paper in these islands were for long met by imports from abroad.

What were these needs?

Paper has three main uses—wrapping, writing, and printing. All are very old, each has played its particular part in promoting the growth of the paper industry, and together they are still the three main uses today.[3]

---

[1] On the very early development of the industry see A. Blum, *Les Origines du papier, de l'imprimerie et de la gravure* (Paris, 1935), pp. 1–49; A. Renker, 'Geschichte des Papiers', *Handbuch der Bibliothekswissenschaft*, vol. i, ed. F. Milkau (Wiesbaden, 1952), pp. 1047 et seq.; Hunter, *passim*; R. Lopez, 'The English and the Manufacture of Writing Materials in Genoa', *Economic History Review*, vol. x, 1939–40; and 'Europe: the Trade of the South', in *Cambridge Economic History of Europe*, ed. M. Postan and E. Rich, vol. ii (Cambridge, 1952), pp. 281, 299.

[2] *Infra*, p. 40.

[3] This remains true in spite of the appearance over a long period of a number of quite different uses. Such modern variants as cigarette papers or chemical filter papers were preceded by some much earlier examples: blotting-paper was known in the fifteenth century; printed or stained paper was coming into fashion for various decorative purposes from the sixteenth century onwards; pressing-paper was in demand by the pressers in the

The first and humblest of these uses has been unjustly ignored. Paper is reported as having been used for wrapping in the Middle East in the eleventh and twelfth centuries, and its use for this purpose was slowly spreading in Europe before the development of European printing in the later fifteenth century.[1] Although the spread of cultures, the extension of literacy, and the widening of communications in the civilized world can all be readily linked with the use of paper for writing and printing, it was nevertheless in the manufacture of low-grade wrapping-paper that the foundations of the industry were laid in this country, and probably also elsewhere. Nor must it be forgotten that its use for wrapping is one mark of expanding and diversifying exchange, especially in retail trade. Consignments of paper imported into England in the fifteenth and sixteenth centuries, for instance, include small quantities of brown paper, and by the early decades of the seventeenth century London was annually importing several thousand bundles of brown paper. In the fifteenth century such valuable imports as fine silks were sometimes wrapped in paper, and so later were such diverse commodities as buckram or 'fruits and conserves'.[2] Much of its use for wrapping purposes was found in such trades as that of the grocer; in the early eighteenth century, for example, a writer described some paper-mills in Kent as making 'a great deal

woollen cloth industry. A galaxy of actual or potential uses for paper entranced the Victorians. (See on this, Labarre, pp. 24–25, 318–26; also *infra*, p. 211.)

[1] See Hunter, pp. 471–3. Paper had of course been used for printing at a very much earlier date in the Orient.

[2] N. S. B. Gras, *The Early English Customs System* (Harvard, 1918): for examples of paper imports at various dates from 1443 to 1526, see pp. 196, 562, 566–7, 573, 578, 580, 606, 609, 632, 640; for examples of other commodities wrapped in paper, pp. 511–12, 513, 695. See also on the latter the examples quoted under 'paper' in the *O.E.D.* For London's imports of brown paper see *infra*, pp. 12–14.

of ordinary Wrapping Paper for Tobacco, Grocery Ware, Glovers, Milliners' Goods, etc.'[1]

A further use for coarse paper arose from the manufacture of pasteboard or cardboard consisting of layers of paper pasted together. The demand sprang partly and indirectly from the growth of printing and book production, for in the sixteenth century pasteboard began to be used in bookbinding, replacing wooden boards. During the next century pasteboard was supplemented by millboard, made directly from the same raw materials as brown paper. Other sources of demand for board included the woollen cloth industry, where it came to be used for packing and in pressing, and the manufacture of playing-cards from the finer sorts of pasteboard.[2]

Yet when all due regard has been paid to the use of paper for wrapping goods or making board there can be little doubt that it was the growth of printing that provided the biggest single stimulus, on the demand side, to the European paper-making industry. The slow spread in use and manufacture of paper in Europe before the mid-fifteenth century gained a new momentum after the great work of Johan Gutenberg.[3] The printed book made demands for paper on a scale which could not readily be met by the continued use of parchment or vellum. More-

---

[1] J. Harris, *History of Kent* (London, 1719), pp. 191 et seq. Cf. S. Hartlib, *Legacy of Husbandry* (3rd ed. London, 1655), p. 150, noting that we then imported from Holland 'a strong brown paper much desired by the Grocers (Although at present, lesse is imported because we have many Paper-Mills lately erected)'.

[2] C. Davenport 'Bagford's Notes on Bookbinding', *Trans. Bib. Soc.*, vol. vii, 1902–4; J. Houghton, *Collections for the Improvement of Husbandry and Trade* (London, 1691–1703, ed. C. Bradley, 1727), vol. ii, pp. 410–11; *The Case of the Bookbinders* (*c.* 1712) and *The Case of the Pasteboard Makers* (*c.* 1712); also *O.E.D. sub* Pasteboard and Millboard.

[3] On Gutenberg and the growth of printing generally, the latest, most compact and readily accessible of the many works on this subject is S. E. Steinberg, *Five Hundred Years of Printing* (London, 1955), esp. pp. 22–29.

over, on the supply side, some improvements both in the techniques of paper-making and in the availability of the linen rags used therein[1] were helping to make paper a more effective competitor to parchment than hitherto. More supple and convenient than parchment, it was now acquiring a new degree of durability. Similarly the high price which had earlier limited its use began to fall, so that it was also becoming cheaper than parchment.[2] As a result the substitution of paper for printing purposes was well under way by the end of the fifteenth century, although parchment continued to be used as well for many years thereafter.

The stimulus given to the paper industry through the substitution of paper for parchment, induced by the demands of printing in this period, has an approximate analogy in the similar stimuli affecting the wood-pulp and paper industries at the end of the nineteenth century, and largely brought about by the invention of the rotary press and the spread of the mass-circulation newspaper. On a much smaller scale and with many differences of detail, printing did for paper in the fifteenth century what newspapers did for wood-pulp and paper in the nineteenth century. This generalization is not entirely

---

[1] *Infra*, pp. 25 et seq., 36.

[2] Blum, op. cit., pp. 33–37; Hunter, pp. 153–5, 473. Both Rogers's and Beveridge's price series show a fall of over 40 per cent. in the price of paper during the fifteenth century and a rise in that of parchment (about 20 per cent. on Rogers's figures and 50 per cent. on Beveridge's). Rogers found moreover that the parchment became inferior in quality. This movement in favour of paper continued in the sixteenth century: during the first eighty years of the century the price of parchment rose a further 70 per cent. or thereabouts, whilst paper prices show an increase varying between 30 per cent. and 60 per cent., according to Rogers and Beveridge respectively (J. E. Thorold Rogers, *History of Agriculture and Prices* (Oxford, 1866–1902), vol. iv, pp. 595, 605–6, 608, 723; Sir William (now Lord) Beveridge, *Prices and Wages in England*, vol. i, p. 857).

For further details on prices see App. III.

accurate,[1] but it may serve to bring out something of the interplay of economic, technical, and cultural factors involved in this substitution. For the printing of Gutenberg's Bible it is said that each parchment copy, consisting of 641 leaves, would need the skins of more than 300 sheep. By the end of the sixteenth century editions of printed books averaged about a thousand copies. As the historian of the English book trade has remarked in this context, 'clearly, for the printed book whose edition was to run to a thousand or more copies, paper was the only possible material'.[2] In the event 180 copies of the Gutenberg Bible were printed on paper and only thirty on parchment, and its production in 1452–6 is a highlight not only in the history of printing but also in the early European use of paper for printing purposes.[3]

In English minds printing and Caxton are for ever linked. But when Caxton set up his printing office at Westminster in 1476, he procured his paper from the Continent. Although his successor in business, Wynkyn de Worde, did use some home-produced paper, the overwhelming majority of books printed here in the sixteenth century used imported paper.[4] The growth of English printing was very slow; Tudor and early Stuart presses were fewer in number and smaller in size than their continental counterparts and the total output of books accordingly much lower. Restrictions imposed by the

---

[1] One of the main reasons for the inaccuracy is that as formulated the analogy takes little account of the extent to which mass-circulation newspapers were themselves dependent on the development of wood-pulp. There was a degree of interdependence between these which was much greater than that between paper and printing.

[2] M. Plant, *The English Book Trade* (London, 1939), p. 190; also pp. 92 et seq.

[3] Ibid., p. 190; and Steinberg, op. cit., pp. 22–29.

[4] Plant, pp. 191 et seq., and E. Heawood, 'Sources of Early English Paper Supply', *Trans. Bib. Soc.*, vol. x (1929–30), pp. 282–307 and 427–54.

State, in the name of security, and by the Stationers' Company, in the name of the powers granted to it by the State in 1557, also hindered the growth of printing.[1] Nevertheless, printing needs were a part, and a vitally important part of the slowly rising demand for paper in Tudor times, a demand which in the seventeenth century was speeded up by the printing of innumerable tracts and pamphlets, by the appearance of the newspaper and by the stimulus to further book printing arising from the heightened intellectual discussion of the time. The *Corantos* of early seventeenth-century England were followed by other periodic news-sheets and in 1665 the *London Gazette* began publication; the Civil War unlocked the flood-gates to a stream of tracts; speculation and discussion on subjects ranging from astronomy to economics combined with such traditional pretexts for publication as theological arguments to swell the volume of printed works, and thereby the demand for paper. Similar developments were taking place, though later and on a smaller scale, in Scotland and Ireland; the first book printed in Edinburgh dates from 1508, though little was done thereafter until the second half of the sixteenth century. In Ireland printing dates from 1551 but little progress was made for many years to come.[2]

Similar factors were at work in helping to bring about the substitution of paper for parchment as a writing material. Lowered cost and better quality matched a demand which widened with increases in literacy, in intellectual enterprise and economic activity, and in the

[1] A. E. Musson, *The Typographical Association* (London, 1954), pp. 4 et seq.; Plant, op. cit., pp. 164 et seq.
[2] H. G. Aldis, *A List of Books Printed in Scotland before 1700* (Edinburgh, 1904); R. Dickson and J. P. Edmond, *Annals of Scottish Printing* (Cambridge, 1890); E. R. Dix, *The Earliest Dublin Printing* (Dublin, 1901); A. S. Green. *The Making of Ireland* (London, 1909), pp. 401–3.

needs of administration. Paper was in use alongside parchment from the fourteenth century onwards and gradually became more and more common, be it for the notes of everyday business or for the details of State affairs. The earliest paper document in the Public Record Office dates from about 1220, but not until Tudor times is paper frequently to be found amongst the records there; from then on there is a tendency, especially in such new classes of documents as the State Papers, for paper sheets in the accepted sizes, loose or bound in book-form, to replace irregular pieces of paper or parchment or the great rolls of parchment membranes on which were recorded the details of so much medieval administration.[1] But parchment lingered on: for example, the series of Exchequer records known as the Port Books and running from 1565 to 1799 are on parchment, although the new series of records of foreign trade, the ledgers of the Inspector-General of Exports and Imports, began in the 1690's as large paper registers. From the fourteenth century onwards there was, too, an increasing use of paper for such purposes as keeping town accounts or records of guilds and colleges,[2] as well as personal diaries and letters or merchants' accounts. Here also the old survived with the new: though the minutiae of correspondence and negotiations which were a part of the great boom in property dealings during Tudor and Stuart times were conducted on paper, the formal evidence in the shape of deeds of sale or mortgage was engrossed on large and unmanageable slabs of enduring parchment.

---

[1] *Guide to the Public Records, Part I: Introductory* (H.M.S.O., 1949), pp. 43–44 n.

[2] J. E. T. Rogers, op. cit., vol. iv, pp. 21, 592, gives examples of the use of paper, and also of parchment, in the records of various Oxford and Cambridge colleges.

It remains to try to put this growing demand for paper into some sort of historical and social perspective. Lest an impression should have been gained of a rising tide of paper slowly submerging the once pre-eminent parchment, and bringing thereby a new and widespread category of demand, it must be emphasized that this was far from the truth. The world of paper and printing was largely an urban world. Outside the universities, the big cities, Dublin, Edinburgh, and above all London, and a handful of the more important provincial towns, paper made its appearance only slowly.[1] Many people had little or no contact with it, and some of the remoter dwellers in the primitive backwardness of sixteenth-century Ireland or Scotland may well have never heard of it. And it never became in this early period an article of common and everyday consumption as it is in modern industrial communities. In Tudor and early Stuart times a quire (24 sheets) of white writing-paper cost about 4d. or 5d.[2] Even today the purchase of paper for writing purposes forms a very small proportion of the total expenditure of an ordinary man or woman. In an age in which the cost of a couple of dozen sheets of writing-paper was about as much as a labourer's daily wage, it is not likely that a great deal of it could have been purchased by any save the richer classes or those concerned with administration and trade. Today a very large proportion of the world's paper output is devoted to the production of mass-circulation newspapers. These did not exist. In short, though the demand for paper was growing, its direct social significance was still trifling. Its indirect significance was greater in that paper was allowing larger

---

[1] Thorold Rogers noted that paper seemed to have been used more frequently in the eastern counties than in the Midlands (ibid., vol. iv, p. 21).

[2] Ibid., vol. vi, pp. 565–9.

editions of books and a multiplication of tracts and pamphlets, vital aids to the spread of ideas.

Demand was met very largely by imports from overseas. Table I sets out quantitative details of paper imports into London from 1560 to 1720. As is only too evident, the statistics are miserably defective before the 1670's. However, they tell, or at least suggest, a tale which is tolerably clear and also readily compatible with what is known of the growth of home production. Two features are unmistakable. First, in the imports of white paper there was a marked rise until the later years of the seventeenth century and thereafter an evident decline. Second, imports of brown paper probably reached a peak in the early decades of the century and subsequently dwindled rapidly to an erratic trickle of a few score bundles after the 1670's.

Obviously not too much credence can be put upon the timing and accuracy of these figures. There are many gaps and isolated years are not necessarily representative. For example, 1640 was a year of general trade depression and the paper imports for that year reflect this. Again, there is reason to suppose that the size of the 'bundle' of brown paper may have altered during the period, thus making it dangerous to compare the earlier and later figures.[1] But even if due allowance is made for this, the

[1] The 'bundle' of brown paper is clearly defined in a Bill of 1699 (H.M.C.: *MSS. of the House of Lords*, vol. iii, pp. 424–34) and in all later relevant legislation as two reams. Before then, however, although brown paper was normally quoted (for instance in the Books of Rates, in the Port Books, and in the overwhelming majority of the Customs entries) by the bundle, no clear indication of the size of the bundle is given. In the 1604 Book of Rates (P.R.O. E. 122/173/3) it was valued by the bundle or ream, thus implying the identity of the two; in another and slightly different version of the 1668–9 import figures, quoted in C. King (ed.), *The British Merchant* (London, 1721), vol. ii, pp. 355–6, bundles are cheerfully added to reams without adjustment. Accordingly, comparison between the earlier figures and those starting in the Inspector-General's ledgers in 1697–8 is

TABLE I

Imports of Paper into London, 1560–1720

(1) Year	(2) White (reams)	(3) Blue (reams)	(4) Other (reams)	(5) Total (reams)	(6) Brown (bundles)
1560	..	..	..	26,432	..
1565 .	..	..	..	24,000	..
1567–8	..	..	..	12,738	4,380
1587–8 . . .	..	..	..	41,389	5,540
*1609 (Alien merchants ONLY)	*13,569*	..	..	*13,569*	*13,035*
1615 (,, ,, ,,)	*28,087*	..	..	*28,087*	*16,876*
1617 (,, ,, ,,)	*19,574*	*212*	..	*19,786*	*5,160*
1621 (English ,, ,,)	*62,959*	*45*	*53*	} [*80,786*]	*16,352* } [*18,302*]
1622 (Alien ,, ,,)	*17,729*	..	..		*1,950*
1624 (,, ,, ,,)	*19,705*	..	..	*19,705*	*4,850*
†1626 (English ,, ,,)	*61,952*	*233*	..	} [*80,012*]	*7,227* } [*7,227*]
1627 (Alien ,, ,,)	*17,715*	*96*	*16*		..
1630 (English ,, ,,)	*95,572*	..	*397*	*95,969*	*8,038*
1633 (Alien ,, ,,)	*27,622*	..	*450*	} [*106,217*]	.. } [*17,058*]
1634 (English ,, ,,)	*78,145*	..	..		*17,058*
1640	75,187	61	..	75,248	1,310
1662–3	118,221	2,173	..	120,394	..
1667	3,253	189	..	3,442	..
1668–9	154,892	1,026	..	155,918	..
1672	119,505	372	154	120,031	250
1676	142,954	1,277	145	144,376	499
1677	155,424	1,043	237	156,704	142
1678	89,182	1,488	147	90,817	12
1679	112,638	657	115	113,410	102
1697–8	51,754	1,346	157	53,257	25
1699	162,908	1,629	606	165,143	65
1700	197,163	946	924	199,033	52
1701	210,699	1,371	482	212,552	200
1702	176,347	812	76	177,235	72
1703	55,670	377	220	56,267	13
1704	145,480	1,548	125	147,153	62
1706	124,702	1,391	31	126,124	50
1707	112,402	973	135	113,510	32
1708	116,222	625	815	117,662	10
1709	91,994	852	385	93,231	130
1710	158,381	767	83	159,231	1
1711	114,724	783	170	115,677	129
1713	100,675	577	152	101,405	12
1714	119,757	1,411	439	121,607	..
1715	103,803	1,214	360	105,437	11
1716	124,011	928	335	125,274	34
1717	106,645	1,395	47	108,087	1,800
1718	108,122	1,756	77	109,955	1,433
1719	110,387	1,258	97	111,742	102
1720	86,973	2,801	20	89,794	61

* The figures in italics cover the incomplete series from 1609 to 1634; the totals in square brackets in col. 5 and col. 6, being aggregates of alien and English merchants' imports for successive years, are only rough approximations to the general magnitude of annual imports.

† 10 months' imports only.

Source: For the sources from which these statistics have been drawn see Appendix I

No attempt has been made to give figures for the late fifteenth and early sixteenth centuries as the total amounts involved were very small and moreover they are not recorded in such a way as to make feasible the comparison with the later period which alone would make it worth while to give such detailed data. The figures for the first two decades of the eighteenth century have been included so as to counter-balance the effects on the statistics of foreign trade of the many years of war during William's and Anne's reigns and thus to bring out more clearly the long-term trend in imports.

trend remains clear and unaltered: brown paper imports
were smaller in bulk than those of white paper and they
began their decline at an earlier date, thus reflecting the
earlier growth in the home production of brown and the
slower growth in the home production of white.

For white paper the annual import totals for the years
before the 1660's may be taken as a very rough indication, ignoring accumulated stocks, smuggling, and the
small amounts sent to Scotland and Ireland,[1] of the
general order of magnitude in white-paper consumption
in England. It is unlikely that the output of such very few
mills as may have produced some white paper would
much affect the total; both exports and re-exports were
virtually non-existent; and the trade in paper by ports
other than London was extremely small. Even by the end
of the seventeenth century London dominated the paper
import trade: for the five years 1699–1703 London's
average share was 97 per cent., the remaining 3 per cent.
representing all the other ports of England and Wales.[2]
A hundred years earlier the percentage taken by these
'outports' may well have been still smaller, for there is no
reason to suppose that paper was any exception to the
dominance which London exerted over English foreign
trade in Tudor and early Stuart times. If then, this is
accepted, it is immediately apparent that paper for
writing and printing was still an unimportant item of

probably dangerous and it may well be that the earlier figures should be
halved.

Similar reasons would confuse the use of still earlier figures. In the early
sixteenth century paper imports were not merely by the bundle and the
ream, the relations between which were not clear, but also by the bale, the
contents of which were not certain (see Gras, loc. cit. and also p. 701).

[1] See, e.g., A. K. Longfield, *Anglo-Irish Trade in the Sixteenth Century*
(London, 1929), pp. 190–1.

[2] The relevant figures (ann. av. 1699–1703) were: London, 162,213
reams, outports 5,337 reams (P.R.O. Customs 3/3–7).

consumption in the community as a whole. An extremely rough estimate of annual consumption per head of white paper, at the turn of the sixteenth century suggests a figure of about $\frac{1}{4}$ lb.; a rather more accurate estimate for the five years 1714–18, and covering all types of paper, gives a figure of $1\frac{1}{2}$ lb. per head per annum.[1] By modern standards these proportions are minute: in 1955 consumption per head of all types of paper in the U.K. was nearly 130 lb.

Within the general classification of 'white', a small number of different types and sizes of paper was distinguished amongst the import data. By far the largest quantities of white paper were those included under the generic term of 'ordinary', or sometimes 'ordinary printing and copy', or 'copy', all with the same formal Customs valuation. Of the 75,187 reams of white paper imported in 1640, for example, 73,172 were described as 'ordinary'; similarly, for the five years at the end of the century, 1699–1703, 'ordinary' paper formed, on the average, 93 per cent. of total white paper imports. Amongst the rest the two most common classifications were the sizes 'cap' and 'demy'.[2]

---

[1] The estimate for about 1600 assumed a total import of 60,000 reams, converted to lb. at the rate of 20 lb. per ream (see Appendix I) and divided amongst an English population of $4\frac{1}{2}$ million. If Scotland and Ireland were included, the consumption would obviously have been even less, almost infinitesimal. The estimate for 1714–18 assumed total imports of 1,100 tons, home production of 2,760 tons, exports of 40 tons, and the resulting consumption of 3,760 tons distributed over a population of $5\frac{1}{2}$ million. For details of home production, &c., see *infra*, pp. 89 et seq.

[2] The names given to sizes of paper are many and varied. For details of them and of their origins see Labarre, pp. 246–72. For examples and details of measurement in the eighteenth century see Appendix II. In this earlier period 'pot' and 'royal' are the only sizes which figure from time to time among the London imports, although at the outports, with perhaps more meticulous Customs officers, there were recorded in the Customs ledgers after the turn of the seventeenth century, such sizes as 'imperial', 'elephant', and 'foolscap', all of which and more besides were provided for in official

Types of paper other than white and brown were of small note, though imports of them seem to have been very slightly on the increase at the end of this period. Blue paper which is specifically described in the Customs ledgers later in the eighteenth century as 'for sugar bakers', was probably being imported for similar grocery purposes in these earlier years. The entries in col. 4 of Table I are almost entirely made up of 'painted' paper, with occasional parcels of 'marbled'. The latter, the fantastically decorated paper still seen today as, for example, end leaves in account books, came into fashion in Europe at the beginning of the seventeenth century. Painted paper was used for such purposes as ornamental box linings and, more important and increasingly, for wall coverings; the declining imports of these in the early years of the eighteenth century are a reflection of the growth of a paper-staining industry in this country, using home-produced paper and satisfying the dictates of fashion in the richer classes of society.[1]

The statistics of imports of pressing-paper and paste-board in these years are so fragmentary that they have been omitted from Table I. Although pressing-paper, used by the cloth-pressers, was provided for in the Customs valuations at the beginning of the seventeenth century,[2] it appears only very rarely among the London

valuations. Other descriptions related to origin, e.g. 'Venice', 'Rochelle', 'Rochelle as large as demi', or simply 'French'. Included also in the category of white paper in Table I are some small quantities recorded as 'unrated' in the Customs ledgers but which can be presumed, by reference to official ratings and later new ratings (see Chap. V), to have been largely white paper.

[1] On marbled paper and on painted or stained paper and wall-hangings see Labarre, pp. 155–8, 318–22. These commodities will not normally be considered in the present study, related as they are to the paper processing rather than the paper-producing industry. Similarly import figures for such items as fan papers or printed paper have been entirely omitted.

[2] Book of Rates, 1604 (P.R.O. E. 122/173/3).

imports, though widely varying amounts appear sporadically among the outport figures.[1] Imports of pasteboard are also unrecorded before 1698, nor moreover was pasteboard included amongst the Customs valuations of 1604 and 1660; the imports were very varied in amount and intermittent in appearance, the outports again seeming to have more regular and frequent imports than London.[2]

Where did all this paper come from?

By his study of watermarks, the late Edward Heawood was able to shed much light on the sources of white paper used in England from the fifteenth to the eighteenth centuries.[3] As might be expected both from the early importance of the industry in Italy and from the economic supremacy of the Italian cities of the time, much of the paper used in fifteenth-century England came from Italy. It came to London or to such ports as Southampton in merchant ships from Genoa or amongst the varied cargoes of the Venetian galleys. But hard on the Italians' heels were the French paper-makers, and bearing in mind the close links between England and France at that time, it is not surprising to find that French paper seems to have been gaining in importance in the later decades of the fifteenth century. Certainly in the following century France was clearly ousting Italy as the main source

---

[1] The only recorded imports into London of pressing-paper in this period were 12,185 leaves in 1718 and 2,900 in 1719. For the outports the totals varied from 300 leaves in 1702 to over 30,000 in 1717, with 2,000 as an average figure (P.R.O. Customs 3).

[2] London pasteboard imports ranged from 2,500 boards in 1707 to 37,031 in 1717. The usual figure was 3,000–6,000, with a rising tendency towards 1720. Outport figures fluctuated from 74,540 in 1715 to 3,083 in 1717, with an average of 7,000–8,000 per annum (P.R.O. Customs 3).

[3] E. Heawood, 'Sources of Early English Paper-Supply', *Trans. Bib. Soc.*, vol. x (1929–30), pp. 282–307, 427–54; also vol. xi (1930–1), pp. 263–99, 466–98.

On the subject of watermarks in general see also Labarre, pp. 328–60, and Hunter, pp. 258–308.

of our paper imports, and there can be little doubt that
France then supplied the greater part of the paper used
for writing and printing in these islands.[1] From this time
onward we hear more and more of French paper in contemporary writings, not simply because it was imported,
but because it was one of the many French commodities
which English economic policy of the time disliked importing. For roughly the first three-quarters of the
seventeenth century France retained her position as
England's main supplier, the chief exporting centres
being Rouen, Caen, Morlaix, Bordeaux, and La Rochelle.[2]

The trade returns offer a check upon Heawood's investigations. Analysis by countries of imports of white
paper for the late sixteenth and early seventeenth centuries shows a clear and gratifying correlation with his
findings. The overwhelming majority of white imports
recorded in Table I down to 1640 came from France.
The largest shipment from Italy was 1,156 reams imported by English merchants in 1621, as compared with
61,684 reams from France in that year. It was the
Netherlands, however, which provided the main alterna-
tive source, especially when Anglo-French trade was
interrupted. In 1567–8 only 1,260 reams out of a total of
12,738 came from the Netherlands, but in 1627, following

[1] *Trans. Bib. Soc.*, vol. x, pp. 282–307, 427–54; Gras, loc. cit.; A. A. Rud-
dock, *Italian Merchants and Shipping in Southampton* (Southampton, 1951),
pp. 75, 175, 190, 228, gives examples of paper imported from Italy at dates
between 1433 and 1518.

[2] Paper-mills were at work in many parts of France, and the French paper
industry was probably the biggest in Europe. The paper-mills of Auvergne
were the most celebrated but many others were to be found, in Provence,
in the Dauphiné, as well as in Normandy, Brittany, and elsewhere in the
north and west. See Heawood, loc. cit.; G. Martin, *La Grande Industrie sous
le règne de Louis XIV* (Paris, 1899), p. 187; E. Levasseur, *Histoire du commerce
de la France* (Paris, 1911), vol. i, pp. 272, 334–5, 337, 342, 344–5, 349; also
evidence of Port Books.

the embargo on French imports imposed in the previous year,[1] alien merchants imported thence 12,220 reams out of their total white-paper imports of 17,715 reams. In brown-paper imports the Netherlands were supreme, virtually all consignments being shipped from there.

Here, however, a note of caution must be sounded. The Port Books from which these figures are drawn record the port from which a ship had come, but they do not name all the ports at which it may have called nor do they distinguish the place of origin of the goods imported. Thus, although most of our brown paper seems to have come from the Netherlands, this does not necessarily mean that it was made in Holland or Flanders; some or all of it may equally well have been manufactured in France or Germany or even Italy. The French had sent writing-paper in the sixteenth century to the great mart of the time, Antwerp.[2] It is equally likely that into Antwerp's seventeenth-century successor, Amsterdam, paper both brown and white was imported for its subsequent re-export. As can be seen from Table I, a substantial quantity of both white and brown was imported into London in the early seventeenth century by foreign merchants, though later in the century their share of total imports fell off markedly.

The last quarter of the seventeenth century marked, as Heawood observed, 'a turning-point in the history of paper-supply to this country'.[3] The changes were various

---

[1] E. Lipson, *The Economic History of England* (4th ed., London, 1947), vol. iii, p. 99 n. It was subsequently lifted.

[2] '. . . Papier à escrire de plusieurs sortes, et d'endroitz divers'—*Guicciardini's description of the trade of Antwerp*, 1560, printed in French, in R. H. Tawney and E. Power, *Tudor Economic Documents* (London, 1924), vol. iii, p. 167.

[3] Heawood, loc. cit., *Trans. Bib. Soc.*, vol. xi, p. 487.

and the reasons for them complex; they affected home production as well as the volume and origin of imports. These aspects are discussed at some length in Chapter III, but meanwhile it will suffice to survey the broad currents of change. Heawood comments on the increase in Dutch paper, and observes that there is little trace during this period of paper from eastern and central France; he notes that after 1680 Italian paper was once again used in England on quite an extensive scale, much of it coming from Genoa; and he finds few indications of paper from elsewhere in Europe, though noting some possibly German paper in the last decade of the seventeenth century.

Again the trade statistics substantially bear out his findings (Table II).

The impact of war and commercial policy shows up very clearly in the stoppages of French imports into England.[1] Supplies of French paper are replaced by imports from Italy, Germany, and Holland. German imports, indeed, appear to have been on a rather larger scale than Heawood estimated.

But once again it is dangerous to jump to too many conclusions from these figures. To the qualifications arising from the nature of the Port Book entries mentioned above, there must be added a further warning. Not only did Amsterdam continue to be the great entrepôt of Europe, thus making it likely that some unknown amount of the paper exported from it was of other than Dutch manufacture, but in addition some paper specifically described as Dutch or apparently bearing Dutch watermarks was in fact made in France. The copying of watermarks was not a new phenomenon: much earlier, Italian marks had been copied by French

[1] See *infra*, pp. 64–65.

TABLE II

Sources of Imports into London of White Paper (reams), 1662–1720

Year	France	Holland	Italy	Germany	Others	Total
1662–3	116,698	. .	1,523	. .	. .	118,221
1667	2,782	. .	. .	. .	471	3,253
1668–9	154,392	. .	500	. .	. .	154,892
1672	114,740	165	2,255	64	41	119,505
1676	138,856	4	3,300	. .	794	142,954
1677	150,911	3	2,334	. .	2,176	155,424
1678	63,647	1,179	23,400	954	12	89,182
1679	300	73,902	36,219	363	1,854	112,638
1685–6	80,685					
1697–8	4,083	39,203	2,758	5,710	. .	51,754
1699	28,301	92,017	31,640	10,950	. .	162,908
1700	15,586	68,677	76,229	36,668	3	197,163
1701	9,576	84,203	85,116	31,804	. .	210,699
1702	2,917	85,597	64,798	23,035	. .	176,347
1703	. .	22,578	21,706	11,386	. .	55,670
1704	. .	102,043	34,137	9,300	. .	145,480
1706	. .	89,387	27,966	7,349	. .	124,702
1707	. .	81,909	15,510	14,983	. .	112,402
1708	. .	86,508	24,972	4,742	. .	116,222
1709	. .	80,564	2,520	8,821	89	91,994
1710	. .	111,387	36,073	9,449	1,472	158,381
1711	. .	107,401	492	6,796	35	114,724
1713	4,412	79,699	16,525	. .	40	100,675
1714	5,329	99,360	14,030	248	790	119,757
1715	890	83,145	17,878	1,950	. .	103,863
1716	7	96,960	24,102	2,942	. .	124,011
1717	111	82,820	21,700	2,014	. .	106,645
1718	10	92,887	14,196	498	532	108,122
1719	3	92,943	17,241	200	. .	110,387
1720	. .	71,173	15,800	. .	. .	86,973

Source—Sources as for Table I.

paper-makers of Troyes.[1] Towards the end of the seventeenth century Dutch capital was being invested in French paper-mills.[2] During the last decades of the seventeenth and the early years of the eighteenth

---

[1] Heawood, loc. cit., *Trans. Bib. Soc.*, vol. x.   [2] Ibid., vol. xi.

centuries, the Dutch industry apparently made rapid strides.[1] The French industry meanwhile seems to have been going through a thin period, suffering perhaps from an excess of regulation as well as a shortage of capital, from the emigration of Huguenot artisans, from a decline in overseas demand, as well as from the general effects of a protracted war upon trade.[2] So it is not perhaps surprising that, whatever may have been the contributions made by the Dutch paper-mills themselves, some paper from this period, bearing the watermarked initials of Dutch factors is known to have been made at mills in Angoulême which were worked by Dutch capital;[3] or that it was complained in England that the Dutch bought French paper cheaply and sold it as their own rather more dearly.[4] In short, then, this difficulty of disentangling French and Dutch paper at this time means that it is quite possible that more paper actually made in France found its way into this country than either trade returns or watermarks would seem to indicate.

The same observations may also apply to the imports, between 1662 and 1720, of paper other than white, for here again Holland was the main supplier. It seems likely, however, that much of this paper may have been

[1] English paper-makers giving evidence to the Board of Trade and Plantations in 1696 commented on the growth of the Dutch industry, as well as alleging that much paper imported from Holland was in fact French (P.R.O. CO. 388/7, 389/14, 391/90).

[2] The Dutch paper industry, like the English, profited from the influx of Huguenots, just as the French correspondingly suffered. See G. H. Overend, 'Notes upon the Earlier History of the Manufacture of Paper in England', *Proceedings of the Huguenot Society of London*, vol. viii (1909), pp. 177–220; also *infra*, pp. 68–80.

[3] Heawood, loc. cit., vol. xi; cf. also Martin, op. cit., p. 140: '. . . Les papiers de Holland jouissaient d'une grande réputation, aussi fabriquait-on, dans les manufactures de France, du papier aux armes d'Amsterdam.'

[4] *Reasons against laying a further duty . . . etc.* (c. 1699). The requirements of the Navigation Acts would also have been conducive to these developments. See Lipson, op. cit., vol. iii, pp. 121 et seq.

made there. Virtually all the brown came from there and so too did the imports of pasteboard and pressing-paper mentioned earlier.[1] Holland also provided most of the blue-paper imports, though here there was some competition from Germany which supplied about 10 per cent. of the total.

To summarize. Britain drew her supplies of various sorts of paper from the Continent to meet the increased demands for wrapping, writing, and printing. Most of these supplies came into London and were consumed in England. The amounts of all types imported rose until the early or middle years of the seventeenth century, when imports of brown paper declined, whilst those of white continued to rise until the end of the century. Italy and France were the main suppliers at the end of the fifteenth century, but France alone became the main source of white paper throughout most of this period. Italy, Germany, and Holland came to replace her, however, towards the end of the seventeenth century and especially after the outbreak of the French wars; at the same time the proviso has to be made that some of the paper apparently coming from the Netherlands may well have been made elsewhere, probably in France.

Meanwhile the home industry was growing, especially in the later decades of the seventeenth century. In the 1540's there was probably no paper at all being made anywhere in the British Isles; yet by 1720 it seems likely that England was producing about two-thirds of this country's total home consumption. To the growth and achievements which this implies we must now turn, after first examining briefly the techniques of early paper-making.

[1] *Supra*, pp. 16–17.

II

Early Techniques and their Economic Significance

DIVORCED from its technical development, the economic development of an industry is meaningless. Techniques and organization go hand-in-hand. Before tracing the growth of the paper-making industry in England, it is accordingly necessary to examine the techniques of paper manufacture in order to see in what way they influenced the economics of the industry.[1]

(i)

The essential chemical constituent of paper is cellulose $(C_6H_{10}O_5)$, the main component of plant tissues. The essence of paper manufacture is that the cellulose fibres should be macerated until each individual filament is a separate unit and mixed with water in such a way that, by the use of sieve-like screens, the fibres can subsequently be lifted from the water in the form of a thin layer, the water draining off and leaving a sheet of matted fibres on the screen's surface. This thin sheet is paper, although it

---

[1] The account of technical processes given in this chapter is based on a number of works and only specific references will be quoted. The main books consulted were Hunter, esp. chaps. vi and viii; R. H. Clapperton and W. Henderson, *Modern Paper-Making* (3rd ed., Oxford, 1947), esp. chap. xvii; and the contemporary or near-contemporary descriptions in Houghton, op. cit., vol. ii, pp. 410 et seq.; C. King (ed.), op. cit., vol. ii, pp. 267–9; J. Evelyn, *Diary* (ed. Bray, London, 1895), p. 401; *The Journeys of Celia Fiennes* (1685–1703), ed. C. Morris (London, 1947), p. 124; J. Imberdis, *Papyrus sive Ars conficiendae Papyri* (1693, English translation by E. Laughton, Hilversum, 1952).

requires pressing, drying, sizing, and finishing before it can be used as such.

This definition excludes certain substances sometimes referred to as paper and sometimes used for the same sort of purposes as paper sometimes. It excludes, for instance, various ancient writing materials made from the leaves, stems, or bark of trees, hammered or flattened and made into sheets in the manner of papyrus;[1] similarly it excludes modern substitutes for paper such as the type of wrapping known as cellophane, a cellulose film made by the viscose process.[2] On the other hand, the definition comprehends all paper which comes within the main historical stream of paper-making in the sense that the fundamentals of manufacture are the same today as they were almost two thousand years ago when what can be called 'true' paper was developed in China. It holds good alike for paper made by hand from linen or cotton rags and for modern newsprint made by machine from wood-pulp. It rests essentially on the joint use of a specific type of raw material and certain basic processes of manufacture. What are these today and what were they in Tudor and Stuart England?

Paper-making offers a long vista of technical developments. In it we can see both continuity in the main process of manufacture and certain landmarks which denote change. A division into three main processes can be traced throughout: (*a*) preparation of raw materials, (*b*) forming the paper, and (*c*) drying and finishing. Within those three categories are subdivisions: bleaching, for example, became in time an important separate constituent of the first, pressing is an integral part of both second and third. In the course of time some of the sub-processes have changed their position: sizing can be in

---

[1] See Hunter, chap. i. [2] Labarre, p. 43.

(*c*) or in (*a*). But the broad outline of the picture remains clear. So too do the landmarks of change. There are three of them. The first landmark is the use of power in (*a*). The exact timing of this initial mechanization is not known, but at least it is quite certain that it was completed well before the period with which this present study is concerned: water-powered devices for raw material preparation are known to have been in use in the paper-mills at work on the European continent from the twelfth century onwards. The second landmark is the mechanization of (*b*). The paper-making machine was introduced into this country during the first decade of the nineteenth century; this development is examined in Part II.[1] Mechanization of (*c*) followed rapidly thereafter. Raw materials feature in the third landmark, which is the successful use after many experiments of esparto grass and wood-pulp as substitutes for rags. These innovations belong to the period between the 1860's and 1880's, and though touched on in Part III their effects fall outside the scope of this book.

The industry with which we are concerned in Part I of this book is thus characterized by the use of water-power in the preparation of raw materials and by hand-labour in the making and finishing processes. Its main raw materials were water and rags. The latter were mainly linen rags, though from the later seventeenth century onwards the use of cotton rags was probably increasing. Old sheets, old clothing, and the like were supplemented by old ropes and sails which were used for the manufacture of the poorer sort of paper.[2] Woollen rags, being fundamentally different in origin cannot be used alone

[1] *Infra*, p. 179.
[2] Waste paper was also sometimes repulped, though the contribution which this made to raw material supplies must have been insignificant. See Houghton, op. cit., vol. ii, p. 411.

for the making of true paper, though there is no doubt that they were used from time to time. An eighteenth-century German paper-maker, Georg Keferstein, observed that rags were mainly of two sorts, linen and woollen; he states that the latter are of little account but adds that they are used in the making of grey paper and scrap paper.[1] In 1678 John Evelyn describes in his diary the use of woollen rags for the manufacture of brown paper, and it is known too that early blotting-paper was sometimes made from woollen rags.[2] In this country where these were so much more common than linen rags it is hardly surprising that efforts should have been made to use them for paper-making, and it seems very likely that in the manufacture of the cruder sorts of brown paper a mixture of old cordage or sails and woollen rags was sometimes used.

The essential feature of the first process is that the raw materials should be reduced to pulp, thereby separating the fibres from other surrounding substances and leaving a mass of macerated fibres in suspension in water. Before the eighteenth century this was carried out in the following manner. The rags were sorted (fine strong linen rags were used for the best white paper; the poorer sorts, such as old canvas, for brown wrapping-paper), soaked in water, washed, put into heaps, and allowed to rot until fermentation set in. Whilst rotting, the piles of rags were turned and watered; the fermentation became apparent by the rags changing colour and becoming hot. Accounts do not agree on how long the process took, and it is evident that there were many variations both in practice and in time taken. That in general it was a process which absorbed an unwelcome length of time is suggested by

[1] G. C. Keferstein, *Unterricht eines Papiermachers an seine Söhne* (1766, Leipzig, 1936), p. 21.   [2] Evelyn, op. cit., p. 401; Labarre, pp. 24–25.

the fact that lime was sometimes thrown on the rags to hasten disintegration. This was, however, regarded as likely to injure the quality of the resulting paper, and in eighteenth-century France, where these methods were still being followed, the use of lime was forbidden.[1]

Fermentation constituted a preliminary stage in the rag-preparation process. It was completed by washing and then pulping in the stamping-mill. This was a water-powered mill which was a logical development of the original method of breaking and pulping the rags by means of a pestle and mortar. Indeed an early drawing of a stamping-mill (1579) shows simply a hand-operated wheel device actuating four pestles in four mortars.[2] However, the normal form throughout the period with which we are here concerned consisted of a row of heavy wooden mallets or stampers caused to rise and fall by means of cams on a mill shaft driven by a water-wheel. Below the stampers was a corresponding row of mortars made from solid blocks of stone or wood, into which the stampers fell, thudding down on the rags. The mortars were kept supplied with running water and had cavities covered by fine sieves, thus allowing the water to run off but retaining the pulped fibres. In its crudest form the mill had only one stamper per mortar, but in the course of the seventeenth century improvements were made by which different types of stampers were used in turn; heavy iron-shod or toothed stampers were used, in conjunction with running water, in order to clean the rags and to start the maceration process; the half-beaten rags were then put under lighter stampers to complete the

[1] Hunter, p. 155. Similar descriptions of this early process will be found in such encyclopaedias as A. Rees, *Cyclopaedia or Universal Dictionary of Arts, Sciences and Literature* (London, 1819), vol. xxvi, where the description of earlier methods of manufacture draws on eighteenth-century French accounts.   [2] Reproduced in Hunter, p. 155.

process, the water being retained. Three stampers per mortar or trough are shown in a German drawing of 1662, and at the peak of its development in the early eighteenth century, the stamping-mill, at about the time when it was just coming to be replaced by the 'Hollander',[1] had sometimes as many as five sets of stampers to each mortar or trough.[2]

At the end of this first process the mixture of water and finely pulped fibres (known as 'stuff') was ready for the second process—that of forming the sheets. The stuff, consisting very largely of water with the fibres in suspension, was conveyed by bucket or by gravity from a storage tank or 'stuff chest' to a large vat at which the paper-maker operated. Attached to the vat was a small charcoal stove to warm the stuff, this being easier to use when kept at an even temperature; at the same time it had to be periodically stirred in order to prevent the fibrous material from settling. Alongside the vat there would be a heavy wooden screw press. Three workmen carried out the making process—the paper-maker or 'vatman', the 'coucher', and the 'layer' or 'layman'. The actual forming of the sheet was done by the vatman with the aid of a tool known as a 'mould'. This consisted of a rectangular wooden frame between two ends of which were stretched, close together and parallel, a large number of fine metal wires, varying from about 25 to 35 to the inch; between the other two sides ran a number of stronger supporting wires, spaced from a half to two inches apart, to which the fine wires were fastened at the intersections. Going with the mould, but separate from it, was the 'deckle', a narrow wooden rim which was placed on the

---

[1] *Infra*, pp. 62–63, 109–11.

[2] A number of illustrations of stampers will be found in Hunter, pp. 156–61. The German drawing of 1662 is also reproduced in Rhys Jenkins, p. 154.

PLATE I

Early paper-making, *circa* seventeenth century

mould to prevent the stuff from flowing off it and at the same time to determine the size of the sheet.[1]

The vatman took the mould with the deckle in position, dipped it into the liquid in the vat, and lifted it out in such a way that an even coverage of the fibrous mass, appropriate to the thickness of paper being made, was deposited on the wires, the surplus water draining off back into the vat. He then gave the mould a peculiar shake so as to ensure that the fibres were thoroughly matted, thus giving to the sheet of paper equal strength in both directions. Removing the deckle, the vatman passed the mould to the coucher who, after allowing the water to drain off, turned the mould over and deposited the wet sheet on a 'felt'.[2] The vatman meanwhile, having retained the deckle, placed it on a second mould and formed another sheet before the first mould was returned to him. In this way the two workmen continued, the coucher making a pile of alternate felts and sheets of paper[3] until a 'post' consisting usually of 144 sheets or six quires was completed.

When this was done the post was transferred to the press and all the workmen then combined to screw it down so as to remove as much water as possible from the pile of wet paper and felts. This being completed, and whilst the vatman and coucher were at work making another post, the layer was busy removing the partially dried sheets from their felts, the latter being returned to the coucher for use in the next post. The separated sheets were then put by the layer into a pile and once again subjected to pressure.

[1] Much detail about and many illustrations of moulds will be found in Hunter, esp. chap. iv.

[2] Originally made of felt, but later of woollen cloth.

[3] Strictly speaking, it is not yet paper but is 'waterleaf'. See Labarre, p. 328, and for an early use, King (ed.), op. cit., vol. ii, p. 267.

The third main process of drying and finishing then began. Still moist, the sheets of paper were taken from the press to the drying loft, at the top of the mill. The walls of the drying loft had shutters which could be adjusted to admit more or less air as was desired. The sheets of paper were hung up on cow- or horse-hair ropes stretched across the loft and left to dry for a period of time varying considerably both with the thickness of the paper and with air temperature. When dried the sheet was ready for sizing. Size made from animal gelatine had come into use in the Italian mills in the thirteenth or fourteenth centuries and marked an advance on the early use of starch or size made from lichens.[1] In the sixteenth and seventeenth centuries it was made at the paper-mill from shreds and parings obtained from tanners, curriers, glovers, and parchment-makers. The pieces of hide were boiled up and the resulting glutinous liquid was strained and allowed to settle; by the end of the seventeenth century alum was being added to the size, although how early this practice was started is not clear. The sheets were dipped into the size, and then pressed again to remove the superfluous gelatine. The paper was then returned again to the drying loft and finally taken to a large room or storehouse known as the 'salle' where it was examined, given such surface finish as was needed, and once again pressed. A smooth surface finish, originally obtained by rubbing the paper with a smooth stone, was imparted in some seventeenth-century European mills by means of a pressing or glazing hammer operated by water-power.[2] After examination of each sheet the

[1] Hunter, pp. 194, 475; Blum, op. cit., p. 31.

[2] Hunter, pp. 197–9; for an example of a 'glazing engine' in an English mill in the early eighteenth century, see A. H. Shorter, 'Paper Mills in Worcestershire', *Transactions of the Worcestershire Archaeological Society*, vol. xxviii (1951).

piles were finally carefully pressed in a 'dry' press of similar construction to the 'wet' press used earlier. It was at last ready for wrapping and the market.

The foregoing description does not claim either to cover every detail of the early processes or to account for the many variations which certainly existed.[1] The manufacture of good quality white writing-paper required greater care in the sorting and preparation of raw materials, greater skills in making, and a longer time in drying and finishing than did that of cheap brown wrapping-paper. Blue paper needed the addition of a dye to the stuff; marbled paper demanded a relatively elaborate finish, wrapping-paper virtually none; blotting-paper was unsized. Between the skill, care, and attention to detail to be found in a mill producing high quality white paper which needed to pass through many hands in its manufacture and the rough and ready methods by which the lowest grades of brown wrapping were turned out there was a substantial gap both in techniques and in organization.

Finally something should be said of the manufacture of board. Strictly speaking the making of pasteboard by the pasting together of sheets of paper was not a part of the paper industry but rather a source of demand for paper. The same is true of the making of board from the 'shavings and cuttings of books' said to have been carried on by the bookbinders themselves in the later sixteenth and early seventeenth centuries. But pasteboard was also made at paper-mills; so too was millboard, the manufacture of which, from old ropes and similar raw materials, clearly forms part of the paper industry. Un-

---

[1] The variations seem mainly to have been in the rag-preparation processes. Comparison of the accounts given in Hunter, pp. 157–63, Houghton, op. cit., vol. ii, pp. 412–14, and Rees, op. cit., vol. xxvi, suggest the existence of different sequences of treatment, and the use of different sorts of stampers.

fortunately for the historian contemporaries did not always bother to distinguish between these different sorts of board, nor between them and scaleboard which was made of wood but was a competing product with similar uses. The early history of board-making is not always very easy to follow.[1]

(ii)

Upon the technical foundations there rested an industrial structure. A number of important economic characteristics of the industry flowed directly from technical needs. It will suffice here to consider the general outlines of these characteristics; in later chapters occasion will arise to examine them in greater detail and to see how their influence has varied from time to time and place to place.

First, the location of paper-mills was very evidently conditioned by water-supply, both for power and as a raw material in manufacture. Once the stamping-mill had appeared on the scene, like the fulling-mill in the woollen cloth industry, it formed a powerful determinant of location [2] As will be shown later, the industry grew up along river valleys, in this country as on the Continent. In paper manufacture water is obviously a raw material of importance, and very large quantities are used. How much was used to make a given quantity in the sixteenth and seventeenth centuries it is difficult to estimate, but there can be no doubt that an ample water-supply from

---

[1] Some details of early board-making and the uses to which board was put will be found in 'Bagford's Notes on Bookbinding', *Trans. Bib. Soc.*, vol. vii; Houghton, op. cit., vol. iii, p. 411; *The Case of the Book-binders* (c. 1712); see also Labarre, pp. 163, 187, 234, and *O.E.D.*

[2] On the rôle of the fulling-mill in helping to determine the location of the early cloth industry see E. M. Carus-Wilson, 'An Industrial Revolution of the Thirteenth Century', *Economic History Review*, vol. xi (1941).

river or spring was of vital importance to the success of a mill. Quantity alone was not enough: not every type of water was suitable. For the manufacture of the poorest sorts of coarse brown it is probable that little close attention was paid to the nature of available water—nor perhaps did this matter very much. But for the manufacture of good quality white rag paper the nature of the water was, and still is, a matter of concern.

Quick streams and clear water: this was the recipe put forward by a representative of the English white-paper makers in 1696.[1] Keferstein's advice to his son in eighteenth-century Germany was similar but more detailed. Should his son contemplate the building of a mill, then amongst other things, he must ensure that he has a supply of clean and clear water. Keferstein then goes on to give a series of comments on the suitability of the water in different parts of his native land.[2] The softness of the water was not (and is not today) as important as its purity. Kent, for example, early became an important centre of English paper-making, and the presence of clear, fairly hard water, free from iron and probably deriving its suitability from its contact with limestone, played its part in determining this location. Similarly in Somerset the early establishment and long-continued existence of paper-mills owed something to suitable water from the porous limestone of the Mendips.[3]

Availability of the other major raw material, rags, was

[1] P.R.O. CO. 391/90.

[2] Keferstein, op. cit., pp. 38–39: '. . . Müsset Ihr auch auf die Beschaffenheit des Wassers, in Absicht seiner Bestandtheile sehen; oder mich noch deutlicher auszudrücken, das es ein weiches, reines und weisses Wasser sey; dass es euren Stoff nicht färbt.'

[3] On location and water-supply see W. W. Jervis and S. J. Jones, 'The Paper-Making Industry in Somerset', *Geography*, vol. xv (1930) and, in general, Shorter, *Historical Geography*. (Since the above was written, Dr. Shorter has published many of the findings of his thesis as *Paper Mills and Paper Makers in England, 1495–1800* (Paper Publications Society, Hilversum, 1957).)

a second important force determining location. The great linen-consuming areas had here an evident advantage; in its earliest days the European paper industry spread outwards from the Mediterranean countries of the Islamic world. There, as Professor Lopez has pointed out, the traveller would find 'great quantities of linen from Egypt, Yemen and South-western Persia'; he added that although 'the manufacture of paper . . . was introduced into Samarcand from China, . . . the method of making rag paper was perfected by the Muslims'.[1] Though perhaps we may cavil slightly at 'perfected', the probable connexion is clear enough. In its spread northward it is no coincidence that it should have arrived comparatively late in England—a major consumer and producer of wool and woollen cloth. The production and use of linen spread but slowly across Europe, and paper followed equally slowly in its train. By the sixteenth and seventeenth centuries the advantage lay with the Continent in linen and paper alike; England imported most of her linens from France, Holland, and Germany, and most of her paper from the same countries.[2] Within the country a close and reliable source of supply of rags was evidently of major importance in determining the site of mills. Rags, being the most important single item in production costs,[3] exerted a commensurate influence on location. So it is not surprising to find many mills springing up at a relatively short distance from the towns, where linen rags were likely to be available. The growth of mills in the Home Counties obviously owes something to this, as well as to the purely economic factor of proximity to a market for the finished product. London was obviously

---

[1] Lopez, in *Cambridge Economic History*, p. 281.
[2] Blum, op. cit., pp. 35–37; Lipson, op. cit., vol. ii, pp. 109–12.
[3] *Infra*, pp. 169–70.

of paramount importance here, controlling as it did the bulk of the country's trade. The use of old cordage and sails probably helped to attract brown-paper mills to the proximity of such ports as Exeter, Dover, and South-ampton.[1]

Two further points arise from the nature of the raw material. First, it gave rise to an ancillary trade which lies at the periphery of our subject: rag-collecting. This offered casual employment for all sorts of poor persons and was thus advanced as a particular merit by early promoters of the industry.[2] In times of plague, however, this merit was less obvious, and during the outbreak of 1636–7 an outcry arose which resulted in the Privy Council ordering the closure of paper-mills in Middlesex and Buckinghamshire until the infection was over. From the correspondence on the subject it is evident that even as early as this rag merchants were to be found in the City buying rags from the poor collectors and selling them on the home or export market.[3] That the rag merchants' trade had become a lucrative occupation is suggested by the observation in the 1690's that of those who dealt in rags 'several there be that have got estates out of them'.[4] In country districts the rag-gatherers often by-passed the middleman by simply taking the rags straight to the mills.[5] Secondly, by the very nature of the product, the supply of rags was—and is—peculiarly

---

[1] On these developments see *infra*, pp. 56–58; Keferstein placed the availability of a good local supply of rags high on his list of priorities in siting a mill (op. cit., p. 38).

[2] See, e.g., *Tudor Economic Documents*, vol. ii, p. 253; *British Merchant*, vol. iii, pp. 267–9.

[3] *Cal. S.P. Dom.* 1636, pp. 119, 122, 126, 290; 1636–7, p. 373; 1637, p. 108; also Rhys Jenkins, pp. 167–8.

[4] Houghton, op. cit., vol. iii, p. 411. See also R. Baxter, *The Poor Husband-man's Advocate to Rich Racking Landlords* (c. 1660, ed. F. J. Powicke, 1926), p. 28.

[5] *British Merchant*, vol. iii, pp. 267–9; Harris, op. cit., p. 191.

inelastic. Though rising prices may encourage the collection of rags, there is very clearly a narrow limit to the
amount of rags available at any given time, or within any
given short period of time. As there was—and is—little
scope for change in the methods of rag-collection, increases in paper-making capacity and hence in the
demand for rags led to sharp rises in rag prices. This
particular characteristic of the rag-paper industry, as
will be seen in later chapters,[1] has been of major importance.

A third economic characteristic which flowed directly
from techniques was the vital place of skilled labour in
the productive process. The work of the vatman was
highly skilled and so to a lesser extent was that of the
coucher and layer. Although less-skilled labour also
found employment, notably in the initial processes of rag-
preparation, the need for the skilled man was of dominant
importance. The vatman's job was thus neither readily
learnt nor cheaply rewarded; apprenticeship became a
normal condition of entry, and the paper-maker's work
and remuneration stand in sharp contrast to those of the
spinners and weavers of the domestic clothing industry
of rural England. Though no doubt there were variations
in the skills of those making the coarsest brown and the
finest white, yet the very nature of the techniques meant
that the industry had to grow slowly; for in an age without a body of scientific knowledge skilled techniques had
to be learnt and transmitted slowly by training and
application. The paper industry could not expand, as did
cloth-making or nail manufacture, on the basis of the
ill-paid domestic labour of thousands of semi-skilled or
unskilled rural labourers—men, women, and children.
Its techniques would not allow it.

[1] Cf. *infra*, pp. 170-4, 337-9.

Fourthly and finally, the capital requirements of the industry were to a large extent dictated by the nature of its processes. Paper-making was essentially a mill industry. The paper-mill belonged to a family which included the corn-mill, the fulling-mill, the slitting-mill, and others less plentifully represented in the English countryside before the Industrial Revolution. The combination of skilled labour, water-power, and the need for some minimum of buildings in which to carry on the processes of manufacture precluded any possibility of the industry assuming the well-known shape of the 'domestic system'. The techniques of cloth-making were ideally suited to a division of labour which allowed the 'putting-out' or 'domestic' system to flourish; those of paper-making demanded centralized work. This in turn implied that a paper-mill represented a more substantial concentration of capital than did the weaver's cottage and loom. Certain opportunities for capital investment thus appeared to be offered by the spread of paper-making. The nature of these it will be part of the task of later chapters to examine.

III

Enterprise, Politics, and Paper, 1495–1720

(i)

ACCORDING to the *Discourse of the Common Weal*, there was at that time (*c.* 1549) neither white nor brown paper made in England. In this set of dialogues on the economic woes of the age, the author causes one of his characters to lament the absence of paper-making in this country and our consequent dependence on imports. But, he adds, 'there was paper made a whyle within the Realme'.[1] This is probably a reference to the mill run by a member of the London Mercers Company, John Tate, for there is no trace of any other mill before the date assigned to the *Discourse of the Common Weal*. Tate's mill, the first for which there is any evidence in the British Isles, was located near Hertford. It supplied paper for a book printed by Wynkyn de Worde in 1495,[2] and is also known to have been at work in 1498 when it was visited by Henry VII.[3] Paper bearing Tate's watermark appears on other occasions in the following years: but in his will, dated 1507, after bequeathing some 'whit paper or other paper', he directed that the mill, together with its appur-

---

[1] [John Hales], *Discourse of the Common Weal of this Realm of England*, ed. E. Lamond (Cambridge, 1929), p. 66.

[2] A. Bartholomaeus, *De Proprietatibus Rerum*, de Worde's edition of which contains the lines:

> 'And John Tate the yonger Ioye mote he broke
> Which late hathe in Englande doo make this paper thynne
> That now in our englyssh this boke is printed Inne.'

[3] B.M. Add. MSS. 7099, p. 47. See also H. R. Plomer, 'Bibliographical Notes from the Privy Purse Expenses of King Henry the Seventh', *The Library*, July 1913.

tenances and the land attached to it, should be sold.[1] The implication is that it had failed.

Not until the 1550's are there signs of a revival in attempts to establish the industry here. There was apparently a paper-mill at Fen Ditton, near Cambridge, in 1557, possibly earlier. This was allegedly set up at the instigation of Thomas Thirlby, Bishop of Ely from 1554 to 1559, with the assistance of one Remegius or Remigeus, a German who presumably supplied that technical knowledge of paper manufacture which bishops do not normally possess. Their enterprise seems, however, not to have been blessed with any lasting success. How long the mill lasted it is impossible to say; it probably fell into disuse and was periodically revived. It was referred to as a paper-mill in a survey of 1599; in the following century Thomas Fuller was possibly referring to this mill when he speaks of paper being made near Stourbridge Fair (which was held in the parish adjoining Fen Ditton) 'in the memory of our fathers'.[2] To the 1550's or 1560's there also belongs, according to John Aubrey, the establishment of a paper-mill at Bemerton, near Salisbury.[3]

[1] Somerset House: Will of John Tate, citizen and mercer of London, made 1507, proved 1508. The relevant passage, and more, is also quoted in Jenkins, p. 157, whose general account of Tate and his enterprise includes a reproduction of Tate's watermark. (He gives the date of Henry VII's visit to the mill incorrectly as 1496.) John Tate, his father and other members of family figure frequently in the *Acts of Court of the Mercers' Company*, ed. L. Lyell (Cambridge, 1936). On Tate's watermark see also Heawood, loc. cit., *Trans. Bib. Soc.*, vol. x, pp. 292, 450.

[2] Thomas Fuller, *The Worthies of England*, 1662 (ed. J. Freeman, London, 1952), p. 48, also quoted in Rhys Jenkins, p. 159, who gives an account of the Fen Ditton enterprise.

[3] John Aubrey, *The Natural History of Wiltshire*, 1685 (ed. J. Britton, London, 1838), p. 95; ibid., *Brief Lives*, 1681 (ed. A. Clark, Oxford, 1898), vol. ii, p. 323. In both works this mill is said to be the second in England. In the *Brief Lives* the mill was of 112 years' standing in 1681, which sets it up in 1569 (not 1596 as by a misprint in Jenkins, p. 160). In the *Natural History* it is 130 years old in 1684, i.e. it would have been started in 1554.

A little later Sir Thomas Gresham interested himself in this new sphere of business enterprise by erecting a paper-mill on his estate at Osterley, Middlesex. But neither Gresham's wealth nor his resourcefulness could apparently make it a lasting venture: the mill was reported as decayed in 1593.[1] A petition for a monopoly of paper-making was submitted by the London stationer, Richard Tottyl or Tottell, in 1585. In this he claims that some twelve years before he and others of his company (presumably the Stationers' Company of which he was an active member) 'seinge the want and dearth of good paper in this Realme and also the disceite that is used Dailye in makeinge thereof did fullie agree to bestowe some labour and cost for the ereccion of a paper mill heare in this lande'.[2] Whether Tottell had ever erected a mill or ever did so is not known. His petition apparently went unanswered, as did also another petition, probably of about the same date, which sought monopoly powers for an incorporated company to make paper.[3] The wording of the quotation from Tottell's petition, together with complaints which he makes against the methods used by the French to impede paper-making in this country,[4] suggest the existence, albeit precarious, of other mills. And the nature of Tottell's own profession implies that it was primarily white paper in which he was interested.

The later decades of the sixteenth century and the

[1] Rhys Jenkins, p. 160. Also T. Burgon, *Life and Times of Sir T. Gresham* (London, 1839), vol. ii, pp. 444–5. It was probably erected in the 1570's.

[2] P.R.O. *S.P. Dom.* Eliz., vol. clxxxv, No. 69. Also quoted in Rhys Jenkins, p. 161. On Tottyl see H. J. Byrom, 'Richard Tottell—his life and work', *Trans. Bib. Soc.*, vol. viii, 1927–8, pp. 199–232.

[3] *S.P. Dom.* Eliz., vol. cxcv, No. 132, quoted in full in Tawney and Power, *Tudor Economic Documents*, vol. ii, pp. 251–4. The unknown author of this cites the example of 'Remigeus in his paper' as one of a number of unsuccessful attempts to set up industries in England.

[4] See *infra*, pp. 52–53.

early decades of the next witnessed the flowering of a number of new enterprises in English economic life. In spite of many years of warfare and of depression in the traditional branches of trade during the 1580's and 1590's, new developments were not lacking either then or during the more peaceful years which followed. Not only were English merchants pushing farther afield in overseas trade but at home there was enterprise amongst the newer industries: in the manufacture of iron, copper, and brass, of salt and glass, in the growth of coal-mining, and in the introduction of such new industries as alum and copperas making. The old-established and overwhelmingly important cloth industry also saw the development of new types of material, the 'New Draperies', often with the aid of foreign immigrants who also contributed their quota of skill or capital to some of the other new ventures.

This is the immediate background against which must be seen the establishment in 1588 of a paper-mill at Dartford, Kent, by John Spilman or Spielman, easily the best-known name in early English paper-making history. The story of Spilman's mill and his monopoly has been told in greater or less detail on more than one occasion.[1] The facts of Spilman's achievement do not so much need repetition as revaluation: his mill and his enterprise need to be put into perspective in their historical setting. It will suffice here to relate the main outlines of the story.[2]

Spilman was a German who having immigrated to England so prospered in his trade or profession that he

[1] Jenkins, pp. 162–7; G. H. Overend, loc. cit., pp. 180–95, who gives probably the most detailed account; Hunter, pp. 119–21 nn.; see also W. R. Scott, *The Constitution and Finance of English, Scottish and Irish Joint Stock Companies to 1720* (Cambridge, 1910–12), vol. i, pp. 116–17.

[2] The account which follows has largely been derived from the sources noted above.

came to occupy the office of 'Goldsmyth of our Jewelles' to Elizabeth I and James I. In 1588 he was granted a Crown lease of two mills in the royal manor of Bignours and situated on the River Darenth near Dartford. The mills seem to have been in Spilman's possession before then, and he carried out extensive repairs and alterations in the course of converting them into a paper-mill, at a cost estimated by a contemporary to have been at least £1,400 or £1,500.[1] Meanwhile he seems to have continued the doubtless lucrative tasks of his office. It must be remembered that the England of the time knew neither a banking system nor funded debt; amongst the props of the revenue in the Crown's chaotic finances were many merchant financiers who combined patriotism with profit by making or arranging for loans to the Crown. Gresham, already an eminent merchant, had risen to greater wealth and fame by his activities as the Crown's financial agent in Antwerp. It seems likely that on a much smaller scale Spilman's official position carried with it similar attractive possibilities both for financial transactions and for dealing in precious stones.[2] The State Papers contain numerous references to Spilman, especially during James I's reign, and are mostly concerned with payments for jewels supplied as well as for 'principal and interest of money due to him'.[3] In 1605,

[1] The former rent of the mills was £10 and in consideration of Spilman's outlay the new paper-mill was leased to him at £4 p.a. In 1597 Spilman was granted a Crown lease of the manor as a whole and in 1605 a Crown grant in fee-farm of the manor (Overend, loc. cit., p. 182).

[2] Spilman was not unique as an immigrant jeweller who rose to wealth on Crown service and finance: Sir Peter Vanlore, for example, a native of Utrecht who was knighted in England in 1624, rose to financial eminence in this country after having been one of the Crown jewellers in 1604; so also did Philip Jacobson, a Flemish immigrant who was one of the King's jewellers in 1624 (R. Ashton, *Government Borrowing under the first two Stuarts*, unpublished Ph.D. thesis (London, 1953), pp. 596–7).

[3] In 1615, for example, he advanced £3,000 on the security of various

at the same time as he secured the freehold of the manor
of Bignours, he was knighted by James I. But not, one
imagines, simply for having set up a paper-mill. He apparently continued his business activities as goldsmith
and jeweller in these later years though we hear nothing
of him as a paper-maker. He died in 1626 and is com-
memorated in Dartford parish church with a tomb, including coloured effigies of himself and his first wife, fit
and proper for a Jacobean gentleman.[1]

Whether Spilman himself knew anything about the
techniques of paper-making is doubtful. In all probability he did not, though as a German he may well have
had a greater chance of being acquainted with the industry than as an Englishman. He was an entrepreneur
who financed the establishment of a paper-mill almost
certainly from the profits of his trade and office and who
arranged also for the importation of the necessary skilled
German workmen to make the paper. And he was seemingly successful. His mill made white paper, apparently
of good quality, though for how long and in what sort of
quantity is not known.

There are two main reasons, apart from this success,
for the attention which has been paid to Spilman's mill.
One is that it was the subject of 44 eight-lined stanzas of
eulogistic doggerel by Thomas Churchyard.[2] Printed in
1588 and dedicated to Sir Walter Raleigh, the poem was

royal diamonds (*S.P. Dom.* Jas. I, vol. lxxx, Nos. 60-63. See also *Cal. S.P.
Dom.* 1581-90, pp. 418, 714; ibid. 1603-10, pp. 574-5; ibid., 1611-18,
pp. 46, 91, 280, &c.).

[1] A photograph of the tomb will be found in Dard Hunter, *Papermaking
through Eighteen Centuries* (N.Y. 1930), facing p. 27.

[2] 'A Description and playne Discourse of Paper and the whole benefitts
that Paper brings, with rehearsall, and setting forth in Verse a Paper-Myll
built near Darthford, by an High Germaine, called Master Spilman,
Jeweller to the Queen's Majestie', in *A Sparke of Friendship and Warme Good-
Will.*

reprinted early in the nineteenth century.[1] It has no obvious literary merit nor has it technical interest save in that it is the first description of paper-making to appear in English. It is platitudinous, repetitious, and probably inaccurate. But it is better than nothing and certain conclusions may very tentatively be drawn from it. Firstly, the mill itself—discounting some of Churchyard's enthusiasm but assuming his description not to be totally fictitious—seems to have been impressive and to have attracted attention:

> This is so fine with workmanship set foorth
> So surely built, and planted in the ground
> That it doth seeme a house of some estate

and

> To which brave mill do thousands still repayre
> So see what things are wrought, by cunning skill . . ..

It was in short something of an exception and curiosity. Like Tate's mill a century or so earlier, it was visited by the reigning monarch.[2] Secondly, all Churchyard's references to what is made there evidently relate to white paper, i.e. he is concerned with the mill as producing white paper rather than brown. Perhaps as befits a poet he thinks of paper only as something for writing and never as something for wrapping. In other words, there may have been several mills making wrapping paper, but Churchyard would probably never have noticed or heard of them.

The other main reason for our acquaintance with Spilman's mill is the fact that he was granted extensive monopoly powers which aroused controversy and dispute. By a patent of February 1589 it was decreed that:

[1] In J. Nichols, *The Progresses of Queen Elizabeth* (London, 1823), vol. ii, pp. 592–602.
[2] When James I knighted Spilman in 1605

(*a*) Spilman should have a monopoly of buying or dealing in linen rags, old fishing nets, leather shreds, &c., '. . . fitt for making all sorts of white paper'; (*b*) all persons were forbidden to build any mill for making any paper, save with the licence and assent of Spilman; (*c*) all persons were forbidden to make any paper in any mills 'alreadye made erected or used for broune paper mills', save with the licence and assent of Spilman. It was also provided that should Spilman use the rags, &c., for making anything other than white writing-paper or should he discontinue its manufacture, then the grant was to become void.[1] In July 1597 on the surrender of the old patent, Spilman was granted a new patent for fourteen years which confirmed his privileges and also granted extensive powers to Spilman or his deputies together with a Constable or other officer to search anywhere they suspected rags or paper to be concealed.

It is clear from the terms of the first grant that the monopoly was originally required to cover the manufacture of white paper; at that stage Spilman was probably not interested in the manufacture of brown save in so far as he was anxious to prevent existing brown mills from attempting to make white. Such mills had apparently been set up, whether then working or no, and the wording suggests that they were regarded as specifically built for the production of brown, i.e. that they were to be distinguished from such as his mill, built to make white. But monopolistic powers, however generous, are not a magic wand with which to dispel all economic difficulties.

That existing mills making brown paper were likely to try to attract away from Spilman the workmen whom he had imported and who were no doubt skilled at making

[1] P.R.O. C. 66/1331.

white paper is suggested, as Jenkins has observed, by the issue of a warrant in 1588 to 'make stay of all High-Germans' who were employed by Spilman.[1] Then in 1601, during a conflict with the City of London over the collection of rags, the City authorities went so far as to emphasize that Spilman was not the first to erect mills in this country, pointing to those set up at Osterley, Cambridge, and in Worcestershire and elsewhere.[2] And at about the same time, in the course of a complaint to the Privy Council that John Turner, Edward Marshall, and George Friend had violated his patent by building a paper-mill in Buckinghamshire and by collecting rags, Spilman wrote in terms that suggested he was beset by the same sort of difficulties which others had met in trying to make white paper in this country:

those accused by him 'doe daily gather upp collect and ingrosse the said comodities and most especially the best and finest stuff thereof, wherewith your Sup[t] doth use to make the white writyng paper, and for want thereof your Sup[t] mills are often in danger to stand still to his exceeding great damage. . . . By gathering and ingrossing into their hands the finest and best of the said comodities this *Petitioner is forced to make browne paper* where otherwise he would make writyng paper, and by means of them and *others* he is like to have small benefitt of her Ma[ts] graunt' [my italics].[3]

Leaving this for the present without further comment it will be convenient now to move on to consider the relevant features of the industry's growth during, roughly, the first three-quarters of the seventeenth century.

[1] *Cal. S.P. Dom.* 1581–80, p. 556; Jenkins, p. 163.
[2] *Cal. S.P. Dom.* 1601–3, pp. 43–44. The Worcestershire mill may have been that which was possibly established at Hurcott in 1600 (A. H. Shorter, 'Paper Mills in Worcestershire', loc. cit.).
[3] Quoted Jenkins, pp. 163–4. See also *Cal. S.P. Dom.* 1598–1601, p. 505.

For this period we have records of the existence of a much larger number of mills than for the sixteenth century and earlier. In his study of the historical geography of the industry in England, Dr. A. H. Shorter has noted the existence of thirty-seven paper-mills between 1588 and 1650;[1] by 1670 the total was probably about fifty or more. The industry was making its mark at last after the false starts of the earlier period. As Fig. 1 shows,[2] many of these mills were concentrated in the Home Counties of Buckinghamshire, Kent, Middlesex, and Surrey, though there were others farther afield. In bringing about this concentration there was at work the powerful magnet of London, the greatest market for paper and the centre of rag supplies.[3] Buckinghamshire in particular came to the forefront in this period, a number of mills springing up in the south of the county between High Wycombe and the Thames, especially along the valley of the little River Wye. The industry also found a foothold in Scotland. Monopoly powers were granted in 1590 to a German paper-maker and his co-partners, and with the financial backing of a leading Scottish merchant, Mungo Russell, a paper-mill was established at Dalry, Edinburgh. It was perhaps from this mill that there came the twenty-two reams of 'Scotis prenting paper' mentioned in a Scottish inventory of 1593. It survived until the seventeenth century and was joined by at least one other mill in the Edinburgh area before 1670.[4]

---

[1] A. H. Shorter, *Historical Geography*, p. 27.

[2] *Infra*, p. 57.

[3] For a detailed discussion of the factors affecting the location of mills in this period, see Shorter, *Historical Geography*, pp. 42–57.

[4] R. Waterston, 'Early Paper Making near Edinburgh', *The Book of the Old Edinburgh Club*, vol. xxv (1945), pp. 55–60. The monopoly of 1590 was granted to John Groot Heres, but in the Dalry enterprise the active figures were Michael Keyser and John Seillar, both named in the original grant,

The great majority of these mills, English and Scottish, almost certainly made brown paper. Some did make white, probably sporadically and of poor quality. There is no evidence to show that any appreciable quantity of white writing- or printing-paper was being manufactured in this country. Of the sixteenth century Heawood remarks that 'marks likely to be those of British makers are extremely rare and apart from Tate's are confined to the last two decades'. Of the following century he has nothing to say concerning possible English watermarks before 1680.[1] That some white was being produced is suggested by observations made during a dispute between the Buckinghamshire paper-makers and the local inhabitants, the latter remarking sourly that 'the paper made is so unuseful that it will bear no ink on one side, and is sold at dearer rates than formerly'.[2] It should be added in all fairness to the paper-makers that this was merely one sour statement amongst many in the course of a lengthy complaint and so should not perhaps be taken too literally. Some similar qualification needs to be given to such remarks as that of Fuller who in 1662 implied that no paper was made in the country,[3] or that of another and later writer who, observing that we had been almost wholly supplied with white paper from France, asserted that in consequence 'no such thing as

and joint lessees of the Dalry mill from Mungo Russell's son Gideon in 1595. See also R. Chambers, *Domestic Annals of Scotland* (Edinburgh, 1858), vol. i, p. 195; W. R. Scott, 'Scottish Industrial Undertakings before the Union', *Scottish Hist. Rev.*, vol. iii (1905).

[1] Heawood, loc. cit., *Trans. Bib. Soc.*, vol. x, p. 454, and vol. xi, pp. 487 et seq.

[2] *Cal. S.P. Dom.* 1636–7, p. 373. An account of the dispute is given in Jenkins, pp. 167–9.

[3] Fuller, op. cit., p. 48: '. . . Pity the making thereof is disused, considering the vast sums yearly expended in our land for paper out of Italy, France and Germany, which might be lessened were it made in our nation.'

manufacture was attempted in the reign of Charles the Second'.[1] Evidently commentators less poetic than Churchyard also commonly equated paper with white paper. In 1684 Aubrey, mentioning two paper-mills in Wiltshire, said firmly that there was no white paper made in that county; in regard to one of these mills, that at Longdeane, near Yatton Keynell, built in 1635 by a Bristol merchant, he observed that 'it served Bristow with brown paper'.[2]

Substitute various other centres of trade and industry for Bristol, and this remark may serve to describe the role of most English paper-mills throughout the seventeenth century. The trend in brown paper imports offers some confirmation of this. Between the 1560's and the 1660's there can be no doubt that the volume of internal and external trade and all forms of economic activity calling for wrapping-paper had increased substantially. And yet the imports of brown paper had dropped to an insignificant trickle, whilst those of white continued to rise. The nature of the demand on which the early English paper industry was first established is obvious enough.

Spilman's complaint that he was forced to make brown paper may thus be seen as a portent of the times. But how far it truly applied to him is not known. The mill apparently continued at work, remaining in the family until the death of his son John in 1641. After this date the family lapsed into poverty and the mill into obscurity.[3] We hear no more of Spilman's fame nor Spilman's paper

[1] John Oxenford, *Essay towards finding the Ballance of our whole Trade, 1698–1719*, quoted G. N. Clark, *Guide to English Commercial Statistics, 1698–1782* (London, 1938), p. 121.

[2] *Natural History of Wiltshire*, p. 95.

[3] J. Dunkin, *History and Antiquities of Dartford* (London, 1844), pp. 305–6. In the 1680's the mill was apparently in the possession of William Blackwell, allegedly a former apprentice at the mill.

until he was rediscovered in the nineteenth century. In brief his success as a maker of white paper was probably temporary, as was that of his predecessors. It may have been of longer duration than theirs but it was still far from complete. In 1640 another patent for the sole manufacture of white paper was granted. The petitioners were Endymion Porter, John and Edward Reade, and John Wakeman. The results of this enterprise are unknown. 'Having learnt how to make white writing paper', the petitioners desired 'to set the art on foot in England'. The Attorney-General reported: 'I have considered this petition and conceive that the art of making writing paper being a new invention not heretofore used in this kingdom, your Majesty may grant the same'.[1] So much for Spilman. He is well known in English industrial history largely because he enjoyed publicity from a poet and patents from a monarch. But neither these nor the money which he invested in building his mill nor the German workmen whom he brought over were ultimately able to overcome the obstacles which then beset all attempts to put on a sound footing the manufacture in England of white paper.

The nature of these obstacles was twofold. First, there was the problem of the requisite skills. To train men to make brown paper was one thing; to achieve the consistent manufacture of white paper suitable for writing or book printing was quite another. It is a testimony to the importance of this factor that efforts should have been made both by this country to bring foreign workers here and, by their countries of origin, to entice them back again. Tottell seems to have attempted to secure the services of French paper-makers; for he was eloquent on the subject of the way in which other Frenchmen had

[1] *Cal. S.P. Dom.*, 1640, p. 226. See also Rhys Jenkins, p. 169.

tried to frustrate their efforts, 'by practisinge the destruc-
cion of the workmen and by writing and calling them
Traytours to their Countrey, and sending men of purpose
to Slaye them, as it hathe byn credeably declared unto
me'.[1] As we shall see later, identical methods were used
a hundred years after Tottell was writing.[2] But an infinity
of skilled workmen would still have been powerless to
establish the industry whilst the second of the main
obstacles remained: an inadequate supply of linen rags.
In the sixteenth and seventeenth centuries in England
this shortage was due to the great importance of the
woollen cloth industry and the widespread use of wool;
to the absence of a native linen industry of any size; and
to the fact that such linen rags as were available tended to
be exported, particularly to France. More than one contemporary writer noted the importance of linen consumption and of a linen industry to the successful growth
of paper-making; perhaps the most specific statement
came from Charles Davenant who, writing at the turn
of the seventeenth century and commenting on the
recent improvements then made in English paper-
making, added that 'we are not come up to the French
perfection (and never can without a linnen manufacture
of our own)'.[3] Complaints about the exporting of rags
are voiced in the *Common Weal* and in Tottell's petition.
It rankled in the minds of the so-called 'mercantilist'
writers that our raw materials should be exported and
then worked up abroad by foreigners: from 'our broken
linnen cloth and ragges' they made 'paper both whit and

---

[1] Quoted Jenkins, pp. 161–2.   [2] *Infra*, pp. 70–71.
[3] C. Davenant, 'A Report to the Commssioners . . . [on] . . . the Public
Accounts of the Kingdom', in *Works*, ed. C. Whitworth (London, 1771),
vol. v, p. 372. Or, as it was put to the Board of Trade and Plantations in
1696, because wool rather than linen was used to dress the people (P.R.O.
CO. 391/90).

browne'.[1] It is a testimony to the importance placed on rag supply that Spilman should have secured such sweeping powers in this respect; they were greater than were normally granted for raw material supply in the industrial monopolies of the time. The author of the petition of 1586 wanted the export of rags forbidden;[2] a century later it was.

The result of these obstacles was simple: it was not economical to produce white paper in England. The actions and motives ascribed to the man (probably Tate) who started and abandoned a mill in this country were probably equally applicable to others: 'At the last, said he, the man perceaved that made it that he could not fourd his paper as good cheape as that came from beyond the seaze, and so he was forced to lay downe makinge of paper. And no blame to the man; for men would give never the more for his paper because it was made heare.'[3]

(ii)

In the half-century between, roughly, 1670 and 1720 the situation was changed. A major expansion in English paper production took place; the industry was developed in Scotland and Ireland; and, the most important advance, we began for the first time to produce white paper in significant quantities. We were still not self-sufficient, exports were trifling, the best qualities were imported and were to be for many years to come; many mills, perhaps a majority of them, still produced brown or the coarser grades of white. But substantial progress was made. The making of white paper was not the only branch of the industry to advance during the period. An

[1] [Hales], *Commonweal of this Realm of England*, p. 63; Jenkins, p. 159.
[2] *Tudor Economic Documents*, vol. ii, p. 252.
[3] [Hales], *Commonweal*, p. 66.

extension of capacity in the existing brown-paper industry may again be deduced from the declining or static
import figures and the certainty of an increased home
demand for wrapping-papers arising from the continuing
growth of trade. The manufacture of blue paper[1] and of
millboard[2] first attracted attention in these years. The
latter innovation provides an early example of competition within the industry by the introduction of a new
process; it was not regarded with much enthusiasm by
those paper-makers who either made pasteboard themselves or sold paper to the pasteboard makers.[3]

The evidence for general advance is diverse. Contemporary comments by economic writers all point in
this direction.[4] They can perhaps best be summed up by
the observation in *The British Merchant* that 'the Manufacture of White Paper is *almost* entirely new in this
Kingdom' and that 'before the Revolution there was
hardly any other paper made in England than brown'[5]
(my italics). The petitions and counter-petitions which
attended the launching of the White Paper Makers
Company in 1686 and the passage of the Act continuing
its powers in 1690 help to confirm the impression that
although white paper was being made by English makers
before that time it was of poor quality.[6] It was this sort of

[1] A patent was taken out in 1665 (see *infra*, pp. 61, 63), though whether
this in fact marked its introduction is not clear.
[2] See Bagford, loc. cit., who says that millboard manufacture was started
at a mill near Windsor.
[3] *The Case of the Bookbinders* (c. 1712), *Case of the Papermakers* (c. 1712),
Case of the Pasteboard Makers (c. 1712).
[4] Davenant, loc. cit.; Oxenford, loc. cit.; Houghton, op. cit., vol. ii,
pp. 401 et seq.; *The British Merchant*, vol. ii, 259–76; *Angliae Tutamen*, p. 25;
Hartlib, op. cit., p. 150; *Reasons humbly offered . . . for laying a further duty . . .*
(c. 1699); Sir Theodore Janssen, 'General Maxims in Trade' (1713), in
Somers Tracts (1751), vol. xvi, pp. 147–54.   [5] Vol. ii, p. 269.
[6] *C.J.*, vol. x, pp. 333, 365, 372, 412–13; H.M.C.: *House of Lords MSS.*,
1691, pp. 74–76; *Cal. S.P. Dom.*, 1700–2, pp. 552–3.

paper, perhaps, that John Evelyn saw being made when he visited the paper-mills at Byfleet, Surrey, in 1678 and described as 'a coarse white paper'.[1] To the evidence of contemporary comment there can be added that relating to the number of mills. Estimates made during this period range from 100 in the 1690's to 150 in 1710 and 200 in 1711–12.[2] Striking as this last figure is, it has the support of the Excise authorities, for at the same time they gave the total of paper-makers as 209 in England and Wales and seven in Scotland.[3] As Fig. 1 shows, the industry had spread farther afield, although the continuing dominance of London had also ensured a large increase in the number of mills in the Home Counties.[4] These were again mainly concentrated in Buckinghamshire and Kent which became the main English paper-making counties. In Scotland most of the early mills were set up, as might be expected, near Edinburgh and Glasgow.[5]

Increasing output and the growth of the industry in such seaboard counties as Kent, Devon, and Hampshire, are reflected, too, in the records of coastwise trade. Though paper was often shipped coastwise, from London and elsewhere, earlier in the century,[6] most of this was probably of foreign origin. Increasingly, however, paper figuring in the coastal trade was noted as being English made. Much of it was still brown, though white was also mentioned. Rochester, for example, in 1699–1700 shipped

---

[1] *Diary* (ed. 1895), p. 401.

[2] P.R.O. CO. 391/90; *Case of the Paper Traders* (*c.* 1696–7); *Case of the Merchants Importing Genoa Paper* (*c.* 1710); *Proposals for raising £40,000 or upwards by laying Additional Duties on Foreign Papers* . . . etc. (*c.* 1711–12).

[3] C. and E.: Excise-Treasury Letters, 1693/4–1721/2, f. 62.

[4] For the sources from which Fig. 1 was derived see App. I.

[5] See *infra*, pp. 77–79.

[6] T. S. Willan, *The English Coasting Trade, 1600–1750* (Manchester, 1938), pp. 109, 130, 141, 154.

FIG. 1. Distribution of Mills to 1720 (England)

to London 3,458 reams of paper and nearly 80 tons of pasteboard and 'parchboard', much of it probably having been made in the Maidstone area.[1] Farther west Southampton shipped paper—brown, white, writing, and blue—from 1685 onwards; sometimes it went to such south-western ports as Falmouth, Dartmouth, and Exeter, and sometimes to London.[2] Small coastal exports of paper from Exeter are recorded from 1700 onwards, mostly to Dartmouth or other local ports and to London.[3]

After 1713 we also have evidence of the scale of domestic production from the Excise returns. These returns and the estimates of production based on them are discussed in greater detail in later chapters. Meanwhile it will suffice to note that the estimate appearing in *The British Merchant* in 1721 to the effect that we were producing 'near two-thirds of what is consumed in Great Britain' was probably not far wrong.[4] A calculation made in 1696–7 suggests that we were producing about 42 per cent. *by value* of total consumption;[5] a calculation based on the Excise returns and the trade statistics and covering the five-year period 1714–18 suggests that we were pro-

[1] Other Kentish ports shipping paper, mainly brown, in increasing quantities during this period were Faversham and Dover (P.R.O. E 190/677/2, 4, 17 and 678/6, 14, 17. Smaller shipments from the same ports are recorded in E. 190/661/17 and 663/13 (Dover 1663–4, 1675–6) and 661/8 (Faversham 1662–3).

[2] Southampton's annual average coastal shipments of all types of paper in 1685–9 were about 370 reams and in 1607–1701 over 1,800 reams (E. 190/834–5 and 840/4).

[3] E. 190/975 et seq. For other references to coastal trade in paper see Willan, op. cit., pp. 109, 116, 124, 127, 131, 148, 157, 158, 162, 168, 175, 185.

[4] Vol. ii, p. 269.

[5] *Case of the Paper Traders.* The authors of the 1696–7 calculation had reason to under-estimate home production and those of the 1721 calculation to over-estimate it. Moreover, calculations by value would further tend to produce a lower percentage for home production as our output still tended to be of sorts of paper inferior in value to those imported. So, allowing also for increases in output between 1696–7 and 1721, the discrepancy may not be quite so great as it at first sight seems.

ducing nearly 300,000 reams or about 71 per cent. *by quantity* from a total consumption of some 418,000.[1] These estimates are all very approximate, but the not displeasing proximity of 66⅔ per cent. to 71 per cent. may perhaps be taken as a rough indication of the ratio of home production to total consumption at the end of the period with which we are concerned. It only remains to consider this in the light of the import figures given earlier for it to become obvious that the decline in imports there revealed was paralleled by a genuine and substantial increase in home production.

What were the forces which brought this about?

Of the stimulus from increasing demand enough has been said in Chapter I. The market was there: it was for home producers to capture it from foreign suppliers. It is thus the problems of supply which call for investigation. How was the production of paper, in particular of white writing- and printing-paper, made a workable economic enterprise in this country?

One of the notable features of the industrial history of later Stuart England is the flood of patents for various sorts of inventions, devices, and projects as well as for many new joint stock companies. The last forty years of the seventeenth century yielded 236 patents for inventions.[2] Their direct significance to industry was not so great as this impressive total might lead one to suppose. Some were curious in name, like that 'sucking-worm engine'[3] for the development of which a joint stock com-

---

[1] See App. I for the methods by which estimates of production have been made and for the sources from which these and the trade figures have been derived; also *infra*, Fig. 2.

[2] K. G. Davies, 'Joint Stock Investment in the Later Seventeenth Century', *Economic History Review*, 2nd ser., vol. iv, No. 3, 1952, p. 285.

[3] Scott, op. cit., vol. ii, p. 481. It was in fact a water pump for fire-fighting.

pany was floated, and some were probably fraudulent. But others were of serious intention and some flowered into promising enterprises. Whatever their true significance, they betoken an energy in economic and technical life evident neither immediately before nor immediately after this period. Not until the dawn of the Industrial Revolution in the 1760's does the flood of patents again rise and then to a new and formidable level. The paper industry did not go unaffected by these bracing winds of endeavour. In the thirty years from 1665 to 1695 twelve English patents were granted for paper-making improvements, and at least six paper-making companies started in England, Scotland, Ireland, and the Channel Isles.[1] In all probability the patents contributed little to solving the technical problems of paper-making; much of the enterprise was ephemeral in its consequences. Only two interrelated ventures seem to have been of any real significance in the industry's history. As is evident from Table III, many of the patents were taken out by men

TABLE III

Patents, Patentees, and Companies in Paper-making, 1665–95

Year	Patentee or Company	Other known interests of Patentee
	1. *For the manufacture of white and/or other paper*	
1675	Eustace Burnaby	Petitioned for linen-weaving patent, 1687.
1682	George Hagar (formed a paper-making company)	Petitioned (with William Sutton) for patent for waterproofing cloth, 1691; company started, 1694.
1685	John Briscoe	Founded National Land Bank, 1695; concerned with Copper Mining Company, 1691.

[1] *Abridgements of the Specification relating to the Manufacture of Paper, Pasteboard and Papier-Maché* (H.M. Patent Office), pt. i, 1665–1857; details of the patents are also given in Jenkins, pp. 170–3; Scott, op. cit., vol. iii, pp. 63–72, 181–5.

Year	Patentee or Company	Other known interests of Patentee
1686	Nicholas Dupin and others (Company of White Paper Makers in England)	(Dupin) founded: English Linen Corporation, 1690, Irish Linen Corporation, 1691, Scots Linen Company, 1691–3, Company for working mines and minerals in Scotland, 1695.
1690	Nicholas Dupin (Irish Paper Company)	
1691	Company for Linen and Paper Manufacture in Jersey and Guernsey	..
1691	Blue Paper Company*	..
1692	Brown Paper Company	..
1695	Nicholas Dupin and others (Scots White Paper Manufactory)	..
	2. For rag-preparation devices	
1682	Nathaniell Bladen	..
1684	Christopher Jackson	..
1691	John Tyzack	Patent for new method of tanning and making imitation Russian leather; company started, 1691. Two patents (with Thomas Neale) one for making Venetian steel, company started 1692; the other for a lead-mining venture, 1692–3. Petitioned for patents for making screens with iron wire, 1693; and for raising ships wrecked at sea, 1691.
1692	Thomas Hutton	..
	3. For manufacture of blue or other coloured paper	
1665	Charles Hildeyard	..
1691	Nathaniel Gifford	..
1692	Patrick Gordon (Ireland only)	..
	4. For manufacture of pressing-paper	
1684	Robert Fuller	..
	5. For a finishing process	
	Peter Oliver	..
	6. Unsuccessful petitions	
1691	Peter Gaultier (for making fine paper)	..
1692	Thomas Neale (for making white, brown, and blue paper without using rags)	Patent for constructing water-works at Shadwell, 1681. Petitions and patents in connexion with schemes for recovering treasure from ships wrecked at sea, 1691–1702. Two patents with Tyzack, as above.

* Possibly associated with Thomas Neale's patent and apparently concerned with paper-staining rather than paper manufacture.

Source: The table has been constructed largely from Scott, op. cit., passim.

who were by no means paper-makers but belonged rather to that mixed group of persons in which the company promoter and the professional inventor are familiar figures. It is quite impossible to say whether the patents were taken out to cover genuine technical inventions or simply to provide a basis for a joint stock company.

In group (1) in the table Hagar's patent covered an improved method of sizing the paper. It seems most improbable, however, that his method came into use,[1] though he certainly went into operation in the industry, leasing a mill at Eynsham, Oxfordshire, and building another at Stanwell, Middlesex; a company was apparently formed and at least £6,000 paid for shares; in 1690 he claimed that for the preceding three years he had 'employed several mills in the County of Surrey'. However, Hagar, who was a dyer, had been made a bankrupt as early as 1677 as a result of his outstanding debts to a cloth factor and the financial basis of his paper-making ventures was decidedly insecure.[2] Of Eustace Burnaby little is known. He is reported as having made printing-paper at a mill near Windsor some time between 1675 and 1678; in 1685 he petitioned the Commons without success for permission to bring in a Bill to encourage paper-making.[3]

The patents in group (2) testify to the inadequacy of existing methods of rag-preparation. It is tempting to see in those of Bladen and Jackson an echo of the 'Hollander', the improved rag-beating engine invented about 1670

---

[1] It entailed the adding of size to the stuff before making the sheet of paper. This anticipated the 'engine-sizing' of a much later period; there is no indication that this came into use in the late seventeenth or early eighteenth centuries.

[2] H.M.C.: *House of Lords MSS.*, 1691, pp. 435–7, 497–8; *C.J.*, vol. x, p. 365; also Jenkins, p. 173, and Scott, op. cit., vol. iii, pp. 63–64.

[3] *C.J.*, vol. ix, p. 744; Jenkins, p. 170.

or 1680 in Holland, known to have been used there in
1682 and in Germany about 1712; it was first described
in detail in 1718.[1] Its principle of operation remains unchanged today. The earliest Hollanders consisted roughly
of a tub or drum in which there was made to rotate, by
wind- or water-power, a solid wooden roller fitted with
iron knives or teeth. The rags, mixed with water, were
macerated between the roll and a metal or stone bed-
plate set immediately below it.[2] Did the English patents
cover such a device as this? Hutton's clearly did not, for
it was 'to worke Eighty or more Stampers at once,
different from all other Mills now used'. Tyzack's
covered 'an Engine to be worked by one or more Men',
which could hardly apply to the Hollander. So Bladen's
and Jackson's remain and the specifications of them are
so vague as to be almost meaningless. In fact there is no
adequate evidence that the Hollander was introduced
into England through these patents or at this time.[3] The
patents may equally well have covered some improved
form of stamper such as was described in Chapter II.

Amongst the other patents Hildeyard's which covered
the making of 'blew paper used by sugar bakers and
others' was supported in 1666 by a proclamation against
the import or sale of foreign blue paper.[4] To judge by the
import figures (Table I), this was not long operative and
Hildeyard could scarcely have met his promise to 'supply
the kingdom sufficiently and at reasonable rates'.[5] On
the fate of Gifford, Gordon, Fuller, and Oliver, history at
present remains silent; Fuller's patent for making paper
and pasteboard to be used for cloth pressing is an evident

---

[1] Hunter, pp. 163–6.
[2] The Hollander made it possible to dispense with the lengthy fermentation process.
[3] On the subsequent spread of the Hollander see *infra*, pp. 109–11.
[4] *Cal. S.P. Dom.*, 1666, p. 558.   [5] Ibid.

reflection of the demands of the cloth industry; he himself was described as a 'bays maker'. Neither the company for making paper in the Channel Islands nor the Brown Paper Company seems to have had any lasting importance.

There remain, therefore, John Briscoe, Nicholas Dupin, and the companies with which the latter was concerned. These ventures merit some detailed attention. But their very existence and indeed the whole growth of paper-making in these islands during this period owed much to three influences which were largely, though not entirely, extraneous to the paper industry: Anglo-French political and economic relations, English commercial policy, and the religious upheavals in France which led to the emigration of the Huguenots.

From the many chapters of antipathy in the story of Anglo-French relations it will suffice to select a few relevant points. French imports had long been viewed with distrust. The goods which France sent us in the sixteenth and seventeenth centuries fell into three clear categories: wines and brandy; silks, linen, and paper; and a multitude of more or less luxurious odds and ends. In the interests of the balance of trade the first and the last could be, and were, frequently stigmatized as unnecessary and demoralizing. To some extent the same argument was applied to silks, but as the seventeenth century progressed the import of the three commodities in the middle category was usually opposed on the grounds that it hampered the growth of the corresponding English industries. The worsening of relations under the weight of mounting tariffs on either side became very marked in the years after the Restoration.[1] In 1663 and 1674 there

---

[1] See in general, on this subject, E. Lipson, *Economic History of England* (4th ed., London, 1947), vol. iii, pp. 99 et seq.; also M. Priestley, 'Anglo-French Trade and the "Unfavourable Balance" Controversy, 1660–85', *Economic History Review*, 2nd ser., vol. iv, No. 1, 1951, pp. 37–52.

appeared two much-publicized calculations designed to show that England annually lost £1 million and more by trade with France.¹ In these circumstances of agitation and protest there was passed in 1678 an Act which prohibited the import of all the major French imported wares, including paper, on the ground that it 'exhausted the treasure of the realm'. The Act was repealed in 1685. But when the peace-time weapons of commercial antagonism were not in operation, those of war were. Thus for one reason or another trade with France was interrupted from 1666 to 1667, from 1678 to 1685, from 1689 to 1697, and from 1703 to 1713.²

The effect of this was both to stimulate home production and to bring about the switch to other sources of supply which was illustrated in Chapter I. Both effects applied to linen as well as to paper. The native linen industry was advancing and linen imports continued to arrive from Holland, Germany, and the Baltic countries; at the same time there was also an increase both in the import of cotton goods and in the home production of mixtures of linen and cotton.³ Moreover, the increased activity of paper-makers helped to attract more rags into the market, although it also raised their price. Most rags came from London; in remote areas, the rags were 'wholly lost'; but wherever there were mills, not a house in thirty or forty miles' radius but was called upon once a week. So, at least, it was claimed in 1696.⁴ It is reasonable to assume that these developments helped to

¹ Samuel Fortrey, *England's Interest and Improvement* (London, 1663), contained a calculation which put the loss at £1,600,000. A document called *A Scheme of Trade as it is at present carried on between England and France*, which was drawn up in 1674 by a number of prominent merchants, put the annual loss at about £1,000,000 (Somers, *Tracts*, vol. iv, p. 537).

² Lipson, op. cit., vol. iii, pp. 104–8.

³ Ibid., pp. 94–98, 109–11.

⁴ P.R.O. CO. 391/90.

alleviate the long-run shortage of rags, although it certainly did not prevent a short-run scarcity as the industry expanded.[1]

Allied to these general tendencies in Anglo-French economic relations were a number of developments which had the particular effect of protecting and encouraging the paper industry. From about the 1690's onwards it is evident that the paper-makers were beginning to be able to make themselves heard as an economic interest. Fortunately for them their views coincided with prevailing anti-French feelings as well as with the desire to foster home industry as a whole. So it is not surprising that these two should have been combined with the ever-present needs of government revenue to justify the raising of Customs duties on imported paper; there was thus created a protective barrier around the English paper industry which was to last until the mid-nineteenth century. Details of this and of its long-run effects are considered in later chapters.[2] Meanwhile it is necessary to outline the commencement of this policy and to indicate the forces which helped to bring it into being.

Up to 1690 paper was normally subject to a 5 per cent. *ad valorem* import duty. In 1690 the rate was doubled on most sorts of paper, increased on others; by 1700 the rates on paper, as on other goods, had been further increased, reaching 15 per cent. *ad valorem*.

---

[1] An Act of 1696 (8 & 9 Wm. III, c. 7 and 8, s. xxvii) claimed that there were enough white linen rags for making writing-paper for the home market and for export if they were not mixed up with other rags and used for making brown paper. This must not be taken too literally, as the Act was secured at the instigation of the White Paper Makers Company (see P.R.O. CO. 388/5, 389/14). The Act ordered that white linen rags should not be used for making brown paper.

The celebrated enactments requiring that the dead should be buried in woollen also had as one of their aims the lessening of the consumption of linen that might otherwise go to the making of paper (see 30 Chas. II, c. 3).

[2] See Chap. V and Chap. XII.

Meanwhile, however, for two years only, 1696/7–1698/9, an Excise on paper was introduced and combined with a substantially higher rate of import duty.[1] Both the passing and the expiry of this Act were attended by a good deal of pamphleteering, the general gist of which was to lament the weight of the Excise and, after the 'New Subsidy' of 1698, the lightness of a mere 15 per cent. on imports. With visions of peace came visions of a flood of paper imports; and as Table I shows, the flood duly arrived. These years were full of lamentations from the newly and recently thriving paper-makers.[2] In 1698 William Blaithwaite, on behalf of the Commissioners of Trade and Plantations, reported to the Commons that imported paper should pay a higher duty than that made at home;[3] in the following year a petition of the 'Principal White Paper Makers' to the Commons said exactly the same thing, adding simply that the duty on all foreign paper, except French, was 'so low that it tends to a vast importation and to the destruction of the English manufacture'.[4] War and the Whigs came to the industry's aid. In 1703 and 1704 the rates on all imports were further raised; in 1712 came a new set of import duties on paper as well as an Excise on home production; two years later

---

[1] An additional 25 per cent. on all imports of paper and books, 20 per cent. on home-produced paper, and 17½ per cent. to be paid by dealers on stocks of paper, with effect from Mar. 1696/7 (8 & 9 Wm. III, c. 7). A further 5 per cent. was added to the import duty by 8 & 9 Wm. III, c. 24, from May 1697 to Feb. 1699/1700. 'The New Subsidy' of 1698 came into effect as from Feb. 1699/1700.

[2] It was alleged that manufacturers were forced to turn to the making of brown instead of white paper. See *Reasons . . . for Further additional duties on Paper*; also *A Proposal for building a Royal Library*; *Case of the Paper Makers*; *Reasons against . . . a further Duty on Paper*; *C.J.*, vol. xiii, p. 184. An attempt to continue a high duty on both home production and imports was defeated in 1699 (*C.J.*, vol. xii, pp. 648 et seq.; H.M.C.: *House of Lords MSS.*, 1697–9, pp. 424–34).

[3] *C.J.*, vol. xii, p. 435.   [4] Ibid., vol. xiii, p. 184.

these rates were increased by 50 per cent. The differential between import and Excise duties was such as to be markedly protective. Furthermore, throughout this time all French goods—when not prohibited entirely—had been saddled with additional heavy duties: 25 per cent. in 1692/3, a further 25 per cent. in 1696/7.[1] And then, finally, Tory attempts to include a treaty of commerce with the French as part of the Treaty of Utrecht were defeated by a combination of the Whigs and all those vested interests, including paper, which had gained by the restrictions on French imports.

The immigration of the Huguenots before and after the revocation of the Edict of Nantes in 1685 brought new influences to bear upon the English paper industry. The story of their achievements and experiences is complex, their significance hard to assess.[2]

In 1685 Adam de Cardonell, Nicholas Dupin, and Elias de Gruchy petitioned the Crown for permission to put the royal arms on their paper. They claimed to have set up a mill in Hampshire and to have imported several skilled French workmen. They produced some paper of their manufacture which duly satisfied the Privy Council, and their petition was granted.[3] These persons, be it noted, were not recently arrived French paper-makers: de Cardonell was a Collector of Customs at Southampton, Dupin a Clerk of the Reports at Plymouth garrison, and de Gruchy a Southampton alderman.[4] In January

---

[1] For details of all these duties see *infra*, p. 124.

[2] On the Huguenots and the paper industry see Overend, loc. cit.; W. C. Scoville, 'The Huguenots and the Diffusion of Technology', *Journal of Political Economy*, vol. lx, No. 4, 1952, pp. 302–3.

[3] P.R.O. Privy Council Reports (P.C. 2/71, ff. 88 and 169).

[4] R. H. George, 'A Mercantilist Episode', *Journal of Business and Economic History*, vol. iii, 1930–1, pp. 264–71; W. Moens, 'Walloon Settlements and the French Church at Southampton', *Proceedings of the Huguenot Society of London*, vol. iii, pp. 63 et seq., 76.

1686 these three together with Marin Regnault, James de May, and Robert Shales petitioned for, and were granted, a patent for 'the art of making all sorts of writing and printing paper'.[1] Meanwhile John Briscoe, whose very similar patent granted earlier in 1685 had contained the significant phrase '. . . for making English paper . . . as white as any French or Dutch paper', had counter-petitioned.[2] Amalgamation was the order of the day. In June 1686 a petition was received from twenty-eight persons including Briscoe, Bladen, de Cardonnel, Dupin, and their associates, and a number of other persons with French names.[3] On the basis of this a charter of incorporation was granted in the following month, setting up the 'Governor and Company of White Paper Makers in England' and granting a monopoly for fourteen years of making all types of writing- and printing-paper.[4] The Company strengthened its position in 1690 by securing the passage of a private Act for 'encouraging and better establishing the manufacture of white paper in this kingdom'. By this its monopoly was confirmed and extended for a further fourteen years, i.e. to 1704, though in deference to the opposition of the 'ancient' paper-makers it was now restricted to the manufacture of paper worth over 4s. per ream.[5] The export of linen rags was

[1] Patent No. 249, Jan. 1686; details also given in Jenkins, p. 172.

[2] P.R.O. P.C. 2/71, f. 274. He claimed here to have spent £10,000 on his 'New Invention of Paper Workes'. His patent, No. 246, July 1685, is quoted in Jenkins, p. 172.

[3] P.R.O. P.C. 2/71, f. 278; S.P. Dom. Entry Book 71, f. 268; the names are given in Overend, loc. cit.

[4] Patent Roll, 2 Jas. II, part 10, No. 17; see Jenkins, p. 175; Overend, loc. cit.; and Scott, op. cit., vol. ii, p. 64. The governor was John Dunston, the deputy governor Nicholas Dupin, and the members included Briscoe and Bladen as well as de Cardonnel, de Gruchy, and others.

[5] House of Lords MSS.: Act to Encourage the Manufacture of White Paper, 2 Wm. & Mary, No. 25. See Scott, op. cit., vol. iii, pp. 65–66, and Jenkins, pp. 175–7.

prohibited in 1686/7 by proclamation[1] and continued by this Act. So, too, were the provisions of a proclamation of 1687 authorizing the Company to empower someone at each of its mills with the rights of a Constable in order to apprehend persons of evil intentions.[2]

Who were these persons? The preamble to the Act stated that the Company had 'erected several mills at great charge and with great hazards of their persons and estates (the said attempts being highly opposed by the ministers and agents of the French King)'. This is an interesting echo of Tottell's complaint of just over a hundred years earlier. There is evidence from both English and French sources that the allegations had some truth. The important French industry was sharply hit by the emigration to Holland, Germany, and Britain of skilled Protestant paper-makers. Many mills are said to have been closed down, thus adversely affecting output and the lucrative export trade.[3] In an age and an industry in which personal skills meant so much it was natural that the French should have taken steps to recover some of those who had emigrated.

Many of these steps were taken or at any rate guided by Barillon, the French ambassador in London.[4] The methods adopted to secure the return of the French workers and the destruction of the English paper industry ranged from bribery to physical violence and included sabotage on the way. Within a few months after the Company's incorporation Barillon was reporting

[1] P.R.O. P.C. 2/71, 11 Mar. 1686/7. It also prohibited the export of items used in making size, e.g. 'Glovers' clippings, Parchment Shreds, Calves Pates and Water Pieces.'

[2] Ibid., ff. 419–20, 29 Apr. 1687.

[3] See Overend, loc. cit., and Scoville, loc. cit.

[4] His activities in particular and this subject in general are examined partly by Overend and more fully by George, loc. cit., from which the account that follows is largely derived.

that he had sent back one skilled paper-maker and several workmen. His success in these activities was in part due to the activities of Daniel Juilhard who was one of the signatories of the original petition of June 1686. He was a skilled paper-maker and had been installed by the Company as head of its mill at Colnbrook. In 1687 the Company brought a successful action against Theodore Janssen, then a young merchant engaged in the French trade and thus in importing paper. It alleged that he had instigated the absconding of Juilhard in November 1686 and had enticed away two other workmen, Stephen Anthoyne and Nicholas Brochard.[1] In 1687 the Company complained that five of its workmen had been enticed away; Juilhard was apprehended and was accused by the Company of various acts of sabotage at the mill. It was these activities that lay behind the proclamation of 1687. That there was justification in the allegations of the Company is evident from Barillon's correspondence. He records paying a special reward to a French paper-maker to come to this country in order to persuade his confrères to leave England, and paying for the passage to France of five workers from the mill at Colnbrook as well as sweetening them with bonuses. He contrived the return to France of another five paper-makers in November 1687, amongst whom were Anthoyne and Brochard. And finally he records the payment of a bonus to Juilhard whose release from jail he secured and who was in time safely sent home to Angoulême.

For a time the Company seems to have weathered these

[1] Janssen, described as a naturalized subject, was presumably the same person who was later to flower into Sir Theodore Janssen, financier, a director of, *inter alia*, the South Sea Company, and a writer on commercial matters (see *infra*, p. 143). He was fined £500 and in June 1687 petitioned against this, claiming that he was 'a young trader, ignorant of the laws'; the fine was reduced to £100.

contrived storms. The original terms of the joint stock provided for a capital of £100,000 of which £20,000 was initially subscribed in £50 shares. The Act of 1690 provided for a new subscription. The only quotations of the stock given by Scott[1] are as follows:

(par=50)

1692	Mar. 60			*1694*	Jan.	94
	May 41			2 & 9 Feb.	98
	June 49			16	,,	105
1693	Jan. 65–67			23	,,	} 120
	Apr. 70			2 Mar.	
	May 69			9	,,	} 150
	July 59			16	,,	
13 Sept. 70			23	,,	
28	,, 80			Apr.	140
	Oct. 90				
	Dec. 94				

These were war years and there is every reason to think that the Company was doing well. Sales were frequently advertised in the *London Gazette* as taking place at the Company's House in Queen Street. Contemporaries wrote fulsomely of the English paper manufacture: its condition was flourishing; its paper, though not quite up to the French standard, was not far off it.[2] But depression was ahead. In addition to the cries against the lowness of the import duties, mutterings were heard against the 'pernicious art of stock-jobbing'. In October 1696 the Board of Trade and Plantations heard evidence for and against the Company's activities, and in November 1696 Blaithwaite told the Commons that the paper manufacture was one which had felt 'the effects of the stock-jobbing management' and was 'not in so thriving a condition' as it might otherwise have been.[3] He repeated

[1] Scott, op. cit., vol. iii, pp. 65–67. A dividend of £500 was advertised in the *London Gazette* (No. 3197) in July 1696.

[2] See, e.g., Davenant, loc. cit., and *Angliae Tutamen*, p. 25.

[3] *C.J.*, vol. xi, p. 595. Similar observations are to be found in a report called 'Reason why the paper manufacture in England has not succeeded' (Bodleian: Locke MSS. c. 30, f. 43). This short, and patently biased, attack

these observations in different terms in 1698,[1] and with that the White Paper Makers Company disappears from our ken until further research can reveal more of its history. To attribute economic troubles to the evils of stock-jobbing was a common gambit of the time; there is little doubt that many contemporary joint-stock companies were highly speculative ventures and that the interests of those concerned with their management often lay more in the making of speculative profits than in sound economic development. There may have been some truth in the allegation, but what is probably more significant is that the Company disappears just at the time when there are to be heard the lamentations over the level of import duties and the likely flood of imports.

It may well have been this that submerged it. Not only was 1698 a year of general depression which saw the disappearance of many joint stock ventures, but for the paper industry the immediately following years did not bring a return to prosperity. Moreover, it is certain that the growing competition for rags was forcing up rag prices,[2] and likely that this worked against the Company.

on the Company, stated also that its operations were uneconomical because, *inter alia*, it paid higher rents and wages than were necessary.

[1] *C.J.*, vol. xii, p. 435. It was in the course of these remarks that Blaithwaite reported that the eight mills of the Company 'make, as we are informed, of all sorts, about 100,000 reams per annum of White Paper'. Scott (vol. iii, p. 68) accepts this statement at face value; not only is it a wildly improbable figure, but in reality the then Governor of the Company, Paul Doeminique, only claimed in his evidence to the Board that the Company sold 50,000 reams per annum (P.R.O. CO. 391/90). Even this is unlikely. Contemporaries seem to have calculated on the assumption that one vat would produce about 2,000 reams per year. So the Company would have had to operate about twenty-five vats, and there is no evidence that they did. For the bases of these calculations see *British Merchant*, vol. ii, pp. 264–70; *Proposals . . . for raising £40,000 or upwards by laying Additional Duties on Foreign Paper*, etc. (c. 1712); and P.R.O. CO. 391/90.

[2] Houghton, op. cit., vol. ii, p. 412, states that prices per ton rose from £3. 10s. to £9 between 1682 and 1699. Similar statements are made in

The Act which the Company secured to prohibit the use of white rags in making brown paper[1] was obviously aimed at the other makers and designed to safeguard its own particular raw materials. It was equally obviously ineffective. Again, the Company was trying to produce the best grades of paper in the face of a continental industry with lower wages[2] and more experience.

The Company is said to have had five mills in 1690 and eight in 1698.[3] A calculation of 1696–7 credits the company with nearly 30 per cent. by value of total home production (the remainder being 'brown paper and the coarsest white').[4] This needs to be taken with some care as it may have been inspired by the Company. Nor do the assertions made in numerous petitions in 1686 and 1690 help to decide precisely what competition it met from other makers. For in spite of the legal monopoly it seems highly probable that before the expiry of the patent in 1704 effective competition had developed.[5]

P.R.O. CO. 391/90. See also *Angliae Tutamen*, p. 25: the author of this work maintained that 'vast quantities of Paper are daily made here', and 'the scarcity of Raggs is great and the young collectors out-do the old and go out in the night to the Dung-hills and Laystalls to tumble them over for this Merchandise which at this time are mightily call'd for'.

[1] *Supra*, p. 66, n. 1.   [2] See *infra*, pp. 143–4.

[3] H.M.C.: *House of Lords MSS.*, 1690, p. 76; *C.J.*, vol. xii, p. 435. The Governor of the Company, however, told the Board of Trade and Plantations on 7 Oct. 1696 that it had eight mills 'besides the new one at Southampton', but on the 14 Oct. 1696 that it had about twelve mills, with twenty vats. His evidence seems very dubious, for he did not 'remember' the location of mills, nor 'remember' the original capital of the company (P.R.O. CO. 391/90).

[4] *Case of the Paper Traders.*

[5] Shorter notes, for example, that a mill at Sutton Courtenay in Berkshire was making paper for bank notes from 1697 onwards; another at Taverham, Norfolk was making printing-paper in 1701; a 'compleat new White Paper Mill' was built at Huxham, Devon, in 1703 (*Historical Geography*, pp. 67–68). There is no reason to suppose that the Company was concerned with these mills, though conversely it must be admitted that it is not known where precisely the Company's mills were. Colnbrook, Southampton, Dartford, and Byfleet are more or less certain locations of mills which at one time or

Some of the statements made by the existing makers far exceeded mere special pleading. It seems improbable, for example, that there was much truth in the contention that 'the Papermakers of this kingdom, since time out of mind, make vast quantities of printing paper, as well for the use of this kingdom as for the English plantations'.[1] However, in some petitions, including that from 'The Mayor, Aldermen and other inhabitants of Chipping Wycombe in the County of Bucks', some distinction is seemingly made, a little ambiguously, between writing-paper and printing-paper. The petitioners claimed to make 'good white printing paper' and scorned the idea that they could not make paper worth more than 4s. the ream. But counsel for the Bill and the patentees relied strongly on such statements as that the exising paper-makers could not make 'any higher writing and printing papers' and even, flatly, 'they can make no writing paper'.[2] It is perhaps significant that in the petition from 'the paper-makers of Kent and Surrey' and from 'the ancient paper-makers of the Kingdom' opposition to the Company is made to rest more on the evils or illegality of monopoly powers than upon extravagant claims of past achievements.[3]

So whatever advances may have been made between, say, Restoration and Revolution, there was probably

another were worked by the Company; Chewton Keynsham, near Bristol, Plymouth, Eynsford, and Thornton-le-dale are other possible locations for their mills. See George, loc. cit.; Jenkins, p. 192; Shorter, *Historical Geography*, p. 35.

[1] *Cal. S.P. Dom.* 1700–2, pp. 552–3; nor does it seem likely that out of the 100 or so mills in the country 'the greatest number always have employed the greatest part of their time in making white printing paper' (ibid.).

[2] H.M.C.: *House of Lords MSS.*, 1690, pp. 74–75. A broadsheet issued by the Company derided the claims of the existing paper-makers to make printing-paper in any quantity, alleging that their product was used by shopkeepers to wrap up their wares (Jenkins, p. 176).

[3] Ibid., pp. 75–76; *C.J.*, vol. x, p. 372.

still a more than adequate field awaiting the Company's endeavours. When such evidence as this is combined with the laudatory comments mentioned earlier, it does seem reasonable to suppose that the Company and its Huguenots did make material improvements in the manufacture of the better sorts of white paper. Some decades later it was observed that William III had granted a patent to 'Mr. Biscoe & Co., who then improved the paper made greatly'. Even though the details were garbled, this at least suggests that the memory of the Company and of at least one of its members had not entirely disappeared.[1] Moreover, the very vigour of the French activities to secure the return of their artisans supports the evidence of statistics and contemporary comment. In the earliest English mills of the Tudor era foreign workmen were obviously the main source of the necessary skills; and inasmuch as any making of white paper here was dependent on this, so far and only so far could immigrants be said to have 'introduced' the manufacture into this country. By later Stuart times there was plenty of native skill though perhaps not much contact with continental improvements such as those in rag-preparation discussed earlier. It is significant that Houghton's description of white-paper making includes an account of a lengthy and careful pulping process similar to that found in the almost contemporary account of French paper-making by J. Imberdis. Moreover it seems possible that Houghton's description was derived from one of the Company's mills.[2] It is just such a

---

[1] *Case of the Papermakers* (*c.* 1737).

[2] Houghton says he derived his information on paper from 'my friend Mr. Million'. This fascinatingly named person was presumably the same as Henry Million who was associated with Dupin in the linen manufacturing company (Scott, op. cit., vol. iii, p. 90) and who also seems to have been in some way concerned with Burnaby's venture (Jenkins, p. 170).

practical improvement as this that may well have been the type of technical contribution which the Huguenots made.[1]

Their contributions were not simply technical and they were not confined to England. The Huguenot immigrants were far from being simply impoverished craftsmen; they included financiers and entrepreneurs of great ability.[2] It is evident that Nicholas Dupin was an active company promoter with fingers in several pies, and the growth of the industry in Scotland and Ireland may owe something to his initiative. The Irish Paper Company was based on a grant to Dupin in 1690 of a patent for fourteen years for the manufacture of white paper in Ireland.[3] Another Irish venture, also for the making of white paper, was the partnership headed by one Colonel John Perry; in 1697 Colonel Perry was petitioning the Irish Parliament, asking for protection against foreign imports and for legislation to prevent the destruction of white rags.[4] It seems improbable, however, that in the then state of Ireland conditions would have been particularly conducive to the growth of white-paper manufacture.

In Scotland the outlook was rosier. The early Dalry venture seems not to have led to any rapid expansion of manufacture; but, as in England, the later seventeenth

[1] Another example of this type of technical advance was the practice of 'parting', designed to improve the surface finish of the paper. This is said to have been invented by the French paper-maker Mathieu Johannot of Annonay, and it is perhaps significant that more than one Johannot is to be found amongst Kentish paper-makers of the early eighteenth century. See Labarre, p. 92; Hunter, p. 186; Rees, op. cit.; A. H. Shorter, 'Early Paper Mills in Kent', *The Paper-Maker*, Oct. 1951.

[2] See, e.g., A. C. Carter, 'The Huguenot Contribution to the Early Years of the Funded Debt, 1694–1714', *Proceedings of the Huguenot Society of London*, vol. xix, 1955. [3] Scott, op. cit., vol. iii, p. 71.

[4] Ibid., p. 72; *C.J.* (Ireland), vol. ii, p. 206. The date is incorrectly given by Scott as 1709.

and early eighteenth centuries saw the setting up of a number of successful mills. They were mainly in the Edinburgh area, but others were established near Glasgow and Aberdeen, and some were making white paper. French paper-makers left their mark at Cathcart and at Dalry where in 1675 the owner of the mill employed 'sevinten Scotsmen and boyes bred up and instructed in these airts be the french'.[1] In 1694 Dupin petitioned for certain privileges in connexion with the establishment of paper-mills in Scotland. These were granted and in the following year he and his partners were given further privileges including the right of incorporation as 'The Scots White Paper Manufactory'. The terms and articles of incorporation being agreed, a capital of £5,000 divided into 1,400 shares was paid up. Dupin and another French immigrant, Dennis Manes, contracted with the Company to supervise the construction of two mills and to train ten apprentices in the art of paper-making. The mills were established at Yester, in East Lothian, and at Braid, near Edinburgh. The Company's claim in 1696 to be producing good white paper in quantities enough to supply the country was followed in 1697, however, by complaints from Dupin that the venture was likely to fail through want of capital, and requests to the Privy Council for more encouragement, in the shape of a monopoly. This it did not get, though securing some support in its efforts to safeguard rag supplies. In 1699 the Company was advertising large stocks of paper for sale; at about the same time, like its English counterpart, it was experiencing various difficulties, and in 1703 the Company let the two mills to other paper-makers. These mills continued to work as producers of white paper in

[1] Quoted Waterston, 'Early Paper Making near Edinburgh', loc. cit., p. 56.

the eighteenth century, long after the Company itself had apparently vanished.[1]

The Huguenots, then, probably contributed both to improving the techniques of paper-making practised here and to the capital and enterprise in the industry. But it was war and economic policy which did much to create the circumstances in which the making of white paper in this country could become a profitable venture.

If it is impossible precisely to distinguish the contributions of different men and differing circumstances, so it is also impossible to know how much was provided by the various companies with which Dupin was concerned, and how much was due to other Huguenots operating outside their ambit. There were a number of immigrants active outside or only partly concerned with the companies. Dennis Manes, Nicholas de Champ, Gerard de Vaux, were amongst others of French origin who were concerned with paper-mills in places as diverse as Devon, Hampshire, and Scotland.[2] De Vaux, whose mill was near Southampton, a town which acquired an important Huguenot settlement, came from Languedoc; so also did Henri de Portal, who, after working at de Vaux's mill,

---

[1] Ibid., pp. 61–68, and 'Further Notes on Early Paper Making near Edinburgh', *Book of the Old Edinburgh Club*, vol. xxvii (1949), pp. 44–47; Scott, op. cit., vol. iii, pp. 181–5, and 'Scottish Industrial Undertakings before the Union', loc. cit.; Spicer, pp. 223–4.

[2] Dennis Manes or De Manes was apparently first interested in 1683–4 in mills near Plymouth and was then concerned with Cardonnel, Dupin, and others, in those near Southampton. He was subsequently caught and imprisoned by the French, but reappeared; he was opposing the grants to the English White Paper Makers Company in 1689–90, but in 1694 he was again associated with Dupin in the Scottish Company (see Jenkins, pp. 190–1; *Acts of the Parliament of Scotland*, vol. ix, p. 429; H.M.C.: *MSS. of the Marquess of Downshire*, vol. i, pp. 157–8; Overend, loc. cit.). Nicholas de Champ is said to have started a mill at Cathcart, near Glasgow, in 1679 (Scott, op. cit., vol. iii, p. 181). The name is spelt as Desham in a confirmatory account of this Huguenot enterprise in *Old Statistical Account*, vol. v, p. 344.

started the famous mill at Laverstoke and began an association with the paper industry which the Portals still enjoy today.[1] Huguenot names were also to be found in Kent and other counties from about this time: Johannot and Galliot, for instance, at Eynsford in the 1690's;[2] and the prevalence of French terms in the hand-made industry testifies to the importance of French influence.[3]

(iii)

What sort of an economic entity was a paper-mill in Tudor and Stuart times? How was the industry financed and organized?

Within any given industry at any given time there are often wide variations in size and capital value amongst its productive units. One of the problems of the industrial historian is to distinguish the untypical, the spectacular exceptions which leave records of their existence precisely because they are untypical, from the ordinary unit, the normal thing which nobody notices precisely because it is too ordinary to merit notice. So it is with paper-mills. Although the techniques of manufacture demanded centralized production and some capital equipment, the average paper-mill of Tudor and Stuart times was not a great absorber of capital. In comparison with the scale of operation of the great landowners or of the naval dockyards, or with the capital tied up in the big seventeenth-century iron-working partnerships, the average

---

[1] For further details of De Vaux and the Portals see Jenkins, pp. 181–2; Overend, loc. cit.; also on the Portal family, *infra*, pp. 159–60.

[2] Shorter, 'Early Paper-Mills in Kent', loc. cit.

[3] e.g. 'coucher' and 'layer' from *coucheur* and *leveur*; *salle* may have come over as it stands from the French or from the German *Saal*. Other continental influences are of course also strong, e.g. in 'deckle' (German *Deckel*) or Hollander (see Labarre, pp. 59, 70, 143, 232–3).

paper-mill was small. As a capital user it lay somewhere between these large-scale enterprises and the tiny units of the cloth industry. It was, in short, a typical 'mill' industry, economically as well as technically.

Many early paper-mills were converted to paper-making from other uses, especially from corn grinding or fulling. Spilman's mill was a conversion from two mills known as 'The Wheat Mill' and 'The Malt Mill'; Buckinghamshire landlords were described in the 1620's as advancing their rents by converting corn-mills into paper-mills. Present or expected profitability was a simple criterion of use: a number of fulling-mills in Kent were turned into paper-mills, as the eighteenth-century historian of Kent, Edward Hasted, observed, 'on the decay of the clothing trade in these parts'.[1] The availability of these mills—with their marked similarity to the stamping-mill—in areas where the cloth industry was on the decline must have been an important secondary factor, given the need for water-power, in shaping the distribution of the industry. There is evidence, too, that old and new uses were sometimes carried on side by side and also that paper-makers were often not simply paper-makers. Six mills on the River Wey, near Guildford, were let in 1679 to three persons all described as millers; the mills were three corn, two fulling, and one paper.[2] In 1704 Thomas Hall of Eashing, Surrey, miller, bequeathed to his wife the rents of his corn- and paper-mills.[3] Gresham's mill was apparently set up under the same roof as a corn-mill already in existence.[4] And over a

---

[1] E. Hasted, *History of the County of Kent* (London, 1778-9), vol. ii, p. 132; Overend, loc. cit., p. 181; *Cal. S.P. Dom.* 1636-7, p. 373; for other examples see *V.C.H. Surrey*, vol. ii, pp. 418-19; *V.C.H. Oxfordshire*, vol. ii, pp. 240-2; Shorter, *Historical Geography*, pp. 43, 96-98.

[2] H.M.C.: *House of Lords MSS.*, 1678-88, p. 123.

[3] *V.C.H. Surrey*, vol. ii, pp. 418-19.   [4] Jenkins, p. 160.

hundred years later, in 1697, when Celia Fiennes went to Canterbury she visited the paper-mill there, saw brown paper being made, and observed, in her inelegant way, that 'the mill is set agoing by the water and at the same time it pounded the rags for the paper and it beat oatmeal and hemp and ground bread together, that is at the same time . . . .'[1]

With such a close link with other types of mill it is natural that the normal financial arrangement was the renting of a mill from a landlord, if necessary for conversion into a paper-mill. Such information as is available does not lead one to believe that paper-mills were especially large or represented in any way striking concentrations of fixed capital. A sample of rents[2] for this period suggests that the usual figure ranged from about

[1] *Journeys*, p. 124. Other examples are given by Shorter and include Darley Mills, Derby, which in 1713 consisted of a corn-mill, paper-mill, fulling-mill, hemp-mill, and a leather-mill (*Historical Geography*, pp. 78–79). It is also interesting to note that one of the machines approved by the Académie Royale des Sciences towards the end of the seventeenth century was a combined paper- and corn-mill ((M. Gallon, ed.), *Machines et inventions approuvées par l'Académie Royale des Sciences* (Paris, 1735), vol. i, pp. 121 et seq.)

[2] Derived from Overend, loc. cit., p. 182 (£4 p.a., 1588); Jenkins, p. 169 (£50, 1638); *Cal. S.P. Dom.* 1636–7, p. 373 (£100–£150, 1637), and ibid. 1700–2, pp. 552–3 (£80–£90, 1690); H.M.C.: *House of Lords MSS.*, 1690, p. 76 (£70–£80, 1690), and ibid. 1691, p. 436 (£150, 1691); *C.J.*, vol. x, p. 372 (£80, 1690); Kent County Archives; Aylesford MSS. (£30, 1718) and Whatman Deeds (£25, 1695); W. H. B. Court, *The Rise of the Midland Industries* (London, 1938), p. 113 (£20, plus various payments in kind for two mills, 1681); also E. T. Finerty, 'History of Paper Mills in Hertfordshire', *The Paper-Maker*, April, 1957, p. 309 (£26, 1660 and 1675).

The lowest figure, £4 paid by Spilman, and the highest figure, £150, were both exceptional. The former was clearly a special concession and a compensation for the £1,400 or £1,500 claimed to have been spent by him on converting the mill (see *supra*, p. 44). The highest figure occurs twice: as the rent assessed in Court for the mill known as King's Mill, Byfleet, which seems to have been something out of the ordinary; and in 1637 in the allegation that the Buckinghamshire landlords increased their rents, by the conversion of mills to paper-making, from £10 or £15 to £100 or £150—suspiciously round multipliers in a document which had every reason to represent the paper-mill rents as high as possible.

£25 to about £90 per annum, thus giving a value at the usual twenty years' purchase, of from £500 to £1,800. These figures agree very reasonably with the £1,500 at which an Oxfordshire paper-mill was valued in the 1680's or the £500 or £1,000 which was estimated as the capital necessary for a paper-mill in the 1580's[1]—allowing for intervening changes in the value of money and for the fact that this was almost certainly an exaggerated estimate.

The cost of conversion was not necessarily very high; such costs, or those of repair, were sometimes borne by the landlord, sometimes by the tenant. When George Gill rented a paper-mill near Maidstone in 1695 from a local landowner, the tenant agreed to pay £200 towards the cost of repair. Alternatively, when John Swinnock leased a mill from the Earl of Aylesford at Boxley, near Maidstone, in 1718, the landlord agreed to pay £300 towards the cost of conversion from fulling to paper-making, Swinnock to pay £30 per annum, this rent later to rise to £52 per annum.[2]

In one sense, then, we may say that an important source of capital was the enterprising landlord desirous of increasing his rents. Many such landlords were often themselves newly successful in trade or finance. Sometimes both capital and enterprise came more directly from those sources: to the examples of Gresham and Spilman may be added that of John Tate who was a citizen and mercer of London and son of a Lord Mayor, and of Mungo Russell, rich merchant and twice Treasurer of the City of Edinburgh. It was both as merchant financiers and as landlords of three corn-mills near Dalry, one of which was converted into the paper-mill, that the Russells

[1] H.M.C.: *House of Lords MSS.*, 1691, p. 496; *Tudor Econ. Docs.*, vol. ii, p. 251.
[2] Kent County Archives: Aylesford MSS. and Whatman Deeds. See also Finerty, loc. cit., p. 310.

helped to establish the paper industry in Scotland.[1] But what sort of persons had started the majority of the hundred or more paper-mills of later Stuart days? Who usually provided the initial enterprise? It was not simply men like Dupin or Hagar. The capital contributions of landlords are only part of the answer. Whence came the savings to contribute towards, or if necessary pay for, the conversion of a mill, to finance the immediate payments for raw materials, for labour or rent? These are difficult questions to answer. The exceptional few we know; as also the Huguenots. The mill built by the Bristol merchant in 1635 and the newly built white-paper mill at Huxham, owned by an Exeter merchant in 1706, point to another line of interest.[2] The stationers certainly came to interest themselves in the establishment of paper-mills, though for this early period there is little evidence to suggest many successors to Tottell's scheme. It was the stationers who bought much of the output of the paper-mills and they may well have helped to provide short-term advances to the paper-makers, as was certainly done later.[3] The bookbinders claimed in 1712 that their initiative (and possibly their capital?) lay behind a mill for making the millboard which they needed;[4] the famous Wolvercote paper-mills are alleged to owe their establishment in part to the celebrated Dr. Fell, seeking paper for the recently established press at Oxford.[5] These all conform to a well-known pattern of economic action. But in the absence of definite evidence its significance

---

[1] *Acts of Court of the Mercers Company, passim*; Jenkins, p. 157; Somerset House: Wills of John Tate (1507) and Sir John Tate (1514); Waterston, 'Early Paper Making near Edinburgh', loc. cit., pp. 56–59.

[2] *Supra*, pp. 51, 74 n. 5; Shorter, *Historical Geography*, p. 78.

[3] *Infra*, pp. 252–3.   [4] *Case of the Bookbinders*.

[5] Quoted Jenkins, p. 170; Mr. H. G. Carter, of the University Press Oxford, kindly pointed out to me that this idea originated with John Bagford, in 1714 (B.M. Harleian MSS. 5901, f. 86).

in the industry as a whole, at this time, must remain a matter of conjecture.

The expenditure of large sums may have meant the creation of much larger mills or may equally mean that the entrepreneur, instead of relying on credit transactions for the initial or subsequent financing of operations, started by making extensive cash purchases. This in turn may imply that the entrepreneur was a rich man willing to lavish capital on risky projects. Spilman was almost certainly in this latter category. Or again, large amounts were spent in order to operate several mills: the White Paper Makers Company advertised in the *London Gazette* their willingness to buy or lease paper- or corn-mills.[1] Dupin, business man and company promoter, was evidently the leading spirit in that enterprise; and with a patent to exploit, with skilled workmen and technical improvements available, and that newly fashionable and speculative instrument—the joint-stock company—at hand, it is natural that he and his associates should have sought to operate on a large scale. Accordingly, neither the £100,000 sought nor the £20,000 initially subscribed tell us much about the amounts normally involved in erecting and running an ordinary paper-mill at this time. This was not the way in which the industry was normally financed and organized. After the demise of the Company nothing more is heard of the joint stock company in paper-making until the days of the limited liability company in the later nineteenth century. The single entrepreneur or the partnership renting the mill, perhaps in time coming to own it, employing wage labour, the extended family business—this is the normal pattern and one which as it becomes clearer in the eighteenth century will be examined in later chapters.[2]

[1] *London Gazette*, No. 2617 (Dec. 1690).
[2] *Infra*, pp. 150 et seq. and Chap. IX.

If the capital needed for paper-mills was not great, neither were the numbers which they employed nor the size in terms of vats per mill. Churchyard wrote of Spilman's mill:

> Six hundred men are set to worke by him,
> That else might starve, or seek abroad their bread.

Now this is not to be taken to mean that 600 workmen toiled inside the mill on the river near Dartford. The figure itself probably owes something to poetic licence, to the exaggeration which so often marks the utterences of the age, and to the inaccuracy which springs from a total lack of acquaintance with quantitative methods. But perhaps more important than any of these is the fact that when contemporaries made statements of this sort they usually included everyone remotely connected with a given activity; the employment of one man came to mean the employment of a whole family. In an age when under-employment and poverty were widespread, it was normal, if one sought to praise an employer or an industry, to exaggerate the numbers which he or it employed. So Spilman's 600 is no more a true estimate of employment in his mill than is the 40,000 poor which an estimate of 1712 said were maintained by the industry.[1] A particular reason for such statements as the latter was the large indirect employment provided by rag-collecting.

Evidence concerning French paper-mills of the seventeenth century shows them to have been mostly very small and employing only a few workmen: three men and an apprentice per vat, four or five women helping to prepare the rags, the master working with his men— about nine or ten in all. For early eighteenth-century France other evidence suggests that the numbers working

---

[1] Quoted Jenkins, p. 180.

in one-vat mills ranged from six to seventeen.[1] These estimates agree closely with the number employed by Keferstein in Germany in the eighteenth century. Three journeymen, two women for rag-washing, one labourer, one servant, and an apprentice made up his total of eight employees for the running of a one-vat mill and household in which he himself and his wife also worked.[2] There is no reason whatsoever to suppose that the average size of British mills was appreciably different. In 1690 the Buckinghamshire paper-makers claimed that the eight mills in the county employed fifty families; another petition of the same time spoke of 100 paper-mills on which were dependent 1,000 families, not including the masters of the mills.[3] If due allowance is made for the tendencies towards exaggeration inherent in these calculations and which were mentioned above, we should arrive at figures for employment of roughly the same order of magnitude as those of the French and German mills. There were, of course, a few large mills in England as on the Continent but the majority were one-vat mills, and such mills could not give employment to more than about fifteen persons each. A statement of 1712 suggests an average of about 1·2 vats per mill and an official calculation by the Excise authorities in 1738 supports this.[4] For the eighteenth century there is further evidence to show the persistence of many small mills; this means that, in spite of the gradual appearance of large mills,

[1] H. Sée, *L'Évolution commerciale et industrielle de la France sous l'ancien régime* (Paris, 1925), pp. 176, 278; G. Martin, *La Grande Industrie sous le règne de Louis XV* (Paris, 1900), p. 206; P. Léon, *La Naissance de la grande industrie en Dauphiné* (Paris, 1954), vol. i, pp. 42, 196.

[2] Keferstein, op. cit., p. 41.

[3] H.M.C.: *House of Lords MSS.*, 1690, p. 74; *Cal. S.P. Dom.* 1700–2, pp. 552–3.

[4] *Proposals . . . for raising £40,000 . . . by laying Additional duties on all Foreign Paper*, &c.; C. & E.: Excise-Treasury Letters, 1733–45, f. 247.

the average numbers employed per mill remained low.[1] At the end of the seventeenth century it is unlikely that the industry directly and regularly employed more than about 2,500 to 3,000 workers, though certainly offering indirect and occasional employment to many more, from rag-collectors to carpenters and millwrights.

This, then, was the paper industry which had grown up in the first two centuries of its existence in these islands: some 150 to 200 mills in England, a half-dozen or so in Scotland, one or two mills in Ireland—scattered over the countryside, along the river valleys, some in remote districts, many near the towns, nearly all small in size and simple in equipment. It is an industry which will not fit easily into either of the main categories which too often seem to dominate accounts of the economic history of this period: it was neither a part of the 'domestic system' nor was it normally 'large-scale capitalist enterprise'.[2]

[1] See *infra*, pp. 149–51.
[2] For some further comments on this see my article 'Industrial Growth and Industrial Revolutions', *Economica*, Feb. 1956.

IV

Growth and Consolidation in the Eighteenth Century

(i)

IT is in some ways a groping and fumbling business to try to reconstruct the growth of an industry without being able to measure its output over the course of the years. In this respect the eighteenth century is kinder to the economic historian than is the seventeenth; the contemporary demands of taxation have left behind them the statistical raw material out of which can be built, at least for some industries, quantitative presentations of industrial growth. The paper industry is amongst those so favoured. Fig. 2 presents in graphical form an estimate of the course of the industry's development, mainly in England, until 1800; the curve of the English production figures from 1713 onwards is supported by those of the corresponding paper imports from 1698 and rag imports from 1725, together with the curve of Scottish output from 1782.[1]

The general picture thus revealed is clear enough. The English industry continued to dominate the scene; although the Scottish industry was evidently growing rapidly in the last decades of the century, its output was still only about 10 per cent. of the English.[2] Between the second decade of the century and its end English output

[1] The sources from which these graphs were derived and in particular the methods by which the output curve was constructed are examined in App. I.

[2] Figures for Ireland are not available before 1801, by which time Irish output was still less than 5 per cent. of English.

multiplied about four-fold; imports of rags rose some twenty-fold; and imports of foreign paper fell off rapidly and strikingly. The proportionate increase in output would no doubt be very much greater were it possible to trace the curve back through the preceding half-century when, as we have seen, a truly striking advance in the home industry took place, though regrettably without leaving a quantitative trail for the historian. But the eighteenth century was mainly a period of consolidation and gradual extension. By comparison with the spectacular rise of the iron, cotton, and pottery industries, paper was slow but worthy. The fear of competition still lingered on: France, Holland, and Italy lurked outside the protective wall. There were neither sensational technical advances drastically to lower costs of production nor sweeping extensions in markets to carry this industry forward in the way that the cotton and iron industries were carried forward.

As Fig. 2 is plotted on a logarithmic scale, the curves show the rate of growth of output and imports. The slow rate of growth shown by the English production curve for the period as a whole contrasts sharply with the rapid rate of change marking the import curves. Moreover it is clear that not until a turning-point marked approximately by the decade 1735–45, does there end a period of virtual stagnation both in output and in imports. After that turning-point, output increases steadily until about 1790 when both English and Scottish production slowed down again until the end of the century. What is the significance of these features? Why was there comparative stagnation at either end of the curve? Why were the turning-points where they were? And what gave rise to the growth that was achieved? In order to answer these questions and at the same time to go beyond the

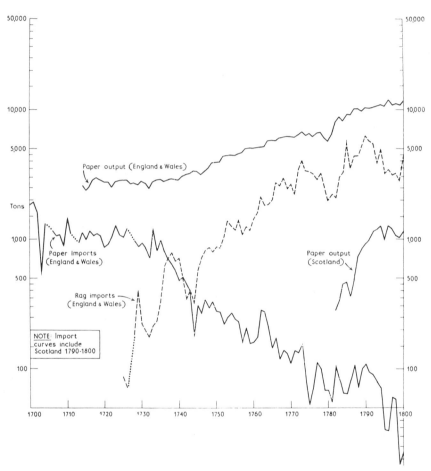

50,000

10,000

5,000

Paper output (England & Wales)

Tons

1,000

Paper Imports
(England & Wales)

500

Rag imports
(England & Wales)

NOTE: Import
curves include
Scotland 1790-1800

100

50,000

10,000

5,000

1,000

Paper output
(Scotland)

500

100

1700   1710   1720   1730   1740   1750   1760   1770   1780   1790   1800

FIG. 2. Output and Imports of Paper and Imports of Rags, 1700–1800 (tons), England and Wales and Scotland (logarithmic scale)

flat, two-dimensional picture which the graphs offer, we must begin by examining the details of production and of imports.

(ii)

In the first half of the century it is certain that this country remained substantially, though decreasingly, dependent on the Continent for the best grades of paper. The impressive proportion of the home market supplied by the English industry conceals the fact that much of this represented the demand for the poorer qualities: wrapping-paper and the cheaper sorts of printing- and writing-papers. Brown paper, of various sorts, formed the largest single class of paper produced not merely at the beginning but throughout the century. In the first years of the Excise statistics (1713–15) the proportion was at least 53 per cent., probably more, in 1782 it was 51 per cent., in 1793 it was 47 per cent.[1] But in the 1780's and 90's the balance of the output included paper of the highest quality; this was far from being so in the earlier years. In 1738 the Commissioners of Excise reported that three-quarters or more of the mills in the country made coarse paper and that the amount of paper worth £1 per ream or more was 'not great'.[2] But if the Commissioners might be thought to have been deluded by the deficiencies of their own statistics,[3] those who lived outside their office saw a similar picture. As early as 1712, Defoe, observing that 'the paper manufacture in Britain is a small but improving thing', added that English mills produced paper 'used in printing small tracts and

[1] These refer to amounts, not values. They are calculated from C. & E.: Quantities, Rates and Amounts of Excise Duties, 1684–1728. For reasons explained in Chap. V, it is not possible to give a continuous analysis of production until after 1781.

[2] Ibid.: Excise-Treasury Letters, 1733–45, ff. 247–8.

[3] See infra, pp. 129–35.

pamphlets, etc. They are not arrived to an improvement able to supply for greater pieces.'[1] In 1747 Campbell wrote in *The London Tradesman*, 'We are but lately come into the Method of making tolerable Paper; we were formerly supplied with that Commodity from France, Holland and Genoa, and still are obliged to these Countries for our best Papers. . . . The French excel us in Writing Paper and the Genoese in Printing Paper, from whom we take annually a great many Thousand Pounds worth of that Commodity.'[2] Similar comments were made in the many commercial and technical dictionaries published in the 1740's and 50's.[3] And it was with Dutch, French, and Italian paper that comparison was normally made by the various Irish paper-makers who from time to time petitioned their Parliament for financial aid in their undertakings. Not until the 60's and thereafter was achievement, real or potential, judged in terms of the English industry and its products.[4]

Still, as Campbell rightly added, imports were lessening. More white paper was being made in England and more books were being printed on it instead of on foreign paper.[5] An advertisement in 1743 from a Gloucestershire mill for a paper-maker who was 'capable of undertaking a white vat,'[6] points to the direction of development. Not only in the Home Counties but in mills farther afield—in Hampshire, Norfolk, Herefordshire, and even

[1] *The Best of Defoe's Review*, ed. W. L. Payne (New York, 1951), p. 83.

[2] R. Campbell, *The London Tradesman* (London, 1747), chap. xxvi.

[3] e.g. *A General Description of All Trades* (London, 1747), p. 158; J. Barrow, *A New and Universal Dictionary of Arts and Sciences* (London, 1751), *sub* Paper; *Case of the Paper Makers* (*c.* 1737).

[4] See, e.g., *C.J.* (Ireland), vol. iv, p. 241, and app. lxxx, p. 526; and vol. viii, p. 32.

[5] Jenkins (pp. 185–6) quotes an interesting example from 1740–1 of a work started on Italian paper and finished on English.

[6] Quoted in Shorter, *Historical Geography*, p. 70.

in so remote a county as Westmorland—white paper was being made.[1] In the printing of certain sorts of books by the Universities of Oxford and Cambridge, and of Scotland, English paper was being used along with foreign in the early years of the century; but from the late 1750's and 60's onwards British paper alone was used for this purpose.[2] From about this time, too, the Scottish industry began to grow apace. In the Edinburgh area there were said to be only three mills in 1763, producing rather over 6,000 reams per annum, but by 1791 there were twelve mills producing over 100,000 reams. Printing paper was then being shipped thence to London, instead of, as formerly, being imported from London.[3] The Irish industry, stimulated perhaps by a few grants of monetary aid to individual paper-makers by the Irish government, also advanced during the century. It seems unlikely, however, that much white paper was made there before the 1730's and 40's. Considerable quantities were imported and, significantly enough, they came not from England but from Holland and France. After the 1770's total imports were declining, but not until the 1790's did England dominate the Irish import trade.[4]

After 1742 the Customs returns make possible an analysis of the nature of paper imports into England.[5]

[1] Ibid., pp. 68–70; *Case of the Paper Makers* (c. 1737); see also *infra*, pp. 147 et seq.

[2] See, e.g., C. & E.: Excise-Treasury Letters 1758–64, f. 188. See also ibid. 1722–33, f. 15, for an example in 1722 in which the paper used for printing, at Oxford, an edition of part of the Septuagint was '24 reams of fine Holland, 434 reams of Dutch demi-second and 309 reams of English demi-fine'. The Universities were entitled to a drawback of Customs and Excise duties. [3] *Old Statistical Account*, vol. vi, p. 595.

[4] *C.J.* (Ireland), vol. ii, p. 206; vol. iii, pp. 227, 232, 269, 272; vol. iv, pp. 241, 245, 526, app. lxxx; vol. v, pp. 17, 18, 19; and *passim*. For Irish imports see *infra*, pp. 96, 144–5.

[5] For the obstacles in the way of using them before then see Chap. V, pp. 124–7.

TABLE IV

Imports of Paper, 1743—England and Wales
(reams, unless otherwise stated)

WHITE

Type	Holland	Italy and 'The Straights'	France	Total
Atlas, fine	9	..	..	9
,, ordinary	19	..	..	19
Bastard	853	..	..	853
Cartridge	3,773	..	..	3,773
Crown, second, writing . .	3,314	1,476	..	4,790
,, ordinary . . .	538	..	..	538
Demy, fine	540	97	..	637
,, Genoa, fine . . .	6	..	..	6
,, second	154	3,011	..	3,165
,, ordinary, printing . .	5,991	..	..	5,991
Elephant, fine	2	..	..	2
,, ordinary . . .	1,057	..	..	1,057
Foolscap, fine	2,195	474	..	2,669
,, Genoa, fine . .	52	..	..	52
,, second	780	5,771	..	6,551
,, Genoa, second . .	517	..	..	517
,, German . . .	117	..	..	117
,, printing, second . .	12	..	..	12
Imperial, fine	128	24	12	164
,, second	37	..	..	37
,, ,, writing . .	..	30	..	30
Medium, fine	267	..	..	267
,, second	45	..	..	45
Post, fine, large, above 15 lb. .	1,526	..	..	1,526
,, ,, small, under 15 lb. .	322	..	..	322
Post, small	27	..	..	27
Pot, superfine	285	..	..	285
,, second	1,085	..	..	1,085
,, ordinary	905	..	..	905
,, Genoa	..	570	..	570
,, ,, second . . .	..	2,770	..	2,770
Royal, superfine	78	..	..	78
,, fine	176	..	1	177
,, second	135	..	..	135
,, ordinary	2,696	..	..	2,696
,, Genoa, second . . .	2	24	..	26
,, Holland, fine . . .	199	..	..	199
,, ,, second . .	269	..	..	269
,, second, writing-super-royal .	5	..	..	5
Super-royal, fine	..	..	1	1
TOTAL WHITE	28,116	14,247	14	42,377

BLUE, BROWN, ETC.

Type	Holland	Italy	France	Germany	Ireland	Total
Brown, by the bundle	209	..	1	..	..	210
Brown, cap . .	91	..	..	..	..	91
Blue, royal . .	115	..	..	..	..	115
„ for sugar bakers	1,116	..	..	..	..	1,116
Painted . . .	7	2	..	32	12	53

Source: P.R.O. Customs 3/43.

Admittedly imports had by this time entered upon their phase of rapid decline. Nevertheless, Table IV may serve to illustrate in detail the nature of our dependence on foreign paper; it may reasonably be taken as representative of the situation in the 1730's and 40's in spite of changes in total amounts. The picture which it offers is remote from that of a half-century earlier and remoter still from that of early Stuart times. The bulk of imports of white paper has shrunk to a mere 42,000 reams and, apart from the naturally small quantities of the most expensive sizes, such as 'atlas' and 'imperial', tends to consist of consignments of better quality printing- and writing-papers in the sizes of crown, demy, and foolscap. Imports of brown are insignificant. Blue is the only paper to have shown any appreciable increase in imports in the intervening years, and it is possible, though by no means certain, that this may have been a reflection of the growth of sugar refining in this country and of the inability of the home industry to meet all demands at that time.[1]

Until her own industry had grown to maturity, Scotland drew much of her paper from England; so Scottish

[1] Unfortunately not until 1743 is the distinction consistently made in the Customs ledgers between paper described as 'blue for sugar bakers' and other types of blue. It is sporadically described in this manner in the 1730's. Imports grew from an average of 1,145 reams annually in 1713–17 to 3,011 reams in 1732–6. In 1743, on the adoption by the Customs of new classifications and values, the imports of blue paper fell off.

imports from abroad were trifling.[1] Ireland, by contrast, with a much lower tariff and an important centre of paper consumption in Dublin, imported heavily from the Continent. The following figures indicate the general course of change in quantity and origin of Irish imports of writing- and printing-paper:[2]

	Reams			Total (incl. small amounts from elsewhere)
	Great Britain	Holland and Flanders	France	
1755–6	504	11,550	15,366	27,420
1763–5	2,330	12,857	21,542	36,729
1771–3	2,205	7,445	6,722	16,376
1793–4	13,020	120	201	13,341

Though France loomed large as a supplier of paper to Ireland, Holland, as Table IV showed, remained easily the largest English supplier in 1743.[3] But even the Dutch were feeling the draught, and the comment of a firm of importers in 1742 offers a nice confirmation of the statistical evidence: 'We are pretty much out of Business and intirely discouraged out of the Paper Trade, which is brought here to a very low Ebb and will decrease more and more by reason of the great quantiteys made in England which Manufactory encreases every Day.'[4]

This prophecy was soon to be proved accurate. Forty

---

[1] About 400 reams p.a. in 1755–6; hardly any in 1793–4 (P.R.O. Customs 14/1a, 12).

[2] P.R.O. Customs 15/59 & 97; *Abstract of the Exports and Imports of Ireland, 1764–73* (being a transcript from the Customs ledgers).

In the Irish imports from Britain, printing-paper predominated. Imports of other sorts of paper were trifling with the exception of pressing-paper which formed the only appreciable imports from England in the earlier years.

[3] Though how much of this paper may have been made in France is another matter. On this point see *supra*, pp. 19–23.

[4] Quoted C. Wilson, *Anglo-Dutch Commerce and Finance in the Eighteenth Century* (Cambridge, 1941), p. 61.

years later imports were an insignificant dribble and home production was booming. The rearrangement of the Excise assessments in 1781 permits an analysis of output. Indeed for the years 1782–93 it is possible, and only then possible, to set out in detail exact quantities of every type of paper as given in the returns to the Excise authorities; and, moreover, there is reason to suppose that these returns are tolerably accurate. Full details for the three years 1782, 1788, and 1793, giving the amounts produced of all the various types, as well as sizes and official values are set out in Appendix II. Meanwhile Fig. 3 provides a general view of output and its breakdown into the five categories or 'Tables' of the Excise assessment schedules used during this period.[1] The percentages of the total output taken up by each of the tables at the beginning and the end of the period were as follows:

	1782	1793
Table 1 .	12	15
Table 2 .	16	15
Table 3 .	15	16
Table 4 .	6	7
Table 5 .	51	47

Just as the situation revealed by the analysis of imports in 1743 differs markedly from that of the seventeenth century, so does the picture offered by these production figures of the 1780's. The five tables cover seventy-seven different types of paper, varying by size, weight, purpose, colour, and quality. This very range in itself suggests improvements in quality and quantity since the 1740's and points to an industry catering for an extensive and diverse market.

[1] C. & E.: Quantities, Rates and Amounts of Excise Duties, 1684–1798. The data refer to England and Wales only.

The constituents of Tables 1 (12 types) and 2 (21 types) comprised the highest grade of writing-, drawing-, and printing-papers. They included the largest and most expensive sizes used for drawings or engravings, the most

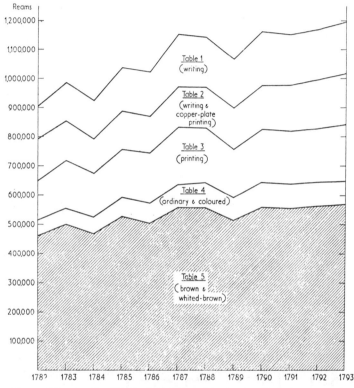

FIG. 3. Output (by 'Tables') 1782–93 (England and Wales, reams)

famous and most expensive being the 'antiquarian' or 'double atlas', valued at £15 a sheet; they also embraced moderate amounts of writing and high-grade printing-papers in such standard sizes as pot and foolscap. Some comment on the timing of the progress made in the manu-facture of these papers of the highest grades is provided by the story of the premium offered by the Royal Society of Arts for the making in England of paper suitable for taking the impression of mezzotints and other copper-plate engravings. The Society offered two rewards, the first for making paper equal in quality to the French paper of the same sort, which was agreed to be the finest, the second for paper which would approximate most closely to the French. The premium was first offered in 1756, but not until 1787 was the first prize awarded. In the meanwhile the second prize had gone to a number of entrants, in 1757, 1763, 1764, and 1786, although in many years no award was made at all. In 1785 the Society had remarked of two entries that neither were equal to the French but that there 'appears to be an evident Improvement in the Manufacture of them when compared with any hitherto produced to the Society'. In the following year the silver medal (£25) went to a Hert-fordshire paper-maker, William Lepard; next year, when John Bates of Buckinghamshire secured the gold medal (£50), the premium was discontinued.[1]

Table 3 (13 types) embraced most of the papers used in ordinary printing. The smallness of the percentage of the total occupied by this table—in 1782 15 per cent. as compared with the 28 per cent. of Tables 1 and 2 and 51 per cent. of Table 5—points to the relatively small role which common, everyday printing then played either in the economic activities of the community in general or, in particular, as a source of demand for paper. In Table 4 were classed three main sorts of paper: those used for wrapping sugar, those in the size known as 'elephant' which went to the paper-stainers to become wall-coverings, and the cartridge paper some of which

[1] R.S.A.: Minutes of Committees, Manufactures, 1763, 1779–80, 1784–5, 1785–6, 1786–7; R. Dossie, *Memoirs of Agriculture and Economical Arts*, vol. i (London, 1764), pp. 14, 91–93; *Transactions of the Royal Society of Arts*, vol. v, p. 231; vol. vi, p. 167.

were destined for wrapping shot, some for more peaceful and prosaic wrapping purposes. Table 5 (18 types) contains the bulk of the ordinary wrapping-papers, in a variety of sorts, weights, and sizes.

The manufacture of board is not susceptible to the same detailed analysis as that of paper. During the century, however, the English Excise figures show an increase in the production of 'Pasteboard, Mill board and Scale board' of from an average of some 116 tons per annum in 1713–17 to 657 tons yearly for the period 1796–1800.[1]

So much, then, for the nature of imports and output. How had these changes been wrought?

(iii)

It will be convenient first to examine the circumstances tending to an increase in the demand for paper.

First and most obvious is the rising population. The 5½ million persons (approximately) who inhabited England and Wales at the end of the seventeenth century had grown to nearly 9 millions by the first census of 1801. Union with Scotland and the extension of Anglo-Irish trade helped to bring the whole of Britain into something approaching a single trading area; in 1801 the population of the British Isles was over 15 millions. In short in the course of a century the population of England and Wales grew by about 60 per cent. and that of the kingdom as whole probably nearly doubled. The output of paper thus certainly more than kept pace with the growth of population.

Increase in numbers is not of itself enough to stimulate industrial production; greater potential purchasing

[1] C. & E.: Quantities, Rates and Amounts of Excise Duties, 1684–1798.

power must be translated into increased effective demand. This link was made, for there can be no doubt that the national wealth and income swelled mightily as the Industrial Revolution got under way in the last two or three decades of the century. The beginnings of mechanization in industry, the first big scatter of factories in the Midlands and north-west, the advent of steam-power, rapid and spectacular increases in the output of cotton textiles, iron, and pottery, improvements in road and river transport, and the start of the era of canal building—such developments as these at once increased the complexity of commercial intercourse and put money into the pockets of many. In indirect and often devious ways this gave people and institutions more money with which to buy paper and more reasons for needing it. Not only was more wanted for wrapping many of the goods which now entered into the rapidly growing trade, both external and internal, but this very expansion of industry and commerce itself needed paper to facilitate its progress; paper for the ledgers and account books of merchants and manufacturers, for bills of exchange and bank notes, for the rising tide of commercial correspondence.

On the whole, however, the growth in its importance during the eighteenth century was more quantitative than qualitative: an extension of demand for existing sorts of uses, a replacement in England of foreign paper by English paper. The demands of industry and trade apart, the printed book be it literary, technical, or scientific, and the written word continued to provide the major source of demand for white paper. Newspapers increased in number, size, and circulation only slowly, though they did provide some extension of demand for the cheaper sorts of printing-paper. An estimate of 1704 lists nine English newspapers with a total circulation of 45,000 per week; there is evidence that in the next few decades, and in spite of the newspaper stamp duty imposed in 1712, the newspaper-reading public grew and both numbers of papers and circulation expanded.[1] These developments were mainly confined to London, though provincial newspapers also started up in this period; the *Norwich Post* of 1701 is now thought to be the earliest, although a daily had appeared in Dublin in 1700. It was followed by others, all weeklies or bi-weeklies, in Bristol (1702), Worcester (1709), Exeter (1707), Nottingham (1710), as well as in Glasgow, Edinburgh, Aberdeen, and elsewhere during the first half of the century.[2]

An important limitation on advance in this direction remained. It has been said that 'the printing industry of 1750 was still almost medieval'.[3] Nor was printing in any way revolutionized in the course of the eighteenth century. Though provincial printing expanded after the lapse in 1695 of the Licensing Acts, and although a few large firms sprang up amongst the London printers, so long as techniques remained what they were, there was no likelihood of any great increase in demand for printing-paper. So that although we must needs pay tribute to this early flowering of the newspaper, we must at the same time recall the mere 15 per cent. of Table 3 (which certainly did not all go to newspapers): it was but a small flower.

It is impossible accurately to assess the role of the ex-

---

[1] *Daily Courant, London Post, English Post, London Gazette, Post Man, Post Boy, Flying Post, Review, Observator.* See J. R. Sutherland, 'The Circulation of Newspapers and Literary Periodicals', *Trans. Bib. Soc.*, vol. xv (1934–5), pp. 110–24.

[2] Musson, op. cit., p. 6; A. and N. L. Clow, *The Chemical Revolution* (London, 1952), pp. 259-60.   [3] Musson, op. cit., p. 16.

port trade in fostering the growth of the paper industry. In 1764 James Whatman claimed that 'the great increase of it (the paper manufacture) in England now depends very much upon the exportation of that commodity';[1] and in 1782 the London wholesale stationers, finding difficulties in securing the drawback in the Excise which was allowed on exports, petitioned the Excise authorities and described themselves as being 'greatly concerned in shipping of Paper for foreign Consumption'.[2] Unfortunately two sources which might be expected to shed light on this can offer but a faint glimmer. For administrative reasons the records of the amounts paid as drawbacks on the exports of paper refer, before 1772, only to ports other than London. These show the payment of very small amounts as drawbacks from 1713 onwards.[3] Secondly, the Customs ledgers did not normally record, during the eighteenth century, the quantities of paper exported separately from the value of what was comprehensively labelled as 'stationery'. At the very beginning of the century some trifling amounts of English paper were certainly shipped abroad and were occasionally recorded as such.[4] Rather larger amounts of foreign paper were re-exported, some 1,400 reams valued at £387 leaving in 1701, and this figure was multiplied about five or six times during the next thirty years or so.[5] Nearly all of it was destined for the American and West Indian colonies; this at once reflects the growth of the English entrepôt trade with that area and points to the

[1] B.M. Add. MSS. 38203, f. 318.

[2] C. & E.: Excise-Treasury Letters, 1779–82, f. 298.

[3] C. & E.: Excise Revenue Accounts, 1662–1827, ff. 130–4.

[4] In 1701, for instance, paper and pasteboard valued at £27 was dispatched to the American plantations and in 1711 the comparable figure was £67; in the latter year some £274 worth was also sent to Ireland (P.R.O. Customs 3/5, 14).

[5] P.R.O. Customs 3/5, 14, 23, 31, &c.

existence of a market which English paper-makers might well have coveted.

After about 1740 the declining imports of foreign paper were naturally matched by a similar decline in the re-export trade. But entries of English-made paper had already disappeared from the Customs ledgers in the 1720's and although there is an increasing export of English-made stationery there is no method of knowing how much paper of English manufacture this embodied. For what it is worth, the following table gives some indication of the increase in the stationery export trade, as well as of its direction:

TABLE V

Exports of Stationery (£)

	Africa	Asia	America, (incl. W. Indies)	Europe	Ireland, Chan. Isles, Isle of Man	Total
1771	159	253	6,706	280	242	7,640
1780		40	9,979	786	554	11,359
1790	291		11,449	924	6,559	19,229
1800	623		24,912	8,198	13,074	46,807

The figures for 1771 and 1780 refer to England and Wales; those for 1790 and 1800 include Scotland.

Source: P.R.O. Customs 3/71, 17/6, 12, 22.

Even when allowance is made for the increase in prices in the 1790's and for the increased coverage of the later figures, these statistics do suggest an appreciably growing export trade in stationery. Add to this the fact that by 1771 no re-exports of foreign stationery or paper were recorded, and it seems reasonable to assume that exports of English stationery included a good proportion of English-made paper. Much of the production of some of the bigger manufacturers, making printing- and writing-papers, may well have gone to overseas markets, especially across the Atlantic. Nevertheless, it is unlikely, in spite of Whatman's contention, that a large proportion of the total English output was exported.[1] For the 1780's and 90's it is possible to compare the amounts allowed as drawbacks on paper exports with total revenue from the paper Excise duty; the former averaged about 9 per cent. of the latter.[2] What weight can be put on this it is hard to say, but as it stands it offers confirmation of other evidence which points to the English industry's growth as resting more upon successful capture and consolidation of the home market than upon any striking ventures overseas.

With this approximate indication of the volume of exports it is now possible to calculate that home consumption of paper (exclusive of board) at the end of the century was, very roughly, 2·5 lb. per head per annum.[3] Again, and even supposing 100 per cent. under-estimation, which is unlikely, the vital fact is brought out that paper was still a long way from being a common item for the common man. Most of the community still lived in rural conditions and more persons still worked in agriculture than in industry. In the circumstances of the time such persons were unlikely to use much paper. It was, in brief, still far from being the ubiquitous thing of our modern urban, industrialized society.

[1] A leading wholesale stationer, James Woodmason, remarked of English paper-makers in 1785 that 'a vast deal of what they make is exported' (C. & E.: Excise Trials, vol. 531, p. 160). But what was true of some of the big makers, such as Whatman or Clement Taylor (see *infra*, pp. 152–7), with whom Woodmason had extensive dealings, was almost certainly untrue of the many small makers who were still responsible for the bulk of British output.

[2] C. & E.: Excise Revenue Accounts, 1662–1827, ff. 132–3.

[3] This estimate refers to England and Wales only. It assumes an estimated production of 11,650 tons (see Fig. 2, and App. I), 10 per cent. as a generous estimate for exports, imports as negligible, and population as 9 million.

(iv)

Matching these limited extensions of demand were certain solid, unsensational, limited changes on the supply side of the industry.

Supplies of raw materials certainly increased during the century. This is true not only of such minor items in production as alum, the ingredients of size, and coal, but also of the major element—rags. The scale of rag imports has been shown in Fig. 2. To what extent rags may have been imported before their first appearance in the Customs ledgers in 1725 it is difficult to say.[1] But in that year,[2] 'for the Encouragement of the making of Paper in this Kingdom', commodities specifically described as 'old Rags, old Ropes or Junks, or fishing nets, fit only for making pasteboard or paper' were allowed in duty free on an entry thereof being made at the Customs house. Germany, as Table VI indicates, was the most important single source of rags during the century, with Italy and Flanders some way behind. The effect of war in interrupting commerce shows up both in the figures for individual countries and in the totals. The arrival of rags from America, Eastern Europe, Scandinavia, and Russia which becomes more frequent in the last decade of the century may be due to stoppages, brought about by warfare, on the normal commercial routes, though it may also reflect a growing scarcity of rags which was making itself apparent by that time.[3]

Home supplies also increased during the period and

---

[1] Consignments of 'old linen', 'old sheets', and the like are listed amongst English imports before 1725, but there is no particular reason to presume that they were destined for paper-making.

[2] 11 Geo. I, c. 7.

[3] It may also owe something to the method of recording the origins of shipments in the Customs ledger (see *supra*, p. 19).

TABLE VI

Import of Rags 1725–1800

(average of five-year periods (tons))

Five-Year Period	Flanders	France	Germany	Holland	Italy and 'The Straights'	Spain and Portugal	Ireland and I. of M.	Channel Islands	Russia and Poland	Denmark, Norway, and Sweden	America (incl. British Possessions)	Total
1725–30	52·4	55·0	18·6	47·4	14·0	..	5·2	..	..	..	..	192·6
1731–35	61·8	15·4	119·4	23·8	6·2	0·8	0·8	1·8	..	..	..	230·0
1736–40	154·0	80·4	266·4	27·4	0·4	35·6	1·2	130·0	..	..	..	695·4
1741–45	75·6	25·0	217·6	11·4	0·4	51·0	2·2	39·6	..	..	..	422·8
1746–50	47·6	5·0	626·0	12·6	5·4	83·2	..	28·8	..	..	..	808·6
1751–55	163·6	6·4	752·0	7·0	71·4	113·2	0·2	28·8	..	..	..	1,142·6
1756–60	130·6	..	1,051·8	11·0	21·0	19·4	12·6	20·6	..	..	..	1,267·0
1761–65	450·0	30·4	1,085·2	199·2	32·8	7·6	5·2	56·8	1·0	..	..	1,868·2
1766–70	668·0	236·4	1,167·6	33·0	258·2	210·2	18·2	94·4	..	..	..	2,686·0
1771–75	604·2	43·2	2,195·4	67·8	285·4	9·0	21·2	59·6	1·0	2·4	..	3,289·2
1776–80	677·8	6·2	1,870·0	29·4	97·4	16·4	10·4	52·0	43·4	2·6	..	2,805·6
1781–85	551·8	137·0	2,220·6	16·0	218·8	2·4	9·6	39·2	5·8	1·8	..	3,203·0
1786–90	811·6	281·6	2,746·0	36·4	573·8	57·4	10·8	45·8	123·2	16·2	26·6	4,729·4
1791–95	314·0	150·2	2,703·2	5·8	1,048·2	44·6	1·0	85·8	234·8	6·8	3·6	4,598·0
1796–1800	108·0	7·2	2,725·2	58·8	303·0	51·8	15·2	68·8	39·0	9·4	18·2	3,404·6

* The figures for 1725–89 cover England and Wales, those for 1790–1800 include Scotland as well; the Scottish imports form a very small percentage of the total.

P.R.O. Customs 3/27–80 (1725–80); Customs 17/7–22 (1781–1800).

this was probably related to the parallel growth of the linen industry and of linen consumption in the British Isles. Cotton rags began to play a part in English paper-making, though the extent of their use is not clear. From the various descriptions of English paper-making in the late seventeenth and early eighteenth centuries there is no indication that cotton rags were distinguished as a paper-making material,[1] nor indeed is there any reason to suppose that they would be, for the amount of cloth made entirely of cotton and used in this country must have been extremely small. Imported Indian cottons and the development of the English cotton-linen industry are likely to have made available more rags from these materials.[2] It was not, however, until after the invention and use of spinning and weaving machinery in the last decades of the eighteenth century that cotton cloth in large quantities began to pour out of the new textile-mills, later to become rags for the paper-mills. So it is likely that even by the end of the century linen rags together with the miscellaneous hempen and flaxen waste of old rope, sails, sacking, and bagging and the like formed the bulk of home, as of foreign, supplies.[3]

What sort of proportion these home supplies bore to total rag consumption it is hard to say with any accuracy. Fig. 2 shows the striking fact that after advancing along parallel courses, the curves for rag imports and paper production diverge sharply in the war-ridden years of the 1790's. This contrary movement continued until about the end of the Napoleonic Wars. It is possible that inaccuracy of the statistics due to war circumstances

[1] e.g. in those quoted *supra*, p. 24, n. 1.

[2] See A. P. Wadsworth and J. de L. Mann, *The Cotton Trade and Industrial Lancashire, 1600–1780* (Manchester, 1931), *passim*; also *supra*, p. 65.

[3] Rees, op. cit., stated in 1819 that cotton rags were then only used in conjunction with other rags in the making of the poorer sorts of paper.

might account for some of the decline; the imposition in 1803 of an import duty on rags[1] may well have contributed both to its realities and to its statistical appearance via an increase in smuggling. Nevertheless it seems improbable that such reasons should be adequate seriously to alter the obvious general conclusion to be drawn from the graphs: that there was a substantial increase in available home supplies which went some way towards counterbalancing the loss of imports. Some proportion of this increase in home supplies may have been due to the introduction of chlorine bleaching,[2] which increased the *effective* supply of raw materials for white paper, though it is unlikely that chlorine was in general use before the very end of the century. Taking the amounts as shown in Fig. 2, it may be estimated that home supplies provided about 63 per cent. of the total before 1790 and about 75 per cent. thereafter.[3] The corresponding decline in imports left its mark however. The slowing down in the growth of output is surely a reflection, in some measure, of the comparative absence of imported rags; the general *relative* scarcity of rags is a part of the limitations of advance at this time and will be discussed in greater detail in Chapter VI.

In the technical progress of the industry the most important item in this century was the adoption of the Hollander. In a petition, possibly of 1737, credit for bringing about a revival of the industry in this country was assigned to Thomas Watkins, a London stationer and paper-maker who, in about 1713 it was said, 'with great trouble and expence in procuring workmen and purchasing engines and other raw materials from abroad

[1] 43 Geo. III, c. 68.
[2] See *infra*, p. 113.
[3] Percentages by weight. Cf. the estimates for 1830–59, *infra*, p. 214.

made further improvements in the art'.[1] There is no especial reason to assume that these 'engines' were Hollanders, although it is perhaps significant that it was by this vague term that they were normally known in the eighteenth century. Unmistakable news, however, of this device in England comes in the 1750's. Discussions stimulated by the Royal Society of Arts, concerning the shortcomings of English paper suitable for copper-plate printing, revealed that whilst the old stampers continued to be used in France, the Hollander was making its way into general English use.[2] For these very high quality papers this was then a disadvantage because the early models of the Hollander were not as efficient as the stampers.[3] Accordingly French paper was superior to ours: 'English Raggs being cut by Engines' whilst 'French Raggs are beat by hammers'.[4]

On the Continent, though the French were slow to use the Hollander, the Dutch adopted their own invention very rapidly; between the two extremes lay the Germans and the Italians.[5] In some mills, in England and on the Continent, both stampers and Hollanders were used: the mill at Astley, Worcestershire, for example, was advertised in 1736 as containing 'one engine and Ten Hammers'.[6] The Dutch example soon became the criterion for the enterprising man: to build 'a new Mill after the best Dutch Manner' was the stated intention of two forward-

---

[1] *Case of the Paper Makers.* Dr. Shorter states that Watkins's mill was probably at Longford, Middlesex. He was bankrupt in 1723 (*Historical Geography*, p. 67 n.).

[2] R.S.A.: Guard Books, vol. iii, pp. 43, 50.

[3] It was claimed, *inter alia*, that the stampers, by their hammering action retained and drew out the long, fine fibres and thus the resulting paper needed less size than its counterpart made with the Hollander which cut and shortened the fibres.

[4] Ibid., p. 43.   [5] Hunter, pp. 163–8.

[6] A. H. Shorter, 'Paper Mills in Worcestershire', loc. cit.

looking Irish paper-makers in the 1730's and 40's.[1] In England there can be little doubt that its adoption was rapid and, in the course of the century, complete; as new mills opened up, most of them would install the Hollander, especially after the mid-century. Its defects for the highest qualities of paper were less apparent for the medium and lower grades; moreover, it was undoubtedly improved in the course of the century. It drastically shortened the rag-preparation process, doing away with the tedious business of fermentation and repeated poundings. 'But lately', as Barrow put it in 1751, 'instead of pounding the rags to a pulp with large hammers . . . they make use of engines, which perform the work in much less time. . . . The engine being carried round with a prodigious velocity, reduces the rags to a pulp in a very short time.'[2]

As this was the only major technical improvement in the industry which came into widespread use it is reasonable to assume that the much greater increase in the output of paper than in the number of mills was due to the higher productivity brought by the Hollanders. Between 1738 and 1800, paper output rose nearly fourfold whilst mills only increased in number by about 50 per cent.[3] Barrow and the correspondents of the Royal Society of Arts make it clear that the beating-engine was in use by 1750. If it had indeed then been 'lately' introduced, say in the 1730's, and it was becoming widespread by the mid-century, then it is not at all fanciful to attribute some part at least of the increase both in output and in rate of growth at that time to the Hollander.

---

[1] C.J. (Ireland), vol. iv, pp. 241, 526. Similarly, in France, as late as 1760–80, to adopt *cylindres hollandais* was a mark of enterprise (C. Ballot, *L'Introduction du machinisme dans l'industrie française* (Paris, 1923), pp. 555–6).

[2] Op. cit. For other comments on the relative performances of the stampers and the Hollander see Spicer, pp. 56–57 and Hunter, p. 163.

[3] See *infra*, pp. 146–7, for numbers of mills.

The motive power of the beater, the new Hollander as much as the old stampers, continued to be chiefly that of falling water. Wind was occasionally, though very rarely, used in this country and steam-power made only a very slight impression on the industry in this century. James Watt's engine and his development of its use in imparting rotary motion opened up new possibilities of power in milling of many sorts from the 1780's onwards. It came into use in flour-mills, malt-mills, iron-mills, and, with great rapidity, in the new cotton-spinning mills. 'The people in London, Manchester and Birmingham', wrote Matthew Boulton to Watt in 1781, 'are steam-mill mad.'[1] The paper-makers were affected by no such enterprising insanity. Boulton and Watt erected only one of their engines in a paper-mill before the end of the century; at Messrs. Howard and Houghton's mill near Hull they installed a 10-h.p. engine in 1786. Not until 1802, when a 20-h.p. engine was put in at Messrs. Brown, Chalmers & Company's mill at Aberdeen, did they make their next installation in the industry.[2] At the very turn of the century another famous engineer, John Rennie, built and installed a steam-engine, for the very big but wholly unsuccessful experimental paper-mill set up by Matthias Koops.[3]

One of the reasons for this comparative slowness in experimenting with steam-power in paper-making probably lay in the converse of the situation which had earlier led the English industry to adopt the Hollander more rapidly than some of its older continental counterparts. The spinning-machines and the mills which housed them were new, almost as new as Watt's engine;

[1] Quoted P. Mantoux, *The Industrial Revolution in the Eighteenth Century* (London, 1928), p. 340.
[2] Birmingham Reference Library: Boulton and Watt Collection, portfolios 16, 235.   [3] See Hunter, p. 336, and *infra*, p. 172.

by that time most of the paper-mills, by contrast, were far older. It was virtually a new industry which was installing steam-engines in cotton-mills; it was not a new industry which was hesitating to do so in paper-mills. There were other reasons for this slowness. The steam-engine could only be used for the one process, driving the Hollander; consequently it would be necessary to have many vats to deal with the stuff produced by a steam-driven beater working more constantly than one dependent on the vagaries of water-power. As many mills were in remote and narrow river valleys and as most mills were very small, the construction of large steam-driven mills remained improbable before the paper-making machine was invented. Some such enterprises, i.e. steam-operated mills making hand-made paper, were developed in the course of time but they remained unusual.[1] A further point militating against the rapid introduction of steam-power was the remoteness from readily accessible coal supplies of the majority of eighteenth-century paper-mills.[2]

A striking example of the application of chemistry to industry came with the discovery of chlorine in 1774 by the Swedish apothecary, Carl Scheele, and its subsequent rapid application, especially in France and Scotland, to the problems of bleaching.[3] Its use permitted the replacement in the textile industry of long, tedious, and time-honoured methods of bleaching; in the paper industry, too, it brought a new process, much needed as the industry expanded.

---

[1] As well as those near Hull and Aberdeen, mentioned above, other mills installing steam-engines but not paper-making machinery included W. Balston of Springfield Mill, Maidstone (1805), and Messrs. Bally, Ellen & Steart of Montalt Mill, Bath (1808) (Birmingham Reference Library: Boulton and Watt Collection, portfolios 327, 846).

[2] See *infra*, pp. 147-9.   [3] Clow, op. cit., pp. 169 et seq.

In the earlier absence of a bleaching agent effective for their raw materials, paper-makers had been restricted in the making of white paper by the limitations of washing and beating and by the original colours of the rags.[1] For the better white papers white rags alone availed. As the demand for rags widened and as cotton rags, often coloured, came to be used, the problem of a truly effective method of bleaching became more acute. Who was initially responsible for its solution it is, as usual, difficult to say. What at least does seem clear is that it was not the earliest patentees. Clement and George Taylor, paper-makers of Kent, were granted a patent in April 1792 for the use in rag-bleaching of 'dephlogisticated marine acid', obtained by the interaction of sulphuric acid, manganese, and common salt.[2] But in Scotland where, under the influence of such men as Joseph Black, important and early advances were being made in chemistry and its application to industrial problems, chlorine is said to have been first used in paper-making at William Simpson's mill at Lasswade, near Edinburgh, in 1791.[3] The Scottish paper-makers not unnaturally objected to the Taylors' patent. They campaigned against it and carried their animosity to the stage of bringing a legal action to have it declared null.[4]

James Whatman, too, had strong views on the subject of the Taylors' patent. In December 1792 he wrote to the Scottish makers that he could prove having had the use of 'dephlogisticated muriatic acid . . . in contemplation for at least three years since to try its effect in my manu-

---

[1] See Hunter, pp. 224–5.   [2] Patent No. 1872 of 1792.
[3] *Old Statistical Account*, vol. x, p. 279.
[4] Clow, op. cit., pp. 265–6; Balston MSS.: J. Barton to Whatman, 3 Dec. 1792. In Feb. 1793 the Scottish paper-makers informed the Taylors that they proposed to disregard the latter's patent (see T. Balston, 'James Whatman, Father and Son', chap. xx, *The Paper Maker*, Dec. 1955, p. 574).

factory and actually purchased all the ingredients for carrying on the process on 13th October 1791'. He did not, however, claim any priority for himself, for he went on further to say:

Several Paper Makers have already manufactured into Paper bleached Pulp and half Stuff done for them by a Mr. Campbell or a Mr. Gardner, particularly Mr. Larking and the Messrs. Curteis's. The latter, at which having got information of an Experiment tried full three years since by the late Mr. Patch of Carshalton with the Dephlogisticated Muriatic Acid on Pulp and Half Stuff, and to whom as far as has come to my knowledge, the Merit is due of the First Application of it in our Manufacture in this Kingdom. I shall trouble you with it at length as stated to me by Mr. Patch, the son, on the 4th Nov. last, in the Presence of Mr. Curteis and Mr. Thomas Curteis, it being a Case intirely in point for the Complete Demolition of the Patent.[1]

He also added that it was on the strength of the skills of one Mr. Willis, a chemist, that the Taylors had secured their patent, as well as on a promise to him of a reward of £500 for success.[2]

---

[1] Balston MSS.: Whatman to Papermakers of Scotland, 10 Dec. 1792. Curteis's mill was at Carshalton, Larking's at E. Malling, near Maidstone. Whatman went on to give:

'Mr. Chris.ᵗ. Patch's Account of an Engine of Pulp and Half Stuff Bleached for his late Father by Mr. Collinson.

That Mr. Collinson took out of the Engine a Quantity of Half Stuff about 96 or 98 lbs wt. which was made from Second Rags: That the said Half Stuff was carried into the Stable and there bleached by Mr. Collinson by some Chemical Process and afterwards brought back to the Mill and put into the Engine again and the said Half Stuff so bleached was manufactured into Thin Post Paper and sold to Mr. Gregs, and likewise that the said Mr. Collinson bleached some Half Stuff made from Third Rags, such as was then working into Coarse Letteris and brought that Half Stuff to a most beautiful colour equal to Fine Half Stuff, and that to the best of his Recollection the above was done about three years since.'

[2] For some further details of this dispute and of Whatman's own experiments in bleaching see Balston op. cit., in *The Paper Maker*, Dec. 1955, pp. 572–4.

No doubt there was a goodly share of the sourer sort of trade jealousy in all this, as well as some measure of the commonly occurring multiplication and coincidence of similar inventions. But that Campbell had some responsibility for the dissemination in England of the use of chlorine in rag-bleaching is clear both from Whatman's remarks and from the granting of a patent to Hector Campbell in November 1792 for a process similar to, though not identical with, that of the Taylors.[1] Campbell had apparently been much in contact with the Taylors and his experience with them had not been very happy: in April 1792 he remarked in a letter to another papermaker that it was his intention 'not to remain any longer in obscurity'.[2] The Taylors' patent covered, in effect, bleaching by chlorine in the form of hypochlorite solution; the rags were treated with this in a revolving drum, after having previously been washed in a beater with an alkali. Campbell, who claimed to have been for some time engaged in bleaching textiles by means of a hypochlorite solution, stated that in 1791 he applied it to rag-bleaching but found that the result was imperfect.[3] His patent was for bleaching by gaseous chlorine produced, as before, by the heating of a combination of salt, manganese (manganese dioxide, in fact), and sulphuric acid. The resulting gas passed into one or more chambers containing the rags which had previously been boiled in a caustic lye. It is not clear what method was being used in Whatman's description of the process which he had seen at Carlshalton. Moreover, to complicate matters further, some Irish paper-makers at about this time are said to have been using potassium hypochloride ('oxy-

---

[1] Patent No. 1922.
[2] Balston MSS.: Campbell to J. Larkin, 18 Aug. 1792.
[3] Patent No. 1922.

genated muriate of potash' or *Eau de Javelle* as it was then called).[1] Though primacy of innovation may not be clearly assignable, it seems clear, however, that it was Campbell's process which was successful. The process of bleaching by chlorine gas went into general use and continued to be employed until it was later superseded by the use of chloride of lime.[2]

Initially the use of chlorine was probably both costly and unsatisfactory. Whatman records that 'on my asking Mr. Patch the reason why his father did not go on with it he told me he found the waste of the stuff so great and the price expected by Mr. Collinson per cwt. being, I think, Twelve Shillings, over-ballanced all the advantages to be derived'.[3] A further effect in the early days was that the paper produced thereby was sometimes of fine appearance but questionable substance, so that printers found it difficult to use.[4] Improvements seem to have been fairly rapid, though its spread into general use properly belongs to the new era ushered in by the machine.

In the making and finishing processes only one innovation of the eighteenth century possessed major significance: the introduction of wove paper. The essence of this was the use of a mould consisting of a very fine woven wire mesh in lieu of the parallel wires of the 'laid' mould. This had the effect of producing a smoother and more even surfaced paper on which, of course, the lines watermarked by the impression of the laid mould were no longer visible. It was particularly desired for very high-grade printing- and drawing-paper. It has also a quite different, indirect significance in that it was an

[1] Clow, op. cit., p. 190.
[2] Rees, op. cit.; Spicer, p. 77; see also *infra*, pp. 215–16.
[3] Balston MSS.: Whatman to Papermakers of Scotland, Dec. 1792.
[4] Rees, op. cit.

endless woven wire mesh of this sort which was later to form the essential feature of the Fourdrinier machine. The responsibility for the introduction of the wove mould into England, and indeed into Europe, remains obscure. The earliest known European book printed on wove paper was an edition of *Virgil* printed by the celebrated Birmingham printer, John Baskerville, and published in 1757. This work was much acclaimed both in England and on the Continent, alike for the printing and for the paper; on no very conclusive evidence Baskerville has accordingly been credited with the introduction of wove paper. More recent research into the subject has suggested that Baskerville may have perhaps proposed the use of woven wire moulds—a Birmingham printer might well have had a particular acquaintance with metal-working and the problems to be faced in constructing such moulds—but that the execution was carried out elsewhere, possibly at Turkey Mill, Kent, which was worked by the Whatmans, father and son, from 1740 to 1794.[1] In 1768 the second James Whatman remarked in a letter enclosing some specimens of paper that one of these was 'made upon Wove Moulds and is the same sort of Paper I made (for) Mr. Caples Prolusions'.[2] This was a reference to a book compiled by Edward Capell, entitled *Prolusions; or Select Pieces of Ancient Poetry*, which was published in 1759. Moreover, there are traces of the Whatman watermark on this and on other examples of wove paper in the 1760's, including that in another book printed by Baskerville, though there are none in the *Virgil*. From these rather tenuous links, reinforced by the eminence of Whatman's position in eighteenth-century English paper-making, the Turkey Mill has

[1] J. Wardrop, 'Mr. Whatman, Papermaker', *Signature*, vol. ix (1938).
[2] Quoted ibid.

become a candidate for this honour. In 1759, however, the second and more famous James Whatman was only eighteen years of age, and thus only sixteen when Baskerville's *Virgil* was published. Young Whatman, as will be shown later, was certainly both precocious and successful, but credibility demands that we should make other assumptions. It is possible that the Turkey Mill made the wove paper for the *Prolusions*, but not for the *Virgil*, i.e. some other maker may have been involved. Alternatively, and this seems the most probable answer, the credit belongs to the elder James Whatman who died in 1759. Very little is known about him but it is at least clear that he was an enterprising and successful paper-maker, capable of an innovation of this sort.[1]

For another, and far less important, innovation in the making process, the second James Whatman seems to have a better claim to priority: the manufacture of a particularly large size of paper which has come to be known as 'antiquarian'. He was approached in 1772 by the Society of Antiquaries for a sheet $52\frac{3}{4}$ in. $\times$ $31\frac{3}{4}$ in. for an engraving. This was far bigger than the largest mould normally in use, the 'grand eagle or double elephant' of about 40 in. $\times$ 26 in. However, by means of 'a Contrivance I have thought of', Whatman indicated that he would attempt the task and sent in a provisional estimate of 16 to 18 guineas per ream. This was later reduced to, and accepted at, £15 per ream, the Antiquaries having ascertained that 'no paper of the size and sort wanted was made at any of the Mills in Europe'. In the following year Whatman delivered the paper, the engravings were

[1] As much as is known about the elder Whatman will be found in T. Balston, 'James Whatman, Father and Son', chap. iv, *The Paper Maker*, Apr. 1955, pp. 292–3. A painting of him is reproduced in *The Paper Maker*, May 1955, p. 385. For further information on the Whatmans see *infra*, pp. 151–5.

very successful and an export demand developed for this sort of paper.[1] The importance of this feat has almost certainly been exaggerated in the suggestion that Whatman's export of paper of this type marked 'a turning point in English paper making',[2] for it was not upon the limited demand for these very high quality and very specialized papers that the English industry was built. Nor was the 'contrivance' by which it was made—an arrangement of levers to facilitate the lifting of the mould, together with a larger than usual crew of men at the vat—of any serious importance in the development of the industry.[3] From a technical and historical viewpoint it is an interesting symptom of the problem of size, posed by the limits of human manipulation, which restricted manufacture before the arrival of the machine.

(v)

It will be evident from the foregoing that the major advances within the industry were in the preparatory process. It was in rag-preparation that higher productivity was being achieved. So long as the making and finishing processes remained virtually unchanged, and so long as demand was growing, tensions were being set up in the industry which could only result, sooner or later, in radical change. By the later years of the century certain problems were pressing acutely for solution. These will be examined in Chapter VI in the context of

[1] Wardrop, loc. cit.

[2] Jenkins, p. 186.

[3] It is possible, that this device had been anticipated in France, though not apparently for sheets so large as 'antiquarian'. See *The Paper Maker*, June 1955, p. 478. Details of the Whatman's 'contrivance', as it continued to be used in Messrs. W. & R. Balston's mill, may be found in *The Paper Maker*, Apr. 1956, pp. 344–5.

the industry's organization and the activities of some of its major entrepreneurs.

Meanwhile, however, there is one aspect of the industry's growth throughout this early period which demands detailed investigation: the influence upon it of a network of Customs and Excise duties.

V

Taxation and Protection

THE Customs and the Excise duties[1] together made up a tangled thread of taxation, on paper as on other commodities at this time. To unravel its complexity became a problem for contemporary administrators and remains one for historians. These duties demand examination for several reasons. They influenced the supply of foreign paper and the volume of home production; the schedules of papers listed for taxation and the returns themselves provide valuable evidence of the nature and quantity both of imports and home production but have to be used carefully because of various administrative snags; they shed some light on the difficult question of paper prices and values; and the disputes which arose in regard to the administration of the Excise illuminate a number of interesting problems affecting the paper-maker and trader. In addition they provide some illustrations of the difficulties of adapting taxes to so heterogeneous a commodity as paper.

(i)

Until the later seventeenth century, paper normally paid, as a Customs duty, the usual 5 per cent. *ad valorem* subsidy of tonnage and poundage.[2] It was valued for this

[1] The duties examined in this chapter were those in force in Great Britain. Ireland had a different taxation system, and not until 1798 was there any Excise on the production of paper. The Irish customs on paper are discussed briefly, and not in any detail, *infra*, p. 144, n. 3.

[2] The duty on paper, as on other commodities, was sometimes temporarily raised as, for example, by the impositions of Charles I and James I. It is possible that these may have had some slight protective effect on the home industry, at any rate so far as brown paper was concerned.

purpose in the Book of Rates. In 1507, for instance, three types are mentioned:[1]

> paper called wyte, the balle
> paper called wyte, the reme
> paper called browne, the bundelle.

Passing by later issues of the Book of Rates it will suffice to draw together the following three issues to show the general range of papers which the Customs authorities chose to notice at that time and the values which they put upon them:

TABLE VII

Valuations in Books of Rates, 1604–60

(All by the ream unless otherwise stated)

Type	1604	Interregnum	1660
Blue	4s.	10s.	10s.
Brown, by the bundle . . .	1s.	3s.	3s.
Cap	2s. 6d.	7s. 6d.	7s. 6d.
Demy	4s.	12s.	12s.
Ordinary printing and copy .	2s. 6d.	2s. 6d.	4s. 6d.
Painted	6s. 8d.	20s.	13s. 4d.
Pressing, by the hundred leaves .	6s. 8d.	20s.	13s. 4d.
Rochelle, as large as demy . .	3s.	9s.	9s.
Royal	6s. 8d.	20s.	20s.
Morlaix	..	2s. 6d.	..
Paper of Caen and Rouen, ordinary	..	4s. 6d.	..

Source: P.R.O.: E. 122/173/3; C. H. Firth and R. S. Rait (eds.) *Acts and Ordinances of the Interregnum* (London, 1911), vol. ii, p. 1216; 12 Chas. II, c. 4. On Books of Rates generally see Gras, op. cit., pp. 121–9.

These values were not necessarily market values. As the basis of an *ad valorem* duty they could be altered to provide greater or less revenue or protection. Although the values bore some general relation to market prices, it may nevertheless be supposed that the discrepancy, for instance, between the rise of 200–300 per cent. shown by

[1] Gras, op. cit., p. 701.

most papers and the mere 80 per cent. of 'ordinary printing and copy' owes more to the need for imports of the latter, and to the inadvisability of taxing them too highly, than to any real market changes.

The increase in tariffs between 1660 and 1714 has already been outlined in Chapter III. The first stages may be summarized thus:

TABLE VIII

Import Duties, 1660–1704

1660[1]	'The Old Subsidy of Tonnage and Poundage'	5 per cent. *ad valorem* on rates quoted in Table VII
1690[2]	Impost	+5 per cent. on all types except the following flat rate additions: Royal +2s. per ream Blue, demy & painted +1s. 6d. per ream Brown +2d. per bundle
[1696/7–1698/9[3]	[for two years only]	[+25 per cent.]
[1697–1699/1700[4]	[May 1697 to February 1699/1700]	[+5 per cent.]
1698[5]	'The New Subsidy' commenced February 1699/1700	+5 per cent.
1703[6]	'One Third Subsidy' }	+5 per cent., i.e. percentage duty *ad valorem* in 1704 = 20 per cent.
1704[7]	'Two Thirds Subsidy' }	

All percentages were calculated on the 1660 Book of Rates valuation (see Table VII). The 'new subsidy' of 1698 was simply a repetition of that of 1660. In addition to the above duties French goods were also subjected to a 25 per cent. impost in 1692/3,[8] and, for 21 years only, a further 25 per cent. in 1696/7.[9]

[1] 12 Chas. II, c. 4.   [2] 2 Wm. & Mary, sess. 2, c. 4.
[3] 8 & 9 Wm. III, c. 7.   [4] 8 & 9 Wm. III, c. 24.
[5] 9 Wm. III, c. 23.   [6] 2 & 3 Anne, c. 9.
[7] 3 & 4 Anne, c. 5.   [8] 4 Wm. & Mary, c. 5.
[9] 7 & 8 Wm. III, c. 20.

A protective policy having been agreed upon under the combined stimuli of industrial pressure and fiscal need, the lists of dutiable goods should, in theory, be complete. But in fact the nine items of the Old Subsidy (and the New) formed a totally inadequate list of the types and sizes of paper in use.[1] This was partly rectified with the imposition of the 'New Duties' of 1712, for they were levied at flat rates varying according to a schedule covering some thirty-seven types of paper.[2]

The imposition of these duties did not of course cancel the old *ad valorem* duties. Accordingly, by this date, all paper imports paid both the New Duties and the five *ad valorem* duties surviving from 1660 to 1704, the payments being based on the valuations of the Old and New Subsidies.[3]

The range of paper covered was still far from complete and it is scarcely surprising that much paper was recorded under the heading of 'Unrated'. Paper which the Customs officials could be persuaded to enter in this category was charged for all *ad valorem* duties according to a valuation given on the oath of the importer. (The New Duties of 1712 contained a 20 per cent. *ad valorem* duty on unspecified types.) So attractive a notion for lessening the burden of duty received its due tribute. The percentage of 'unrated' gradually increased: from 4·6 per cent. for the 5 years 1699–1703 it rose to 11·6 per cent. in 1706–10 and 13·3 per cent. in 1719–23.[4] In 1725 this leak in the revenue was stopped. An Act was passed in that year to rate goods previously admitted unrated.[5] The preamble complained that 'some Persons (were) greatly undervaluing the same, to the Detriment of the Revenue and Discouragement of the Fair Traders'. It

---

[1] Its inadequacy is very apparent when compared with a list from 1674 covering sixty-seven different types, sizes, or qualities of imported paper offered for sale at that time (R. W. Chapman, 'An Inventory of Paper, 1674', *Trans. Bib. Soc.*, vol. vii (1926–7), pp. 402–8).

[2] 10 Anne, c. 18.

[3] The valuations were the same.

[4] P.R.O. Customs 3 (England and Wales only).

[5] 11 Geo. I, c. 7.

was no doubt because of the knowledge of this pending legislation that in 1724 the percentage of 'unrated' soared to 49·3.[1] The sudden leap in the level of total paper imports in that year was also probably almost entirely due to this fact.[2] In 1725 the percentage sank to 4·3 and thereafter the category disappeared.[3] The Act rated fourteen types and sizes of paper for the Old Subsidy and also dealt with the New Duties. These had been raised by 50 per cent. in 1714[4] but here, too, the *ad valorem* category (now 30 per cent.) was providing a useful loophole for importers. Another clause of the same Act of 1725 accordingly rated seventeen sorts of hitherto unrated paper for this duty.

So by this time provision had been made for the payment of duties on imported paper in accordance with the following confused categories:

I. The old *ad valorem* duties (1660–1704) were paid on two bases:

  (i) For the types quoted in Table VII, on the valuations there given which were those of the Old Subsidy.

  (ii) For the fourteen types rated in the Act of 1725 at the valuations then given.

II. The New Duties were paid:

  (i) In accordance with the flat rates of 1712 and the 50 per cent. increase on these in 1714.

  (ii) *Ad valorem* (30 per cent.) on the basis of:

    (*a*) The valuations for the seventeen types given in the Act of 1725.

    (*b*) The oath of the importer, for any unenumerated papers.

---

[1] P.R.O. Customs 3/26.   [2] See Fig. 2.
[3] P.R.O. Customs 3/27.   [4] 13 Anne, c. 18.

Confusion was to be further confounded by three more moves in the game. By far the largest class within group I (i) above—indeed in the imports as a whole—was that of 'ordinary'. A concentration of the declining imports into this comparatively lowly rated category had sooner or later to be broken up in the same manner as the 'un-rated' had been in 1725. In 1743 a new, long, and com-prehensive list of types and values makes its appearance in the Customs ledgers.[1] The all-embracing 'ordinary' category disappears. In this way the revenue was assisted and the protective barrier reinforced. Thereafter they were further strengthened and the complexity of the duties heightened by a series of percentage increases. These owed much to the need for revenue posed by war: the years 1747, 1759, 1779, and 1782 each saw 5 per cent. increases on all import duties.[2] And then in 1784 ten specified types or sizes of paper were singled out for various flat rate increases.[3]

By this time imports had shrunk to a trickle of some 7,000–8,000 reams per year. But the duties on paper, as on other goods, had grown into a monstrous and idiotic jumble. What this meant, even by the mid-century, can be gathered from the following extract of two examples taken from a guide to the Customs published in 1752 (Table IX). And on to this were to be piled the additions of 1759, 1779, 1782, and 1784 before reform came. By that time a foreign merchant importing French

[1] P.R.O. Customs 3/43. It is this which makes possible for the first time a comprehensive, detailed, and reasonably reliable analysis of imports. See Table IV, *supra*, p. 94.

It should be added that the values given in the Customs ledgers were not always the same as those on which *ad valorem* duties were charged.

[2] 21 Geo. II, c. 2; 32 Geo. II, c. 10; 19 Geo. III, c. 25; 22 Geo. III, c. 66.

[3] 24 Geo. III, c. 18.

TABLE IX

Aggregate Import Duties on two Types of Paper, 1752

Type	Rate	Old subsidy 1660, 1/20th of the rate (discount 5%)	New subsidy 1699, 1/20th of the rate (discount 5%)	1/3rd subsidy 1703 · 2/3rds subsidy 1704	Subsidy, 1747, 1/20th of the rate (without discount)	Impost, 1690, 1/20th of the rate (discount 6¼%)	New duties, 1712 & 1714 (net)	Total duties (British)	Aliens duty over and above British duty, 1/80th of the rate (no discount)
	£ s. d.	£ s. d. 1/100	£ s. d. 1/100	£ s. d. 1/100	£ s. d. 1/100	£ s. d. 1/100	£ s. d. 1/100	£ s. d. 1/100	£ s. d. 1/100
Demy, fine	0 12 0	0 0 6·84	0 0 6·84	0 0 6·84	0 0 7·20	0 1 4·875	0 3 9	0 7 5·595	0 0 1·80
Brown, cap	0 7 6	0 0 4·275	0 0 4·275	0 0 4·275	0 0 4·5	0 0 4·21¼	0 1 6	0 3 3·54⅞	0 0 1·12½

Source: T. Daniel, *The Present State of the British Customs* (London, 1752).

paper would have paid duties calculated under thirteen different heads.[1]

Pitt's tariff reforms hacked a way through this tangle of paper import duties as they did through other import duties. The various subsidies, imposts, and duties on paper were swept away in 1787 and a set of new net duties replaced them.[2] These covered some fifty-six types and sizes of paper together with an *ad valorem* duty of 55 per cent. on unenumerated types. Imports increased very slightly for the few years during which these duties were in force, though still remaining at an insignificant level. But this was the last time that the clumsy apparatus of enumerating types and sizes was to be used. In 1794 these duties were repealed and the principle of assessment by weight was at last introduced for both Customs and Excise.

(ii)

The Excise of the Interregnum introduced in 1643 a sales tax on paper to be paid by 'the first buyer thereof from the merchant or importer'.[3] The 5 per cent. duty which it imposed made no distinction between English or foreign paper; paper was included, for rating purposes, not amongst home-produced goods but in the list of imported foreign wares.[4] Neither this tax nor the short-lived experiment of 1696-8 need detain us.[5] Not until 1712 does the Excise on paper truly begin. The same Act that imposed the New Duties on imports also laid down

---

[1] See E. Hoon, *The Organization of the English Customs System, 1696–1786* (N.Y. 1938), pp. 27–28 n.

[2] 27 Geo. III, c. 13.

[3] *Acts and Ordinances of the Interregnum*, vol. i, p. 277.

[4] Ibid., vol. ii, p. 848.

[5] 8 & 9 Wm. III, c. 7. It combined a 25 per cent. duty on imports of paper and books with a 20 per cent. tax on home paper production and 17½ per cent. tax on dealers' stocks.

the following duties on home production and made detailed provision for their collection:

TABLE X

Excise Duties, 1712

(per ream unless otherwise stated)

Demy, fine	. .	1s. 6d.	Pots, fine	. .	1s.
Demy, second	. .	1s.	Pots, second	. .	6d.
Crown, fine	. .	1s.	Brown, large cap	.	6d.
Crown, second	.	9d.	Small ordinary brown	.	4d.
Foolscap, fine	. .	1s.	Whited brown (per bundle)		6d.
Foolscap, second	.	9d.	Unenumerated	.	12%
					ad valorem

Pasteboard, Millboard, and Scaleboard: 3s. per cwt.

Source: 10 Anne, c. 18.

This schedule remained the basis of assessment until 1781. Just as the Customs were periodically subjected to percentage increases, so were the Excise rates: by 50 per cent. in 1714, by 5 per cent. in 1779, and again in 1781.[1]

Various provisions were made for the collection of the duties.[2] These arrangements were soon the subject of complaints and of fraud. Early petitions against the im-

---

[1] 13 Anne, c. 18; 19 Geo. III, c. 25; 21 Geo. III, c. 17.

[2] 10 Anne, c. 18. The most important were:

(a) Commissioners were to be appointed with powers in turn to appoint collectors and other officers.

(b) Makers were to report their place of manufacture to local Excise officers.

(c) Makers were to render a return, every six weeks, of types and quantities made.

(d) Duties were to be paid by six weeks after the returns made.

(e) Excise officers were granted powers of entry to mills in order to survey paper, rags, &c., in stock.

(f) Paper subject to the *ad valorem* duty was to be valued on the oath of the maker according to what it would be worth if sold at the nearest market town.

(g) Drawbacks of the duty were to be allowed on exports and for paper used in printing books for Oxford, Cambridge, and the universities of Scotland in the 'Latin, Greek, Oriental or Northern Languages'.

(h) Sundry provisions were made for penalties, forfeitures, &c., in case of non-compliance with the regulations.

position of the duties[1] were succeeded in due time by allegations of evasion. In 1738 Samuel Galliott, a paper-maker, and Richard Parry submitted a scheme to Walpole, 'setting forth the many Frauds practised by the Paper-Makers in General to the great prejudice of his Majesty's Revenue'.[2] They alleged, *inter alia*, that rated papers were now underrated, that unrated papers bearing the *ad valorem* duty were regularly undervalued, and that Excise officers were variously deceived by the makers in regard to the types and quantities made. They put forward suggestions for improved methods of collection. The Excise Commissioners rejected Galliott's and Parry's allegations and generally showed themselves to be complacently content with existing arrangements. Nevertheless their report to the Treasury contained what was in effect a tacit admission of the existence of fraud in regard to the undervaluing of paper rated *ad valorem*.[3]

More weighty criticisms of a similar sort were made in the 1760's. After an earlier memorandum against the duties, a further petition to the Treasury from the 'Committee appointed by a General Meeting of the Paper Makers of Great Britain in behalf of themselves and the rest of the Trade' asked that the duty should be collected 'for this year only with the same Lenity as has been done for many years past'.[4] The petitioners urged this because they affirmed that the Excise officers had lately been directed to collect duties which the trade found intolerable. They promised to produce a plan to 'regulate the Duty so that the Revenue may be increased and an

---

[1] e.g. *Case of the Manufactures of Paper; Case of the Traders in and Exporters of Woollen Manufactures in relation to the duties laid on pasteboard, etc. etc.*, and similar broadsides in the Goldsmiths Library.

[2] C. & E.: Excise-Treasury Letters, 1733–45, ff. 245–6.

[3] Ibid., f. 248.

[4] C. & E.: Excise-Treasury Letters, 1763–8, ff. 134–5.

equitable Duty levied and the fair Trader not injured'. The Excise Commissioners replied that no direction had been given to charge any other duties than usual but admitted that in view of numerous disputes which had arisen about the nature and value of various sorts of paper the collection of the duty had been tightened up slightly. This petition was submitted by Charles Jenkinson (later Lord Liverpool), then Secretary to the Lords Commissioners of the Treasury, to the Excise authorities on 24 May 1765. In December 1764 James Whatman, one of the signatories of the petition,[1] had himself submitted a lengthy memorial to Jenkinson on the subject of the paper duties.[2] He claimed that the notion of valuing paper by what it would fetch in the nearest market town[3] was absurd as there would be no sale in such places for most of the paper then made, and that accordingly the maker merely put his own valuation on it; that most of the paper that was made was not covered by the rated categories; that Excise officers were ignorant of the various sorts of paper, and that false denominations were given. Because of the way in which the duty was levied, because the remoteness of many mills prevented frequent surveys by Excise officers, and because of the possibilities of collusion between masters and men—'at least half the paper that is made pays no duty at all'. He proposed various remedies, and although the precise response to his petition is unknown, some of his ideas were certainly embodied in later reforms of the Excise. Meanwhile, a petition in 1771 from Buckinghamshire paper-makers added weight to the first of Whatman's complaints: they, too, insisted that the clause in the Act

[1] The others were John Vowell, Thomas Wright, George Street, John Bullock, Joseph Portal, Richard Ware, and Robert Herbert.

[2] B.M. Add. MSS. 38203, ff. 317–20.

[3] See *supra*, p. 130, n. 2.

relating to the value at the next market town was quite useless.[1]

That there was substantial proof in all these allegations is apparent from the returns of paper made. The defects of the printed returns and the methods by which these may be remedied by estimates based on the original manuscript returns are set out in detail in Appendix I. Meanwhile Fig. 4[2] shows how more and more paper was switched into the *ad valorem* category—and no doubt undervalued as well—thus serving to ease the full burden of the Excise, and also to give the false impression to the historian that the output of some of the rated types was stationary or declining. Just as the 'unrated' and 'ordinary' categories in the Customs provided loopholes for the importer so, on a larger scale, did the *ad valorem* category operate similarly for the home producer.

When reform came in 1781, it took the shape, as mentioned earlier, of the elaborate schedules of seventy-seven different types of paper, specifying sizes and values.[3] For the government this had the desirable effect of substantially increasing the yield of the duties.[4] But the paper-makers themselves soon came to view it in a very different light. The problems posed by these duties loomed large amongst the subjects discussed in the regular meetings of the paper manufacturers which were coming to be a feature of the industry at this period.[5] The general weight of the duty was very much increased and it was soon made heavier still by further percentage increases in 1782, 1784, and 1787.[6] Moreover, the regula-

---

[1] C. & E.: Excise-Treasury Letters, 1767–74, ff. 197–8.

[2] Constructed from data in C. & E.: Quantities, Rates and Amounts of Excise Duties, 1684–1798.

[3] 21 Geo. III, c. 24.   [4] See Fig. 5, *infra*, p. 141.

[5] These are discussed in detail in Chap. X.

[6] The rates set out in 21 Geo. III, c. 24, were themselves subject to an

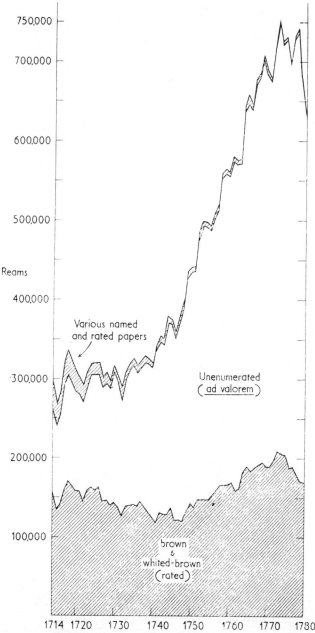

FIG. 4. Output (Rated and *Ad Valorem*, unadjusted) 1714–80
(England and Wales, reams)

tions concerning the wrapping of the paper and its sub-
mission to the Excise officers for inspection were made
more stringent. The sheer complexity of the various
'tables' also made for trouble. Furthermore troubles
differed between manufacturers according to the grade
of paper which they made and the tables with which
they were concerned.

In general it is clear that rising prices were distorting
the valuations and the schedules. Paper as made did not
always precisely correspond to paper as specified in the
schedules. What then was it to be called and what duty
was it to pay? Should it be in a lower or a higher table?
The opinions of Excise officers clashed with those of
paper-makers; paper was seized and fines were imposed.
There were sundry wrangles not dissimilar to those which
have arisen in more recent times about purchase tax.
The elaborate apparatus of the law—judge, jury, learned
counsel, expert witnesses, and detailed pleading—was
set in motion in order to determine such weighty matters
as the exact name, type, dimensions, and value of a
particular sort of paper so as in turn to decide whether
it should pay a duty of, say, $11\frac{1}{2}d.$ or $1s.$ $1\frac{3}{4}d.$ per ream.[1]
In particular it seems that the makers most aggrieved
were those chiefly concerned with papers in the second
and third tables. Rising rag prices combined with the
added weight of the duty to make certain sorts of paper

extra 10 per cent. (being the two 5 per cent. increases imposed by 19 Geo.
III, c. 24 and 21 Geo. III, c. 17). An extra 5 per cent. was then put on in
1782 by 22 Geo. III, c. 66; in 1784 further specific additions were made to
each of the rates, usually amounting to $33\frac{1}{3}$ per cent. on the original rates
of 1781; in 1787 existing rates were repealed and new rates laid down,
consolidating and, in some cases, slightly increasing the existing duties.

[1] These and other sorts of disputes arising from the Excise regulation are
chronicled in the volumes of Excise Trials. See, e.g., C. & E.: Excise Trials,
vol. 531, pp. 128–264; vol. 532, pp. 419–45, 447–99; vol. 544, pp. 51–153,
&c.

unprofitable to manufacture.[1] An example given by William Lepard in 1792 indicates the sort of annoyance which the Act could and did create: 'If a maker of a 2nd Table Imperial makes one worth 50s. or 50s. 6d. he is to pay 7s. 5¾d. duty as the Act now stands; but if his Customer wants one to be made of 2s. or 3s. higher value then he is liable to pay 13s. 9½d. [being brought into Table 1 on price] and so get less of the stuff, tho' a better paper, or else run the hazard of being uneasy in his mind for having exceeded legal limits.'[2]

Pressure exerted by the more influential manufacturers had its outcome in the reforms of 1794 affecting both Customs and Excise duties. These two can now be drawn together and their relation shown clearly as follows:

TABLE XI

Customs and Excise Duties 1794–1801

Class	Description	Excise duty per lb.	Import duty per lb.
1	Writing, drawing, printing, elephant, and cartridge .	2½d.	10d.
2	Coloured and whited brown	1d.	4d.
3	Brown wrapping . .	½d.	2d.
4	Unenumerated . .	2½d.	10d.
5	Pasteboard, millboard, and scaleboard . . .	10s. 6d. per cwt.	20s. per cwt.
	Glazed paper . .	6s. per cwt.	12s. per cwt.

Source: 34 Geo. III, c. 20.

Though simplified in this manner the provisions for wrapping, inspection, stamping, and so forth attained a new and fearsome rigorousness. In addition to the existing regulations for makers and to the duties and powers of Excise officers new and precise methods for wrapping

[1] Balston MSS.: James Greatrake (paper-maker of Hertfordshire) to Whatman, 1792.   [2] Ibid.: Lepard to Whatman, 1792.

the paper were laid down.[1] The amount and class of paper were to be marked on the wrapper and numbered according to the number of such reams or bundles made at the mill in the current quarter. It was to be inspected, weighed, and stamped by the Excise officer.

Penalties were as usual liberally provided. Amongst the new ones were penalties for stationers or dealers receiving any paper not in an entire ream or bundle and duly stamped, or returning old wrappers to makers; wrappers were to be destroyed immediately on receipt.[2]

The duties remained at these rates until 1801 when they were doubled.[3] This new weight of taxation together with the stifling regulations attached to its collection continued to provoke a good deal of vigorous protest. This and the subsequent history of the duties will be considered in later chapters.

Three further matters may be briefly mentioned here: drawbacks, duties on rag imports, and licences. The drawback of the Excise duty on exports, allowed by the Act of 1712, was continued by the later Acts. According both to Whatman in 1764 and to a petition of London stationers in 1782 it was not very easily obtained, but the difficulties seem to have been circumvented judging by the growth of an export trade.[4] Drawbacks on the import duties were not normally given. Rags and similar paper-

---

[1] It was to be 'inclosed and tied up with strong thread or string in several covers or wrappers containing one Ream or Bundle each and not more or less'. It was ordained that 'the different Parts of such thread or string shall pass over and across each other at the middle of the Ream or Bundle of Paper or Parcel of Pasteboard, etc. etc. . . . and where the different Parts of such thread or string shall cross each other, the same shall be passed from thence over and across the Ends and Sides of such Ream or Bundle', &c. &c. (34 Geo. III, c. 20, s. vii).

[2] 34 Geo. III, c. 20, s. x, s. xxiv–xxvi.

[3] 41 Geo. III, c. 8.

[4] B.M. Add. MSS. 38203, f. 318; C. & E.: Excise-Treasury Letters, 1779–82, ff. 298–300.

making materials, as mentioned earlier, were allowed in free as from 1725; they remained thus unencumbered until 1803 when they were subjected to an import duty of 15s. 9d. per ton.[1] In 1784 a licence duty was imposed on paper-makers; each maker had to take out a licence and pay an annual duty for it of £2.[2]

What effect did this complex of Customs and Excise duties have on the production and supply of paper?

(iii)

The ideal data for an evaluation of the effect of the Customs and Excise duties would include prices, domestic and foreign, for precisely comparable types of paper. But the ideal remains at its habitual distance. Price comparisons are particularly difficult for paper and reliable data on this period hard to come by. (For some notes on this see Appendix III.) Such imperfect evidence as exists, however, tends to confirm what might be expected to follow from the differentials between Customs and Excise duties. As is shown by the examples given in Table XII, these were very marked.

The complex Excise schedule of 1782–94 listed different papers in a different way from the schedule favoured by the Customs authorities.[3] Accordingly comparison of the respective duties during this period is difficult. Table XIII offers some sample comparisons of different types in 1787.

The levying of the duty by weight makes comparison much simpler for the remainder of the century. From 1794–1801 in classes 1, 2, 3, and 4 the Customs duty

[1] 11 Geo. I, c. 7; 43 Geo. III, c. 68.
[2] 24 Geo. III, c. 41.
[3] The arrangement in the Customs ledgers was similar to that laid out in Table IV; cf. the arrangement in the Excise tables in App. II.

TABLE XII

Comparative Weight of Customs and Excise Duties, 1714 and 1752

Type	1714		1752	
	Excise duty %	Customs duty %	Excise duty %	Customs duty %
Pot, second	17	67	17	74
Demy, second	17	55	17	63
Brown	25	53	25	58
Brown, cap	10	39	10	44
Unenumerated (ad valorem) . .	18	60	18	65

Source: The percentages for the named types were calculated on the basis of the following estimated values (per ream): Pot second—4s. 6d.; Demy, second—9s.; Brown (per bundle)—3s.; Brown, cap—7s. 6d. For the sources of these estimates see Appendix III.

TABLE XIII

Comparative Weight of Customs and Excise Duties, 1787

Type	Excise duty, %	Type	Customs duty, %
Table 1:		Atlas, ordinary . .	89
Foolscap . . .	26	Blue, for sugar bakers .	78
Pot	26	Brown . . .	48
Thick Post . .	27	Foolscap, Genoa, fine .	61
Table 2:		Demy, second . .	117
Foolscap . . .	21	Double copy or Bastard .	88
Copy of Bastard .	24	Fine large Post, over	
Elephant . . .	25	15 lb. wt. . . .	61
Table 3:		Unenumerated . .	55
Demy, single . .	23	(ad valorem)	
Unenumerated . .	20·7		
(ad valorem)			

Source: Percentages calculated on the following bases: Excise—rates and valuations as given in 27 Geo. III, c. 13; Customs—rates as given in 27 Geo. III, c. 13 and valuation as given in the Customs ledgers (P.R.O. Customs 3) during the period 1743-79. These were (per ream): Atlas, ordinary—43s. 6d.; Blue, for sugar bakers—9s. 3d.; Brown (per bundle)—6s.; Foolscap, Genoa, fine—7s. 8s.; Demy, second—8s.-10s.; Double Copy or Bastard—6s.; Fine large Post, over 15 lb. wt.—14s.

per lb. was four times the Excise duty; in class 5 it was twice the Excise duty.[1]

On the whole, then, import duties averaged some three or four times the amount of the Excise duty. In practice the differential was often still greater until after 1781, because of the channelling of much home-produced paper into the Excise *ad valorem* category and the persistent undervaluing and/or evasion which went on. Bearing in mind Whatman's observations quoted earlier, we may be certain that most of the paper produced in this country paid an Excise duty, before the reforms of 1781, of well under the *ad valorem* rate of 18 per cent. To a papermaker complaining in 1792 of the weight of the duties then in force those of 'Queen Anne's Act' were 'very trifling'.[2] The situation can be indicated in graphical form. Fig. 5 shows the relationship between the growth of paper output and of the revenues collected from the paper Excise.[3] Until about 1730, as can be seen, revenue did not even keep pace with output, but after that it maintained a consistent relationship with output at a ratio which, did we know the true value of all paper produced during that period, would almost certainly prove to be very low, probably not more than about 6 or 7 per cent.[4] Confirmatory evidence of such a percentage

---

[1] 34 Geo. III, c. 20.

[2] Balston MSS.: Greatrake to Whatman—April 1792.

[3] Sources: production curve as for Fig. 2; revenue curve—C. & E.: Quantities, Rates and Amounts of Excise Duties, 1684–1798; Excise-Treasury Letters, 1784–7, ff. 252–3; *First Inland Revenue Report* (1857). This last-named source has been used for the revenue figures after 1770. Before that date it is misleading as it includes duties on stained paper along with those on paper.

[4] Evidence on paper prices (see App. III) suggests that an average value for paper produced in England might be about 6s. per ream in the middle of the century. On this assumption the relation between gross revenue and output in reams then gives a figure of about 6 per cent. as a very rough indication of the weight of the Excise.

appears in a surviving Whatman ledger. Here the sharp increase after 1781 is very marked: in 1781 the amount he paid in Excise duty was approximately 4 per cent. of his total production expenditure, in 1785 it constituted

FIG. 5. Output and Excise Revenue 1714–1800 (England and Wales) (logarithmic scale)

22 per cent.[1] It seems clear, therefore, that before 1781 the effective weight of the Excise was scarcely ever such as seriously to impede the over-all advance of home production.

It must be said in qualification, however, that the Excise probably did have a discriminatory effect within the range of types of paper made. There were obviously

[1] Balston MSS.: Whatman Ledger, 1780-7.

certain limits to the scope of under-valuation, and any serious attempt to make large quantities of the highest qualities of paper, the true value of which could not be indefinitely concealed, were bound to be penalized. It is no accident that it should have been Whatman, whose interests and subsequent fame were bound up with high-quality paper, who wrote in the 1760's of the desirability that 'an equitable duty (should be) levied and the Fair Trader not injured', and who complained that 'at present almost the whole Burthen falls on People of Credit'.[1]

After 1781, as Fig. 5 shows, the position altered radically. In these later years of the century the paper-makers were in fact having to pay the sort of percentages, 20 per cent. and over, which the authorities had prescribed. After the reorganization of 1794 the effective weight of the Excise became still heavier; between 1770 and 1800 the output of paper rather less than doubled whilst the yield of the duty multiplied just over eleven-fold. There can be little doubt that this was another of the factors which contributed to that slowing up in the expansion of the industry in the later years of the century illustrated in Fig. 2.

The relationship between the Customs and the Excise rates meant that the paper industry grew up in the eighteenth century as an extremely sheltered industrial child. While the importer had to watch the loopholes in the Customs barrier being stopped up in 1725 and 1743 and the barrier further strengthened thereafter, so the home producer was finding effective means of easing the full burden of the Excise. And reform when it came did not bring an end to protection.

In the years around the beginning of the century the

[1] B.M. Add. MSS. 38203.

arguments of protectionists and anti-protectionists revealed the situation as it seemed to them. Those more
interested in the merits of 'free trade', or of cheaper
paper, than in the virtues of drubbing the French
claimed that two-thirds of the ordinary printing- and
writing-paper rated in this country at 4s. 6d. cost 1s. 3d.
to 3s. overseas.[1] Or they observed, as did one com-
mentator in 1713, that 'there is hardly a Manufacture
erected by us in Britain in the memory of man, but that
if the high Duties laid upon Foreign Goods of the same
kind were taken off, or (put) within 2 or 3 per Cent of
what they were before, would be ruin'd, and the Under-
takers thereof must lay them down: if the Manufacturers
of Paper, Linnen, Cloth, Canvass or Sail Cloth and many
other things were heard to this, it is believed they would
all acknowledge the Truth of it'.[2] The protectionists,
though with different intentions in mind, were equally
certain about the reality of this situation. At about the
same time Sir Theodore Janssen wrote:

Since the high Duties laid on foreign Paper, and that none hath
been imported from France, where 'tis cheapest, the making
of it is increased to such a Degree in England, that we import
none of the Lower Sorts from abroad, and make them all ourselves: But if the French Duties be taken off, undoubtedly most
of the Mills which are imployed in the making of White Paper,
must leave off their Work, and £30 to £40,000 a year be re-
mitted over to France for that Commodity.[3]

The superior competitive power of the French industry was normally ascribed to cheaper provisions,
lower wages, and depreciation of currency. The lowness
of wages was particularly stressed; it was alleged that

[1] *Reasons . . . against laying a further Duty upon Paper* (c. 1699).
[2] *Extracts from several Mercators, being Considerations on the state of the British
Trade* (Dublin, 1713), p. 7.
[3] 'General Maxims in Trade', in *Somers Tracts*, vol. xvi (1751), p. 152.

French rag-sorters were paid less than the equivalent of 1¼*d*. per day as against 4*d*. in this country.[1] Although it was to keep out French paper that the protective wall was most wanted by the English paper-makers, and for this the extra duty on French goods was especially useful, the wall was amply strong against other country's products. The Dutch industry grew in stature along with our own. In spite of the stout protective barrier the fear of foreign competition persisted throughout the century and the Dutch came more and more to figure as the bogy.[2]

Further evidence of the efficacy of protection was the sustained preference shown by the Irish for importing paper from the Continent rather than from neighbouring England, despite the preference which British wares enjoyed in the Irish tariffs.[3] The desire for continental paper doubtless owed something to its superior quality, but there can be no doubt that price was an important element here. In 1763–4 Ireland drew over 90 per cent. of her white-paper imports from France and Holland,

---

[1] Ibid., p. 150. A similar ratio appears in 1701 when the paper-makers here were, as usual, petitioning for protection; they claimed that they could not 'hire servants' under 8*s*. or 9*s*. per week, though foreigners could hire them for 3*s*. to 4*s*. (*C.J.*, vol. xiii (1699–1702), p. 474).

[2] Whatman, speaking as one interested in the export market, wrote in the 1760's that 'the rivalship of the Dutch (who can already undersell us) makes it necessary that we should afford ours at a Foreign Market as cheap as possible' (B.M. Add. MSS. 38203, f. 318).
Examples of fear of foreign competition amongst those concerned with the paper and paper-staining trades in the 1780's and 90's will be found in C. & E.: Excise-Treasury Letters 1784–7, ff. 126–7 and 1790–2, ff. 225–9.

[3] By the Irish statutes 15 Chas. II, c. 8, an import excise of 5 per cent. *ad valorem* was imposed on paper, as on other goods, the duty to be paid by the first buyer or importer; and by 15 Chas. II, c. 9, a Customs duty also of 5 per cent. This arrangement continued in operation though the rates were increased from time to time, e.g. by 33 Geo. II, c. 1, when an additional 1*s*. per ream over and above existing duties was imposed on imported paper (excluding that from G.B.) of a value over 5*s*. per ream. It did not, however, acquire so strongly protective a character as the British tariff. By various Acts in the 1790's the duties were consolidated and new rates drawn up.

yet at the same time those two countries together accounted for only 11 per cent. by value of Ireland's total overseas trade whilst England's share was 67 per cent.; ten years later, when the combined French and Dutch share of the total had fallen to 7 per cent. and England's risen to 70 per cent., still 89 per cent. of the white paper imports came from the two continental countries.[1] Moreover by that date England's own imports of paper were almost insignificant and there is every reason to suppose that much of her home-produced paper was equal in quality to that of the Continent.

Be it by accident or by intent, then, heed seems to have been paid to the notion that 'Wise Nations' were 'fond of encouraging Manufactures in their Infancy'.[2] In the short run the home consumer paid for this policy by paying more for his paper. Perhaps the slowness of the industry's growth for most of the century may be in part due to this brake upon demand. Yet an industry was developed, albeit a high-cost industry reared in an atmosphere of duties and surrounded by a deal of conservatism. But it did exist and might well not have done without protection. Something survived from the early struggles to receive, at the end of the century, the impetus of the Industrial Revolution. And this industry then forged ahead of its continental rivals. This is the classic case of the 'infant industry' argument for protection.

[1] *An Abstract of the Exports and Imports of Ireland, 1764–73.*
[2] Janssen, op. cit.

VI

The Organization of the Industry and its Problems on the Eve of Change

(i)

THE industrial structure which was fashioned as the industry grew up in the eighteenth century under these various formative influences did not differ greatly from that of the previous century. The influences which bore upon it and the technical changes wrought within it carried revolutionary implications neither for output nor for organization. It remained an industry of many and widely scattered units, mostly small, rented from landlords and worked within a family or partnership organization assisted by a small amount of hired labour. Yet if this was the basic theme which persisted, it was one upon which many variations were played.

The number of mills rose in the course of the century. In 1738 the Commissioners of Excise put the number in England at 278.[1] From 1785 onwards we have records of the number of Excise licences issued to paper-makers and pasteboard-makers; the figures for England and Wales and Scotland up to 1800 are shown in Table XIV. The rate of growth which they exhibit is hardly rapid. To some extent this may simply reflect increasing productivity in existing mills, though the mounting burden of the Excise and other difficulties in these last decades of the century probably checked the entry of new firms into the industry.

---

[1] C. & E.: Excise-Treasury Letters, 1733–45, f. 247.

TABLE XIV

Number of Licences issued to Paper-makers, 1785–1800 (G.B.)

Year	England and Wales	Scotland	Year	England and Wales	Scotland
1785	381	27	1793	395	33
1786	377	28	1794	398	30
1787	382	28	1795	407	39
1788	394	27	1796	419	33
1789	392	32	1797	428	34
1790	389	35	1798	420	37
1791	392	29	1799	422	33
1792	382	33	1800	417	32

Source: *First Inland Revenue Report* (1857), app. 30.

In the location of these mills there was both a marked spread into new areas and a consolidation of the dominant positions gained in the earlier period by Kent and Buckinghamshire.[1] By the end of the century the former had about forty mills at work within its boundaries; in the latter a remarkable concentration of mills developed along the little River Wye, between Wycombe and Bourne End. Hertfordshire, Berkshire, and Surrey also witnessed the growth of paper-mills, and these counties combined with Kent and Buckinghamshire to form a solid core of the industry in the Home Counties, engaged in supplying the London market; on the outer edge of this group was the important paper-making county of Hampshire. In the west Devon forged ahead from some four or five mills in the first decade of the century to about twenty-five in the last decade;[2] Somerset, too, came to occupy an important place in the industry of the

[1] Shorter, *Historical Geography*, *passim*.
[2] See, in particular, A. H. Shorter, 'The Historical Geography of the Paper-Making Industry in Devon, 1684–1950', *Transactions of the Devonshire Association for the Advancement of Science, Literature and Art*, vol. lxxxii (1950), pp. 205–16.

West Country. But perhaps the most striking development was the extension of the industry in the West Midlands: Monmouthshire, Shropshire, and, to a rather less
marked extent, Gloucestershire, Worcestershire, and
Herefordshire all saw a substantial growth in the number
of paper-mills during this period; those of Shropshire,
for instance, increased from about three at the beginning
of the century to eleven or more by the mid-century.[1]
In the north Lancashire added to its representation in
the industry, though less markedly than did Yorkshire.
Coming down again into the Midlands, Derbyshire,
Nottinghamshire, Northants, and Oxfordshire all had
their paper-mills, and a sizeable group of pasteboard-
makers had grown up in and around Birmingham. There
were, in short, few English counties without some paper-
mills. Those without, or with only a very few mills, fell
normally into one or other of two clear categories: the
East Anglian counties without, on the whole, adequate
water-power from the slow running streams of that area,
and those remote from both markets and raw materials.[2]
In Scotland the later decades of this century saw the
establishment of a number of mills south of Edinburgh,
on the Leith and the Esk. In addition to those already in
existence around Glasgow and Aberdeen, others were
established at such relatively distant places as Dal-
beattie, Kirkcudbright, and near Perth.[3] The Irish in-

---

[1] L. C. Lloyd, 'Paper-Making in Shropshire, 1656–1912', *Transactions of
the Shropshire Archaeological and Natural History Society*, vol. xlix (1937–8),
pp. 121–87, and vol. liii, part ii (1950), pp. 153–63; also Shorter 'The
Excise Numbers of Paper-Mills in Shropshire', ibid., pp. 145–52.

[2] In the former group were such counties as Suffolk, Norfolk, Rutland,
Lincolnshire, Huntingdonshire, Cambridgeshire, Bedfordshire, and Essex;
in the latter group were the remoter Welsh counties and those in the extreme
north of England.

[3] *Old Statistical Account*, vol. v, pp. 323, 344; vol. vi, p. 595; vol. ix, p. 592;
vol. x, pp. 279, 422, 617; vol. xi, p. 75.

dustry developed mainly in the vicinity of Dublin, though mills were also established in Cork and Antrim.[1]

In many of the areas where there was a rapid growth in the industry a major stimulus came from the rising demand from other industries for wrapping-paper, pasteboard, and various special sorts of paper. A number of mills in such counties as Devon, Gloucestershire, and Yorkshire made wrappings, board, or pressing-papers for the cloth industry.[2] The growing metal trades in Birmingham, and in the West Midlands generally,[3] undoubtedly encouraged the manufacture of wrapping-paper and pasteboard in that region. The rising importance of Bristol and of Liverpool as ports and centres of processing industries, such as sugar refining, similarly had its effect upon, respectively, Somerset and Lancashire; in the latter county the striking rise of the cotton industry and the growth of such towns as Manchester, Bolton, and Bury, stimulated the demand for paper for a variety of purposes. Though the largest concentrations of white-paper production were around London, Dublin, and Edinburgh, and especially in Kent and Buckinghamshire, some of the remoter mills, as we have already seen, were by no means confined to wrappings and board. And there is reason to think that towards the end of the century a number of larger mills were coming into being which were capable of turning out various types of paper in comparatively large quantities.

On this question of the size of mills or of the number

[1] *C.J.* (Ireland), loc. cit. According to a report in the *Dublin Journal* (No. 1543) in 1741 there were twelve near Dublin, six or seven in the north, and five in Munster.

[2] The Mill at Moreton Hampstead, Devon, for example, which was still equipped with stampers in 1776, made pasteboard used in packing bales for serge (Shorter, 'Historical Geography of the Paper-Making Industry in Devon', loc. cit.; and *Historical Geography*, pp. 426–8).

[3] Court, op. cit., *passim.*

of vats per mill it is safe to say that most establishments remained small, one- or two-vat mills, though a few large mills of three, four, or more vats were at work. In 1738, when the Excise Commissioners reported the existence of 278 mills, they put the number of vats at 338, i.e. an average of 1·2 vats per mill.[1] Spicer estimated the number of vats in the United Kingdom in 1805 to be 762; in that year 461 paper-makers' licences were issued in England and 47 in Scotland; on this basis, and ignoring Ireland, the average would still have been approximately 1·5 vats per mill.[2] As for Ireland, an Irish paper-maker asserted in 1757 that the biggest mill in the country had only three vats and most had only one;[3] Dr. Shorter's investigations of individual English mills confirm these impressions culled from different sources, for he records less than a dozen mills with three or more vats in the eighteenth century, and all from the 1770's and later.[4]

In most mills little capital and few workers remained the rule, as in the previous century. Much of the wrapping-paper which accounted for so large a proportion of total output was made, as a petition of wholesale stationers put it in 1802, in remote places by 'men of small capital'.[5] These small mills, employing scarcely more

---

[1] C. & E.: Excise-Treasury Letters, 1733–45, f. 247.

[2] Spicer, p. 249; *First Inland Revenue Report* (1857), App. 30. Even allowing for the inclusion of a number of pasteboard-makers without mills the average would not be materially different (see *infra*, pp. 217–19 & nn.

[3] *C.J.* (Ireland), vol. v, p. 30.

[4] *Historical Geography*, pp. 432–4.

[5] C. & E.: Excise-Treasury Letters, 1801–4, ff. 320. The average per mill of all the amounts *claimed* to have been spent by ten Irish paper-makers between 1747 and 1769 on the establishment of their mills works out at not much more than £1,000; so we may be sure that the true amount per mill for most mills was appreciably less (*C.J.* (Ireland), *passim*, loc. cit.). In England and Scotland values were higher, but even towards the end of the century £2,000 would probably have covered the value of the average mill.

than a dozen workers, were by no means confined to remote areas. At a mill making coarse paper near Glasgow in the 1790's 'eight men usually find employment'; and at Mill End, Rickmansworth, Hertfordshire, in 1788, the 'general average number of people about the Mill' was five men and a boy.[1] Employment was not constant: women and girls were taken on periodically for rag-preparation; at other times the mill was not working, as when water was short. So that when some contemporary is found claiming that his little mill employed twenty to forty persons weekly,[2] this may refer to periods of peak activity or it may simply owe more to optimism than to experience. A more realistic observation was that made about the Rickmansworth mill mentioned above: as well as five men and a boy there were 'sometimes more, sometimes less, sometimes girls, sometimes women and sometimes men'.[3]

Nevertheless there were some large mills even at the beginning of the century, though evidence of their existence is more common for the later years. As early as 1719 there is the following description of a mill near Maidstone:

And about Three Quarters of a Mile Eastward from the Town there is one [i.e. a Paper mill] which makes very good White Paper. 'Tis situated on what they call the Little River which, coming from Leeds, Hollingbourn, etc., runs into the Medway at this Place: It drives a Fulling Mill at Bersted, and two or three Corn Mills before it comes to this Place. Here it

[1] *Old Statistical Account*, vol. v, p. 344; C. & E.: Excise Trials, vol. 542, p. 313 (Attorney General v. Mary Dell and Mark Howard). The second statement was made by Richard Howard, the brother of one of the defendants; there were four men and a boy besides himself. Shorter, *Historical Geography*, p. 81, mentions three mills in Cumberland in the 1790's of which none employed more than fifteen.

[2] See, e.g., *C.J.* (Ireland), vol. vi, p. 29; vol. vii, p. 211; vol. viii, pp. 32, and App. cccxxvi.   [3] loc. cit.

turns three over-shot Wheels of about 8 feet in Diameter, which moves the whole Work; the Water-Boards are about two Feet and a half long, and the Trough delivers a Stream of Water of Six Inches deep. 'Tis a very large Work, and they could easily make much greater Quantities of Paper, if there were demands accordingly. . . . The Brown and White Brown Paper which they make here is chiefly from old Ropes, Sails, etc., and this Matter doth not require above 12 Hours beating; but the fine Rags require 36 Hours before they are fit to make White Paper. And Mr. Gill told me when I went to see his Mill, that he could not make his Paper fine and White, till he brought into his Work a Collection of fine, clear Water from two or three Springs, which rise in a Field adjoining to the Mill.[1]

This mill was almost certainly that which subsequently became one of the biggest and most famous paper-mills of the eighteenth century, Whatman's Turkey Mill. This is perhaps a convenient place to trace the outline of the history of this mill and its owners.[2]

One of the signatories of the petition of 'ancient paper makers' in 1690[3] was George Gill. In 1695, and probably earlier, he was the tenant of a paper-mill, formerly a fulling-mill, near Boxley, Kent.[4] It passed into the hands of his son William who was presumably the Mr. Gill referred to by Harris, for in 1716 William Gill insured two paper-mills in that area, at Sandling and at Boxley.[5] The Gill family was not, however, destined to be the proprietors of what the Kentish historian Edward Hasted was to describe in 1778 as 'the most extensive and curious manufacture of paper perhaps in Europe', for in 1729

[1] J. Harris, *The History of Kent* (London, 1719), p. 191.
[2] Further details of this subject will be found in a series of articles by T. Balston, 'James Whatman, Father and Son', in issues of *The Paper Maker* for Apr. 1955 to Apr. 1956 (since published in book form as *James Whatman, Father and Son* (London, 1957)).   [3] See *infra*, pp. 69, 75.
[4] Kent County Archives: Whatman Deeds.
[5] A. H. Shorter, 'Early Paper-Mills in Kent', *The Paper Maker*, Oct. 1951.

William Gill went bankrupt.[1] The mill subsequently found its way into the hands of Richard Harris, paper-maker of the neighbouring village of Hollingbourne. In due time, and after rebuilding the mill, Harris died and bequeathed to his widow, Ann, 'All that Messuage or Tenement with Paper Mill . . . wch. said Mill was formerly Fulling Mill but some time then since converted into a Paper Mill by George Gill father of . . . William Gill and was then commonly known by the name of Turkey Mills.'[2] In 1740 Ann Harris remarried, her second husband being James Whatman, the son of a prosperous local tanner. Whatman was already interested in the mill as a trustee; it passed into his use and eventually the Whatman family became the owners.[3]

Of this member of the family—James Whatman, senior, to distinguish him from his more famous son—little is known, though evidently some part of his son's reputation properly belongs to him or, at any rate, was built upon the solid foundations which he laid.[4] In 1762, when his son took over the business, the annual wage bill was about £1,000; it was only £1,268 in 1780 when it was probably the biggest mill in the country.[5] It seems likely therefore that Turkey Mill was already an out-standing enterprise under the elder Whatman.

When his father died in 1759, James Whatman was 18 years of age. He came into possession of the mill when he reached the age of 21; it was already a very prosperous business and he was an active and enterprising young man. At 23 he was corresponding with Charles Jenkin-son, then Secretary to the Treasury, in regard to Excise matters and in a manner which suggests that he was a

---

[1] Ibid.; Hasted, op. cit., vol. i, p. cxxiv.
[2] Quoted in Wardrop, loc. cit.   [3] Ibid.
[4] *Supra*, pp. 117–19, for his possible role in the development of wove paper.
[5] See *The Paper Maker*, Apr. 1955, p. 292.

leading figure in the industry; at 26 he was High Sheriff of Kent.[1] Under his hand the enterprise grew. In 1768, when William Hickey visited Turkey Mill, he wrote of the 'great paper manufacturer, who entertained us in a princely style';[2] and three years later Whatman claimed, on oath, to make more paper than any other manufacturer in England.[3] As the rewards of his enterprise and of his father's were reaped so did the Whatmans rise in the social scale. Landowner, Sheriff of the County, country gentleman, and prosperous industrialist, in 1776, after the death of his first wife,[4] he married Susanna Bosanquet and thereby became connected with a rich and powerful family of merchants and financiers. In the 1780's he bought from Baron Ongley the estate of Vinters, near Maidstone, as well as other property in that area. He died in 1798 having in 1794 sold his mills to Thomas Robert and Finch Hollingworth, who then worked them for a short time in conjunction with William Balston who had previously been employed by Whatman.[5]

Enough has been said of his achievements and enterprise in this and earlier chapters. The scale of his activities merits some attention. Apart from Turkey Mill, he also at one time or another owned, leased, or otherwise controlled Poll Mill, Loose Mill, and Hollingbourne Mill, all in the same area.[6] During the period 1780–7, for

[1] B.M. Add. MSS. 38203, f. 316; Hasted, op. cit., vol. i, p. xcviii.
[2] Quoted in *The Paper Maker*, May 1955, p. 384.
[3] Ibid., p. 390.
[4] At the age of 21, he had married Sarah Stanley, daughter of Edward Stanley, Secretary of the Commissioners of Customs and a noted antiquary (ibid., p. 382).
[5] Ibid. July 1955, pp. 40–42; Oct. 1955, pp. 341 et seq.; Jan. 1956, pp. 34 et seq.; Feb. 1956, pp. 122 et seq.
[6] Ibid. Aug. 1955, p. 130; Oct. 1955, pp. 344 et seq.; Jan. 1956, pp. 40 et seq.

which there has survived one of his ledgers covering Turkey and Loose Mills, his expenditure was running at about £10,000 per annum and his receipts at some £14,000. His wage bill averaged about £1,200 per annum at Turkey and £225 at Loose.[1] In 1782 he paid about 4·6 per cent. of the entire paper Excise revenue and 10 per cent. of all the revenue collected in Tables 1 and 2;[2] these percentages dropped as the industry grew and in 1787, when he paid £2,831, they were 3·6 and 8 respectively.[3] When he sold his mills in 1794 Turkey Mill probably had five vats, Poll two, and Loose one; the eight vats all told were valued at £20,000.[4]

Although Turkey Mill and the Whatmans were in many ways untypical of the industry, facets of their story are nevertheless faithfully reflected in the general picture of the industry at that time. The tendency for mills to get larger and for paper-makers to own more than one mill, the rise and fall and the complex interlocking of family interests in the business—such characteristics as these can be found all over the country.

The growth in scale of operation almost certainly owed much to the Hollander, the greater productivity of which rendered multi-vat mills economical. At the foundation in 1803 of the United Society of Paper Makers the resolution creating the Society was signed by deputies representing 120 makers, being 'the Proprietors of near 400 vats':[5] a ratio of 3·3 vats per maker. This organization

[1] Balston MSS.: Whatman Ledger. See also *The Paper Maker*, Aug. and Sept. 1955.

[2] i.e. the first two 'Tables' in the Excise Schedules (see *supra*, p. 98), comprising the better quality papers in which Whatman specialized.

[3] Ibid. and C. & E.: Quantities, Rates and Amounts of Excise Duties, 1684–1798.

[4] i.e. as going concerns, at £125 per annum per vat at 20 years' purchase (*The Paper Maker*, Jan. 1956, p. 36).

[5] Balston MSS. See *infra* Chap. X.

was undoubtedly overweighted by the larger manufacturers of the south; and of course the ratio of vats per
makers reveals nothing of the size of individual mills.
Nevertheless it points to the same situation as does
scattered evidence of a different sort.

In 1790, for example, the mill at Hurcott, Worcestershire, was offered for sale, and it is evident from the advertisement that the plant was substantial: the equipment included two engines (i.e. beaters), four vats, and
four iron presses and the buildings included a warehouse,
drying-rooms, a rag-house four stories high, and seven
tenements for workmen. Power was derived from an
overshot wheel fed from a pool covering twelve acres.[1]
In Surrey at the end of the century the Curteises controlled three vats at Carshalton.[2] In Lancashire sundry
members of the Crompton family were rising in the industry, building the foundations upon which Thomas
Bonsor Crompton was to achieve his wealth and make
his important contribution to the industry in the next
century.[3] In Kent more than one generation of Taylors
brought enterprise to the industry and wealth and position to the family, the most eminent member of which
was Clement Taylor who became M.P. for Maidstone
from 1780 to 1796.[4] As a paper manufacturer contemporaries evidently ranged him with Whatman as one of
the leaders of the industry. In 1793 he had entered into
a partnership with the aim of investing in paper-making

[1] Shorter, 'Paper Mills in Worcestershire', loc. cit.
[2] Balston MSS.: Curteis & Sons to Hollingworth & Balston, May 1801.
[3] V.C.H. Lancashire, vol. ii, pp. 406–7, and vol. v, p. 34. See infra, pp. 194, 238–9.
[4] This was the Clement Taylor concerned with the chlorine experiments (supra, pp. 114–16); his father, also Clement, secured prizes from the Royal Society of Arts, including one for copper-plate printing-paper in 1757 (Dossie, op. cit., vol. i, p. 14; R.S.A.: Guard Books, vol. iii, ff. 31, 87; vol. iv, f. 17).

in Ireland, but in the stormy economic seas of those years he overreached himself and sank. He was made bankrupt in 1797 and his five-vat mill at Tovil, near Maidstone, was offered for sale. John Taylor, however, was still operating four vats in 1801, though by this time his neighbours in Kent included such large concerns as Edmeads & Pine who controlled seven and Hollingworth & Balston with ten.[1]

A striking example of family connexions and also of apprenticeship in the industry is provided by tracing a chain beginning with the Quelch family, alleged to be descendants of a German paper-maker at Spilman's mill. Edward Quelch was a signatory of the 'ancient paper makers' petition of 1690, and in 1698 John Quelch was in possession of a mill at Dartford. This in time passed to William Quelch who died in 1775 at the mature age of 96. Meanwhile he had apparently blossomed into paper-making in other parts of Kent. As William Quelch of Wrotham, paper-maker, he took apprentices in 1733 and 1741, and as William Quelch of Loose he insured a paper-mill there in 1741 and took an apprentice in 1743. All these apprentices later became paper-makers on their own account. In 1739 Quelch also insured a mill at Hollingbourne, then in the occupation of John Terry who had been a journeyman of Quelch and who had married Quelch's daughter. In the course of time the mill at Dartford passed to William Quelch II. Meanwhile Clement Taylor (father of the Clement Taylor,

[1] W. E. Bridge, *Some Historical Notes on the Basted Paper Mills* (Basted Paper Mills Co. Ltd., 1948); *The Paper Maker*, Oct. 1955, pp. 344–53; Dec. 1955, pp. 573–4; *C.J.* (Ireland), vol. xviii, pp. 24–25 and app. ccccxiv; C. & E.: Excise Trials, vol. 531, p. 160; Balston MSS.: Meeting of Master Papermakers of Kent and Surrey, 1801.

The Basted mill with which the Taylors were long associated in the eighteenth century was near Wrotham.

M.P.) had married a daughter of William Quelch of Dartford. William Quelch II died in 1797 and the mill found its way, after an intervening change of ownership, to the Budgen family, Mrs. Budgen being the daughter of John and Eleanor Terry and thus the niece of William Quelch II. It descended in time to John Budgen, and this story of family ramifications can be brought to an end with John Budgen's insolvency in 1820.[1]

In Buckinghamshire the Spicer family—a name still famous in the industry today—can be traced in the industry from the seventeenth century. Edward Spicer was another of the signatories of the 1690 petition and at that time was a tenant of a mill near High Wycombe. In the 1760's Ralph Spicer was one of the signatories of the petition of Buckinghamshire paper-makers to the Treasury in regard to Excise matters. Thirty years later Freeman Gage Spicer was an important paper-maker of the district, along with S. and R. Spicer, and in 1816 the family operated three mills in the Wycombe area.[2] The Midlothian paper-making area of Scotland owed much to the enterprise of Charles Cowan and other members of the family which built up the modern firm of Alexander Cowan & Co. Ltd. The Valleyfield mill at Penicuick, established in 1709, was bought by him in 1779 and the business then so prospered that by the turn of the century

[1] H.M.C.: *House of Lords MSS.*, 1690, p. 76; Dunkin, op. cit., pp. 306–9; Shorter, 'Early Paper Mills in Kent', loc. cit.; W. E. Bridge, op. cit.; C. & E.: General Letter (1816).

A Thomas Quelch was living at Wolvercote, Oxford, in the 1660's and a Mr. Quelch of Wolvercote supplied the University Press with paper in 1694 (ex. inf. H. G. Carter). It seems possible therefore that another member of the family was at an early stage associated with the famous and then only recently established Wolvercote mill.

[2] H.M.C.: *House of Lords MSS.*, 1690, p. 76; *C.J.*, vol. x, pp. 412–13; C. & E.: Excise-Treasury Letters, 1767–74, ff. 197–8; Balston MSS.: Meetings of Buckinghamshire papermakers, 1796, 1799, and of Master Paper Makers in London, 1803; C. & E.: General Letter (1816).

it expanded to include two neighbouring mills. Cowan
himself, with the help of an Edinburgh chemist, William
Cunningham, took out a patent for an improved method
of chlorine bleaching in 1794.[1]

Perhaps the most romantic of the success stories of the
industry during the Age of Reason was that of the Portal
family. Originally a Huguenot refugee, Henri de Portal,
after working at Gerard de Vaux's mill near Southampton, was naturalized in 1711. He prospered, and in 1718
took a lease of a mill at Laverstoke and rebuilt it. Six
years later he obtained the monopoly of making Bank of
England notes, a very specialized branch of paper-
making which shaped the destinies of the Laverstoke mill
and of the Portals for many years to come and helped to
bring wealth and fame to the family. Henry Portal died
in 1747, and was succeeded by Joseph. As with the Whatmans so with the Portals.[2] Though their origins were very
different, their courses were not dissimilar. As the grandson of the Kentish tanner became landowner and Sheriff,
so did Joseph Portal buy the estate of Laverstoke and in
1763 served the office of High Sheriff in Hampshire. On
his death in 1793 Joseph was followed by his son John,
whose letters show him to have been a forceful person
with an independent turn of mind. In various disputes
around the turn of the century other paper-makers
found the Portals[3] often taking a line of their own, and
the monopoly of Bank of England notes was not always
kindly regarded. 'I w^d not have acted', so a less favoured
Hampshire paper-maker remarked in 1803 in reference

[1] Clow, op. cit., p. 257; D. Bremner, *The Industries of Scotland* (Edinburgh,
1869), p. 322; Patent No. 2026.

[2] Joseph was a co-signatory with Whatman of the 1765 petition to the
Treasury on Excise matters (C. & E.: Excise-Treasury Letters, 1763–8,
ff. 134–5).

[3] At this time the business was carried on as Portal & Bridges.

to a certain action of Portal & Bridges, 'as they have c^d. I have earned guineas as well as made Bank Notes. . . .' In 1822 when William Cobbett rode past that stream which ran through Whitchurch and saw that it turned 'the mill of 'Squire Portal . . . which mill makes the Bank of England note-paper', he was characteristically moved to pages of furious eloquence on the dire effects of paper money. The little river, simply by turning a wheel and setting certain machinery in motion 'produced a greater effect on the condition of men [than] all the other rivers, all the seas, all the mines and all the continents in the world'. He looked around him and saw the ancient landed properties in the hands of bankers, merchants, and manufacturers. He was much annoyed. If he could have lived till 1901, he would have been distressed to note the creation in that year of a new baronet—Sir Wyndham Portal.[1]

A different pattern of enterprise is presented by the activities of those who ran a mill at Hopton Wafers in Shropshire. In 1756 Joseph Oldham of Bewdley, a hop merchant, leased a mill from the local Lord of the Manor and carried on business as a paper-maker in partnership with Thomas Compson whose sister he married. The business thrived; Oldham was successful both as a hop merchant and as a paper manufacturer, he purchased the local manor, and in 1789 became Sheriff of Shropshire. His partner and brother-in-law was himself a landowner and he was Sheriff of the county in 1792.

---

[1] Jenkins, pp. 182–3; S. Smiles, *The Huguenots* (London, 6th ed. 1889), pp. 273–5; C. & E.: General Letter (1816); Balston MSS.: various letters, especially J. Hooke to W. Balston, Aug. 1803, and also those quoted in *Economica*, Feb. 1954, pp. 47–49; W. Cobbett, *Rural Rides* (1830, Everyman ed. 1912), vol. i, pp. 39, 302–4. See also Shorter, *Historical Geography*, p. 68, where it is noted that the insurance on Portal's mill rose from £300 in 1719 to £1,200 in 1727.

Such men as these were almost certainly not themselves practical paper-makers: they were successful entrepreneurs. The same is true of Thomas Botfield who purchaed the property in 1798. He had made money in the coal and iron trades and although he continued as a paper manufacturer—he controlled three mills in Shropshire in 1816—he wrote of himself in 1803 as being largely engaged in the iron trade.[1]

These examples lead on to two aspects of the industry's organization at this time which demand further illustration. One is the converse of the continuity of successful families: the comparative rapidity with which some mills changed hands and some entrepreneurs entered and quitted the industry. The other is the existence in one entrepreneur or partnership of a diversity of industrial or commercial interests.

Some mills were bought and sold or, more often, let and re-let, at frequent intervals. At least six different names were associated, for instance, in the running of Hurcott Mill, Worcestershire, during the course of the eighteenth century; Poll Mill, near Maidstone, passed through a similar number of hands during the same period. Between 1727 and 1753 at least seven Kentish papermakers were declared bankrupt or otherwise failed in business. Some of the many fulling- and corn-mills which were converted into paper-mills found their way back to corn-grinding or were put to other uses. Spilman's mill became a powder-mill in the early eighteenth century; fulling, corn-grinding, and powder-making were activities traversed by some of the early Surrey mills; the eighteenth-century fate of an early-established paper-mill on

---

[1] L. C. Lloyd, 'Paper-Making in Shropshire, 1656–1912', loc. cit.; C. & E.: General Letter (1816); Balston MSS.: Botfield to Magnay & Pickering, Aug. 1803.

the River Cart, near Glasgow, was to be converted to the manufacture of snuff.[1]

A diversity of interests was characteristic of much of early trade and industry; paper-making duly reflected this. For Oldham, the hop merchant, to invest money in paper manufacture was perhaps not very different from the enterprise of Spilman, the Crown jeweller, or of Gresham, merchant and financier; of John Larking, eighteenth-century banker and timber merchant of Maidstone who had a paper-mill in the neighbouring village of East Malling, of Joseph Sexton, merchant of Limerick who in the 1750's built a paper-mill nearby, or of the London insurance broker who in 1778 had paper-mills in Cambridgeshire.[2] Similarly partners in the partnerships of the time could, and did, come from very diverse walks of life. The very common use of the mortgage or the loan on bond as sources of capital at this time often brought people into contact with trades and industries with which they normally had little or no connexion. Thus, for instance, a paper-maker of Houghton Mills, near Grantham, Lincolnshire, borrowed £500 on mortgage from a local druggist; in 1799 the latter became his partner, advancing £600 as his share of the capital in the paper-making venture.[3]

But the diversity was sometimes more complex than this and arose out of different circumstances. The similarity of technical processes between rag-beating and

[1] Shorter, 'Paper Mills in Worcestershire', loc. cit. and 'Early Paper Mills in Kent', loc. cit.; Balston in *The Paper Maker*, Oct. 1955, p. 344; Dunkin, op. cit., p. 306; J. Hillier, *Old Surrey Water Mills* (London, 1951), *passim*; *V.C.H. Surrey*, vol. ii, pp. 418–20; *Old Statistical Account*, vol. v, p. 344.

[2] *The Paper Maker*, Dec. 1955, p. 573 n.; *C.J.* (Ireland), vol. v, p. 96; Shorter, *Historical Geography*, p. 95, who also quotes a number of other and similar examples, p. 80. For some Scottish ones see *Old Statistical Account*, vol. ix, p. 592; *New Statistical Account*, vol. i, pp. 353–4, 600–1; Bremner, op. cit., p. 322.   [3] C. & E.: Excise-Treasury Letters, 1801–4, ff. 16–22.

corn-grinding brought successors to that mill at Canterbury which as Celia Fiennes saw, was able to do both.
It is no coincidence that the baker or the miller appears
on more than one occasion in the eighteenth century to
have been connected with paper-mills. The mills at
Cattershall, on the River Wey in Surrey, for example,
embraced both corn and paper, and in 1794 Joseph
Chandler of Guildford, baker, held a moiety of these
mills. In the 1760's, at Horton, Buckinghamshire,
Thomas and James Pearson carried on in partnership the
'severall trades or businesses of a Paper Maker, Miller,
Mealman and Farmer'.[1] Such mills as these not only
changed their function in the course of the years, but it is
quite likely that they were switched from job to job in the
short run, according to the relative profitability of the
goods which they produced or the supply of the relevant
raw materials. To the irregularity of production induced
by the unreliability of water-power must be added that
of multiple uses. How many of the little paper-mills of the
time consistently turned out paper all the year round?[2]

By far the most important combination of activities,
however, was that of stationers and paper-makers. Sometimes this went farther in one direction and was a link
between booksellers, publishers or printers and the
paper-maker, sometimes it went farther in the other
direction and joined the paper-maker to the stationer and

[1] *V.C.H. Surrey*, vol. ii, p. 419; Wiggins, Teape MSS.: Chartham Deeds.
See C. & E.: Excise-Treasury Letters, 1733–45, ff. 324–7, for an example
of a baker's interest in a Derbyshire paper-mill.

[2] In this context it is significant that around 1700 contemporaries
reckoned on a working year of about 200 days, and admitted that they
could not work during frost nor size during the winter (P.R.O. CO. 391/90).
In 1738 the Excise authorities wrote of "the many Interruptions" which
affected paper mills from "a Redundancy or Deficiency of Water, want
of Materials, Intervention of Holydays, and other Contingencies"
(C. & E.: Excise-Treasury Letters, 1733–45, f. 247).

the rag merchant. In any event it forms a clear example of economic integration and is of considerable importance in the history of the industry.

A number of printers and publishers were closely connected with the establishment of paper-mills in Scotland: in 1742, for instance, two Edinburgh printers, who were also publishers of local newspapers, together with a bookseller, started making paper at Springfield Mill on the North Esk.[1] But the stationer seems to have been a more important and enduring figure in eighteenth-century papermaking enterprise. As early as 1747 it was observed that

The Wholesale Part of them [i.e. the stationers] are partly Merchants or Importers; and to make their Home-made Goods they either employ Mills of their own or of others, or buy them up in large Quantities of the Makers, which they dispose of either to the Retailers, Booksellers, Printers, etc. This is a very genteel Employ, to which they do not take an Apprentice under 50 L.

The Retailers and Working Stationers not only sell all Sorts of Paper in small Parcels, with all the other Necessaries for the Business of Writing, but bind and stitch up all manner of White Paper Books for Accompts, etc. . . .[2]

Entry into the retail trade was easy. The wholesale trade, on the other hand, required a fair amount of capital: it was a likely source from which money might flow into manufacturing. The wholesale stationers not only bought the maker's output but the bigger London stationers also controlled such export trade as there was.[3]

An early example of these interconnexions is provided by that interesting eighteenth-century figure, William

[1] Waterston, 'Further Notes on Early Paper Making near Edinburgh', loc. cit., p. 55, also pp. 48–49, 51.

[2] Anon., *A General Description of all Trades* (London, 1747).

[3] C. & E.: Excise-Treasury Letters, 1779–82, ff. 298–9; and Excise Trials, vol. 531, p. 160, where James Woodmason, one of the leading wholesale stationers, replying to a remark by Counsel that Whatman 'deals considerably for exportation', contradicted him flatly with the assertion: 'The

Hutton, who started his working career as an apprentice at Lombe's silk-mill in Derbyshire and finished it in prosperous circumstances as a respected antiquary and the author of a well-known history of Birmingham, having made his money largely as a paper merchant and as a land speculator.[1] In 1749 he became a bookseller and retail stationer in Southwell, near Nottingham; in the following year he migrated to Birmingham where he set up shop in the same trade. His business prospered in a small way and in 1756 he records that

> Robert Bage, an intimate friend, and a paper maker,[2] ... proposed that I should sell paper for him, by commission or purchase, on my own account. As I could spare two hundred pounds, I chose to purchase, appropriated a room for its reception, advertised, and hung out a sign: The Paper Warehouse— the first in Birmingham. From this small hint I followed the trade for forty years and acquired many thousand pounds.

Prospering in this new trade, Hutton was moved to write in his diary two years later, 'if there was a profit to the seller, I concluded there must be one to the maker. I coveted both. Upon this erroneous principle I wished for a paper mill.' He then set about acquiring knowledge of paper-making, had a model of a mill constructed, took a lease of two acres of land and started to build. But for reasons which he does not make clear his plans mis-

paper makers don't deal for exportation at all, they only supply stationers.' This relationship continued well into the nineteenth century, see *infra*, p. 257.

[1] The following account is derived entirely from Llewellyn Jewitt (ed.) *The Life of William Hutton and the History of the Hutton Family* (London, 1872), which largely consists of Hutton's own diary.

[2] Robert Bage, described here by Hutton as a paper-maker provides yet another example of miller-cum-paper-maker, for in the same year Robert Bage, of Elford, Staffordshire, miller, insured his paper- and corn-mills under one roof (Shorter, *Historical Geography*, p. 78).

There can be little doubt that this was the same man, for Jewitt notes that Robert Bage set up as a paper-maker at Elford.

carried. By 1761 he had abandoned the idea; the next year he sold the mill.

Though Hutton failed in his paper-making venture, others did not. The position of the stationer in relation to the paper-maker at this time was interesting. The mills were scattered over the country and often in remote areas. By contrast the wholesale stationers were urban dealers, sometimes operating on a large scale, especially in London. The market was unquestionably a seller's market; demand was expanding, and a stout tariff wall kept out the winds of competition. The dealers could thus sell virtually all the paper they could lay their hands on, the makers could dispose of virtually everything they could make. Stationers wanted to be sure of adequate supplies of what they sold; makers had to have adequate selling outlets, and in these economic circumstances they were amply provided by the stationers who were evidently willing to hold such stocks as accumulated from time to time, in the knowledge that in the longer run sales were continually expanding. Stationers relied on a number of mills for their supplies and spent much time travelling from mill to mill.[1]

As the paper-maker was thus dependent on the stationer for selling outlets, and the stationer on the paper-maker for supplies of paper, so in turn there was another link of dependence between the paper-maker and the rag merchant. As demand expanded and output grew, the maker needed all the rags he could find; rags were far and away the most important single item in his costs of production.[2] Now although some rags still found their

---

[1] The partners in the firm of Jones, James & Leventhorp, stationers of Aldgate, for instance, made regular journeys in the late eighteenth and early nineteenth centuries to Kent and other south-eastern counties, to the West Country, to the Midlands, and to the North (Wiggins, Teape MSS.: ledger I, 1798–1813).   [2] *Infra*, pp. 169–70.

way haphazardly to the mills, the trade as a whole was controlled by rag merchants. Itinerant rag-and-bone men collected the rags, mostly in the towns, the great centres of linen consumption; the rags were then bought by the merchants, who had them sorted and stored in warehouses.[1] The rag merchant, then, like the wholesale stationer, was an urban dealer; on both of them the paper-maker was in some way dependent.

In these economic circumstances it is hardly surprising to find that stationers were sometimes rag merchants, that stationers tended to become paper-makers, that, less frequently, paper-makers became stationers, and that sometimes a firm was all three at once.

Amongst the London firms who, at the turn of the century, were both stationers and rag merchants were Jones, James & Leventhorp; Fourdrinier, Bloxam & Fourdrinier, the leading firm of wholesale stationers, of whom more will be said later; and George Bangley, who described himself as 'Wholesale Stationer and Importer of and Dealer in Rags'. Elsewhere Benjamin Smith of Liverpool, for example, kept a 'Paper and Rag warehouse' and dealt in both commodities.[2] In the 1780's Wright, Gill & Dalton, one of the three main firms of wholesale stationers to whom Whatman sold his paper, often sold him small quantities of rags; conversely, Stephen Horncastle, one of his main rag suppliers, was a London wholesale stationer.[3]

---

[1] Rees, op. cit., Vol. xviii. As in the previous century the poor were periodically exhorted to go about collecting rags, thereby to relieve their unemployment and at the same time assist the paper industry.

[2] Wiggins, Teape MSS.: Johnson Gore Invoice Books (these were the property of a Liverpool stationer and contain large numbers of invoices, receipts, &c., from paper-makers, stationers, rag merchants, and others from all over the country); Fourdrinier Papers.

[3] Balston MSS.: Whatman Ledger; P. Barfoot & J. Wilkes, *The Universal British Directory* (London 1791).

Examples of the union of stationer and paper-maker include William Lepard, stationer of Newgate Street and paper-maker of Oxhey, near Watford;[1] Fourdrinier, Bloxam & Fourdrinier, who launched into manufacture at the beginning of the nineteenth century; Thomas Creswick of London and Hatfield; Thomas Curtis of London and Buckinghamshire; and a number of others of varying importance.[2] Diverse examples from the provinces include, in Westmorland, William Pennington, printer, bookseller, and paper-maker of Kendal; and in Nottinghamshire, George Stretton who combined the activities of paper-maker of Basford, stationer of Nottingham, and editor and publisher of a local newspaper. Finally, an example of the truly comprehensive embrace is supplied by Williams, Cooper & Boyle who, in 1808, labelled themselves on their letter heads as 'Stationers, Paper Makers, Dealers in Rags and Paper-Hanging Manufacturers'.[3]

This integration was almost certainly not universal in the industry. Plenty of paper-makers large and small were unconnected with stationers save by the ordinary ties of business, just as plenty of stationers were not rag

[1] The son of a Baptist bricklayer, Lepard had started up as a stationer in Southwark in 1757. In 1766 his trade card told prospective customers that he sold 'all sorts of stationery wares, paper hangings, Bibles, Testaments, spelling books, etc., wholesale and retail', and that he gave 'the best prices for all sorts of rags for paper making'. In 1780 he took a lease of the mills at Oxhey and soon became a respected and able manufacturer (Lepard & Smith MSS.).

[2] Balston MSS.; C. & E.: Excise-Treasury Letters, 1779–82, ff. 288–9; ibid., 1814–22, ff. 375–433; B.M. Add. MSS. 15054; Fourdrinier Papers. Shorter, *Historical Geography*, p. 95, quotes an example of a London stationer, Thomas Haydon, who had both corn- and paper-mills under one roof at Stanwell, Middlesex. An instance of a partnership involving stationers and a paper-maker is given by that which led to the present-day firm of Spalding & Hodge; in 1789 Thomas Spalding and Henry Routh, both stationers of the Strand, went into partnership with Thomas Hodgson, stationer, of the Strand and paper-maker of Arborfield, Berkshire (*Spalding & Hodge Ltd.* (150th Anniversary Souvenir, 1789–1939)).

[3] C. & E.: Excise-Treasury Letters, 1815–17, ff. 391–2; Wiggins, Teape MSS.: Johnson Gore Invoice Books.

merchants and vice versa. But the tendency to integration, especially between paper-makers and stationers, was strong and important.[1]

(ii)

Within this industrial structure various forces were at work creating problems which, by the last decade of the century, were extremely pressing. The attempts made to solve these problems left lasting impressions upon the industry.

A useful avenue of approach to the economic problems of an industry is offered by an analysis of the costs of production. There is reason to think that the following figures are not untypical for the industry as a whole:[2]

Percentages		
Whatman, 1784–5 (average)		*Keferstein, 1765*
Raw materials:		
Rags . . . 47·5 } 59		38 } 50
Others . . . 11·5		12
Wages . . . 14·0		21
Excise . . . 21·5		7
Carriage . . . 1·5		4
Miscellaneous . . 4·0		12
Rent . . . . —		6
100·0		100

These figures are not strictly comparable and the special

[1] Financial relations between stationers and paper-makers are discussed in Chap. IX in the context of both the late eighteenth and the early nineteenth centuries. See pp. 251 et seq.

These financial relations were sometimes the cause of unions between stationers and paper-makers, mills coming into the hands of stationers as a result of the failure of paper-makers to whom they had lent money. William Gill, for instance, mortgaged Turkey Mill to a London stationer, James Brooke, in 1729, and in 1738 Brooke became possessed of the mill, though it was worked by Richard Harris to whom it was later sold (*The Paper Maker*, Apr. 1955, pp. 289–90).

[2] Balston MSS.: Whatman Ledger; Keferstein, op. cit., pp. 40–41.

nature of Whatman's business has to be borne in mind.[1] Nevertheless they do reveal clearly that in two quite different enterprises, a small mill in Germany and a large one in England, rags and labour were the two main items in production outlays.[2] The very high percentage of the Excise in the English mill is also noteworthy.

It is precisely these three items—rags, labour, and taxation—which were posing the most acute problems to English paper-makers by the end of the century, because the cost of each was rising sharply. The economy as a whole, especially after 1790, was being swept along by a strong inflationary current; between 1790 and 1800 wholesale prices rose by roughly 50 per cent., and this rise had become about 100 per cent. by 1814.[3] But the paper industry had its particular troubles.

Shortages of rags with accompanying increases in price (and sharp ones, too, in a commodity with particularly inelastic supply conditions) have continually recurred; and, from an early date, this chronic raw material problem led men to experiment with substitutes as well as to devise legislative arrangements for conserving or encouraging supplies. The increased consumption of rags in the eighteenth century brought about by the expan-

---

[1] The Whatman figures are calculated direct from his ledger on the basis of his total expenditure annually. The Keferstein figures come from a calculation designed to show in general what went into the cost of making a specific quantity of paper: thus his 'miscellaneous' heading includes a large allowance for maintenance, not allowed for or incurred to any large extent in the Whatman figures. 'Wages' in the Whatman figures makes no allowance for costs of Whatman's own labour; the Keferstein figures allot an amount to 'dem Meister und Frau vor die Direction'.

[2] Even in the lowest grades of paper and board the figures are similar: it was estimated at about the same time that the cost of old ropes used in making brown paper and pasteboard accounted for about 35 per cent. of the selling price (*Transactions of the Royal Society of Arts*, vol. vii (1789), pp. 111 et seq.).

[3] A. D. Gayer, A. J. Schwartz, and W. W. Rostow, *Growth and Fluctuations of the British Economy, 1790–1815* (Oxford, 1953), vol. i, pp. 471–2.

sion not simply of the English but also of the continental paper industry gave rise to pervasive fears of a permanent shortage. As early as 1684 a plan had been put forward in this country for making paper from asbestos and in 1716 the use of raw hemp in paper-making was advanced in a work published in London.[1] But the Continent was the scene of the most famous of these early inquiries into rag substitutes. Réamur's observations of the activities of the wasp in making filaments out of wood fibre led him to advocate the use of wood in paper-making. In 1719 he noted that rags were not an economic raw material and that they were becoming rare.[2] The use of various vegetable and other substitutes for paper-making was recommended by J. C. Schäffer and other continental writers. Schäffer published a detailed account of his experiments and included in his book specimens of paper made from various plants and sundry materials ranging from turf to wasps' nests.

His work attracted a good deal of attention in places well distant from his native Regensburg. In England a correspondent of the Royal Society of Arts, observing the rising price of rags, had suggested the use of nettles, hops, and the like, and in 1768 the Society, impressed by Schäffer's work, awarded him a silver medal for his experiments. Later the receipt of two of his volumes prompted the Society to encourage similar researches in this country. Noting in 1781 that the consumption and the price of paper was 'every day encreasing', it offered a reward for the making of paper from vegetable substances which had not previously been made into cloth.

[1] Hunter, pp. 312–13. [2] Ibid., p. 314.
[3] *Versuche und Muster ohne alle Lumpen oder doch mit einem geringen Zusatze derselben Papier zu Machen* (6 vols. Regensburg, 1765–71). These were collected and published in one volume as *Sämtliche Papierversuche* (Regensburg, 1772). See also Hunter, pp. 317–28.

Awards were made shortly afterwards to Thomas Greaves, paper-maker of Mill Bank, near Warrington, who submitted paper made from the bark of withies. In 1797 a pamphlet was published by a London bookseller, advocating the making of paper from jute; four years later, Thomas Wilmott, one of a family of Kentish paper-makers, secured an award of 20 guineas from the Society of Arts for some paper manufactured therefrom. In spite of these experiments none of this paper ever reached commercial production. The same is true of the efforts to make high-class drawing-paper out of silk rags which the Society of Arts encouraged in the 1750's and 60's and for which it awarded premiums to four paper-makers.[1] It is true, too, of the one known experiment at this time in the large-scale manufacture of paper from a substance other than rags.

In 1800 and 1801 Mathias Koops took out three patents. The first covered a method of extracting ink from old paper and of repulping the paper; the second and third were for making paper from straw, hay, thistles, and the like. At the same time he produced a book printed on paper made from wood or straw and from repulped paper. Armed with the patents, he set about forming a joint-stock company and erected a mill for the manufacture of paper from straw 'and other vegetable substances without the admixture of rags'. The enterprise was conceived on a large scale, the company having a capital of some £71,000; the mill itself was evidently far larger than the ordinary paper-mill of the time, for its equipment included twenty vats and two steam-engines, one of 80 h.p.; the celebrated engineer John Rennie had been responsible for making some of

[1] *Transactions of Royal Society of Arts*, vol. vi, pp. 159 et seq.; vol. vii, pp. 111 et seq.; vol. xix, pp. 235 et seq.; Dossie, op. cit., vol. i, p. 14; vol. iii, p. 457; R.S.A.: Guard Books, vol. ii, f. 65; vol. iii, f. 31; Loose Archives B 2/48, Sewell; Hunter, pp. 329–30.

the presses and other plant. Although some paper was made, within two years the company was bankrupt; in 1804 the premises were put up for auction. Thus ended rapidly what was obviously an over-capitalized, over-ambitious, but ingenious project.[1] In May 1802 Koops had petitioned the Treasury in regard to the question of what duty should be paid on the paper; he stated that over £60,000 had been spent on the buildings and plant and also complained of the

> Opposition which your Memorialist has already met with and still expects to meet with from the powerful Wholesale Dealers in Rags and Paper who remit large sums of Money to the Continent for the Importation of Rags to the detriment of this Country, and who have raised the price of raw Materials to an unprecedented height. . . .[2]

The price of rags had indeed been rising alarmingly meanwhile. In the 1780's the average price of fine rags varied from 35s. to 37s. per cwt. A temporary sharp increase in 1783 to 41s. had the effect of pushing up the percentage of Whatman's expenditure on rags, in relation to the total, to 55 per cent. in that year. By 1792 fine rags were not to be obtained under 42s.; in 1799 the price was 45s., in 1803, 56s., and in the next year, 58s.[3] The problem was not met by direct technical change in the sense of finding a practical substitute for rags. It was not, in fact, solved at that time; it was postponed to a later date by means of an indirect solution—the introduction of chlorine bleaching. This enabled a much wider range of

---

[1] For further details see Hunter, pp. 330–40.

[2] C. & E.: Excise-Treasury Letters, 1801–4, ff. 317–20.

[3] Balston MSS.: Whatman Ledger and various letters. This price rise (about 60 per cent. from 1780 to 1804) was greater than the increase in general wholesale prices (40 per cent.) as shown in the Silberling's price index (N. J. Silberling, 'British Prices and Business Cycles, 1779–1850', *Review of Economic Statistics*, 1923, pp. 232–3).

rags to be used in making white paper and undoubtedly went a long way towards counterbalancing the deficiency in supply at a time of sharply increasing demand. Obviously, however, it took some time for this new method to be put into general use, and meanwhile attempts to meet the problem took the form of combined restrictive action on the part of a large number of paper manufacturers, designed to push down rag prices.

This was a powerful force in helping to weld together the employers. And their actions in attempting to combat the other two pressing problems—taxation and labour—followed the same lines. To the growing burden of the Excise in the decade from 1781 to 1801 was added the threat to protection implied by the negotiations for the Eden Treaty of 1787. Throughout these same years the general rise in prices, especially of foodstuffs during the war years after 1793, pushed up the cost of living and provoked organized action by combinations of workers in the industry. By the later decades of the century a trade association had been created for concerted action on all these matters.[1]

Meanwhile these various increases in production costs combined with the general upward movement of prices drastically to force up the price of paper. A sharp rise had already occurred with the passing of the 1781 Act, but a further steep advance took place in the 90's. One sort of printing demy doubled its price from 13s. 6d. per ream in 1793 to 27s. in 1801; a grade of writing demy advanced from 27s. per ream in 1794 to 41s. in 1801, during which time the Excise payable on it rose from 19 per cent. to 24 per cent. of its price per lb.[2]

---

[1] Details of this and of the struggle with the men's association are given in Chap. X.

[2] *Report of the Committee on the Booksellers and Printers Petition* (*B.P.P.* 1801-2, vol. ii).

(iii)

These, then, were the circumstances in which the industry was operating towards the end of the century. The pressures imposed by these three specific problems, as well as those mentioned earlier, which arose from the differential rates of advance within the processes of manufacture, combined with the swirling currents of inflation and of economic change to make it a difficult and dangerous period.

With this in mind we may now revert to the questions posed early in Chapter IV concerning the shape of the production curve during the century. The reasons for the apparent stagnation in the early years of the century and for the upward move in the 1740's are admittedly not much nearer to elucidation. The spread of the beating-engine may have contributed to the change; but in general terms it is worth noting that the trends exhibited here, in paper-making, are reflected in many other aspects of the economy. The striking relationship between the import and output curves has its parallels in indices from other industries and branches of trade; the timing of change seems also to reflect, however dimly it may yet be seen, the probable course of population growth. In short, the upward movement of paper output just before the mid-century may well have been simply a reflection of the general setting into motion of the economy. This new movement followed a period of comparative stagnation which itself followed on the rapid and vigorous economic upsurge which marks the last decades of the seventeenth century, an outburst of activity in which the paper industry shared.

The flattening out of the curve in the last decade of the eighteenth century is more readily attributable to the factors which we have now been able to examine—the pressure of particular problems and the rising prices which may well have caused a relative slackening of demand. But it is also clear that this slowing down in the rate of growth was accompanied by a period of re-assessment and of new ideas; it was a halting place preparatory to a new surge forward, preparatory in this particular instance to the great new advance which mechanization was to bring in the nineteenth century.

PART II

THE INDUSTRIAL REVOLUTION

PLATE II

Bryan Donkin and Henry Fourdrinier
(detail from 'Men of Science Alive in 1807-8' in the National Portrait Gallery, London)

VII

Mechanization

A N invention may be a response to a challenge; but before it can gain success as an industrial innovation, favourable circumstances must smooth the way for its adoption. From the initial posing of the problem to the final response there may be a long and tortuous path. Many discoveries have been made at the same time and in different places. But if one man and one country get the esteem of posterity, it is often because that man solved the final problems of practical application, or that country had the economic circumstances which favoured development. In the years around 1800 a number of enterprising men were trying to develop paper-making machinery; amongst the machines that which was finally to come into general use was invented in France and developed in England. It owed its initial invention to the problems of the French industry and to the mechanical ingenuity of a French clerk; it owed its eventual appearance in practical production to the existence of similar problems in English industry, to the money and enterprise of a firm of London wholesale stationers, and to the skill of an English engineer.

The dependence of paper-making upon skilled labour has already been mentioned, as has also the growth of labour disputes in the English industry in the later eighteenth century.[1] In the widespread and old-established French industry conflicts between masters and men can be traced back to earlier centuries. By the eighteenth

[1] *Supra*, pp. 38, 170, 174.

century, tension between the many small masters and the powerful *compagnonnages* had become acute in spite of government action; strikes in various areas were not uncommon; labour costs were rising.[1] In France, then, these labour troubles constituted a strong pressure driving the industry towards some change in the method of making the sheet of paper which would be labour-saving.[2]

In 1799 Nicholas-Louis Robert received, in France, a patent together with a monetary reward for his newly-invented paper-making machine.[3] He had been working on it intermittently during the previous three years whilst employed, in a clerical capacity, at the important paper-mill owned by Leger Didot at Essonnes, near Paris. Didot had encouraged Robert and helped him to obtain the patent. But little progress was made with the machine and soon Robert sold the patent to Didot for 25,000 francs; the latter, however, defaulted on his payments and after legal proceedings Robert recovered possession of his patent in June 1801. Meanwhile, news of the machine had been taken to England, the one country in the world which at that time possessed the capital, the enterprise, and the skill necessary to develop

[1] C. M. Briquet, 'Associations et grèves des ouvriers papetiers en France aux XVIIᵉ et XVIIIᵉ siècles', *Revue internationale de sociologie*, vol. v, no. 3 (1897).

[2] The role of these labour troubles in stimulating change both in France and in England is considered in greater detail in Chap. X.

[3] The following account of the introduction and development of the Fourdrinier machine has been put together chiefly from these sources: Fourdrinier Papers; Library of H.M. Patent Office: YV 38 (John Gamble, *Documents relative to the Invention and Introduction of the Paper Machine*); *Four-drinier Committee* (1807); *Fourdrinier Committee* (1837); *A Brief Account of Bryan Donkin, F.R.S. and of the Company he founded 150 years ago* (The Bryan Donkin Co. Ltd., 1953). See also Hunter, pp. 341–9; J. Strachan, 'The Evolution of the Fourdrinier Paper Machine', in *The Paper Maker* (Suppl.), May 1931; and V. Sanguinetti in *World's Paper Trade Review*, Mar. 1931.

industrial mechanization. Didot had communicated in 1800 with his English brother-in-law, John Gamble, then employed in the office of the British Commissioner for exchanging prisoners-of-war in France. Didot proposed to Gamble that the latter should take out an English patent for the machine and should share in the expected profits. Gamble left Paris in March 1801 and an English patent for the paper-making machine was taken out in Gamble's name in April of the same year.[1] In London he was introduced to Henry and Sealy Fourdrinier of the firm of Bloxam & Fourdrinier, the leading firm of London wholesale stationers, and interested them in the invention. Returning to France, Gamble arranged with Didot and Robert for the original working model of the machine to be sent to England; in 1802 Didot arrived here and met the Fourdriniers; work then began on the task of turning Robert's invention into an efficient and economical piece of industrial machinery. At this stage France and Robert disappear from the scene, to be replaced by the British engineer Bryan Donkin.

Donkin, who became one of the leading engineers of his time, had been apprenticed in 1792 to John Hall, millwright and engineer of Dartford. The Fourdriniers approached Hall for assistance in the development of the machine, and for some six months in 1801–2 he experimented with it under the direction of Gamble and Didot, but all to no avail. Hall told the Fourdriniers, in effect, that they were wasting their money. Donkin, meanwhile, had been working under Hall, and his ability presumably so impressed itself on the Fourdriniers that in 1802 he started to work for them on his own account. An engineering workshop was set up at Bermondsey, financed by the Fourdriniers and with Donkin as manager; for the

[1] Patent No. 2487 (Apr. 1801).

next five years and more, Donkin worked on the machine there and at the mills which the Fourdriniers opened up at St. Neots, Huntingdonshire, and at Frogmore and Two Waters, Hertfordshire. Machines were installed at these mills, but it was not until 1806 that one of the Hertfordshire machines gave promise of success both economic and technical. In 1806 the new invention was first offered to the trade under the terms of the patents which covered it. Experiments continued and improved versions were produced. By this time the new invention was proving itself and a number of machines were at work in various mills in the United Kingdom.

In this success story it is not easy to distinguish the part played by the leading figures—Donkin and the Fourdriniers, Gamble and Didot, not to speak of Robert. Claims and counter-claims stand side by side with patents and apparently conflicting patents. The evidence offered to the historian is various and contradictory: different sources allot the credit to different persons. What follows is an attempt to strike some sort of balance.

After the initial patent of 1801 Gamble took out a second patent in 1803 for improvements.[1] Meanwhile he entered into various financial arrangements with the Fourdriniers, the upshot of which was that by 1804 he was a partner with them in the St. Neots mill but had assigned both patents to Henry and Sealy Fourdrinier.[2] In 1807 Parliament granted an extension of the terms of the patents for 15 years, the Act vesting the sole right of making and selling the machine jointly in the Fourdriniers and Gamble as partners in the St. Neots enterprise.[3] In 1808, however, Gamble assigned to Henry and

[1] Patent No. 2708 (June 1803).
[2] *Fourdrinier Committee* (1807); *Fourdrinier Committee* (1837), p. 1; Fourdrinier Papers, *passim*.   [3] 47 Geo. III, c. 131.

Sealy Fourdrinier all rights to which he was entitled under the Act of Parliament, though continuing as partner in the St. Neots business until 1811.[1] But meanwhile, the Fourdriniers, who had evidently financed all the work in developing the machine and in setting up the mill at St. Neots, were getting into deeper and deeper waters financially. They were withdrawing large sums from the London stationery business in order to finance the experiments with the machine, and they were doing so against the wishes of, and later without the consent of, their partners. In 1803 William Bloxam left the firm because he disagreed with their policy, and in the ensuing years there were other changes in the partnership.[2] For the year ending 30 June 1801 the firm's profit as stationers had been over £14,200; in December 1809 their balance sheet, in spite of assets valued at over £230,000, showed a loss approaching £6,000.[3] In that year they made over their share in the St. Neots mill to Mathew Twogood.[4] In November 1810 the Fourdriniers were bankrupt.[5] As a result they found difficulty in

[1] *Fourdrinier Committee* (1837), p. 1; 'History of the Paper Machine by John Gamble, 1855', in *Documents relative to the Invention and Introduction of the Paper Machine* (Patent Office Library).

[2] Fourdrinier Papers: especially No. 6, a ledger of the firm showing for 30 June 1809 a transfer from H. & S. Fourdriniers' joint account to Bryan Donkin's account of the sum of £13,204. 6s. 4d., noted as having never been agreed to by either of the partners; Nos. 26–37, 46–54. J. B. Hunt, W. Abbott, and F. Morse became partners in 1809 and the firm in late years traded as Hunt & Fourdrinier.

[3] *Fourdrinier Committee* (1837), p. 2; Fourdrinier Papers, No. 23.

[4] Mathew Twogood, senior, and Mathew Twogood, junior, both entered the firm as partners sometime between 1803 and 1809, possibly in connexion with advances made by the banking house of Langston, Twogood, Cazalet, and Amory. In 1809 Twogood, senior, retired from the partnership, retaining the lease of St. Neots; in 1814 his son also withdrew. The Twogoods later developed the St. Neots mill successfully (Fourdrinier Papers, Nos. 6, 7, 11, 46–54; see also 'History of the Paper Machine by John Gamble').

[5] *Fourdrinier Committee* (1837), p. 3.

collecting any patent dues and their assigns and former partners became involved in lengthy and costly litigation which dragged on until well after the patent had expired in 1822.[1]

In 1837 Henry and Sealy Fourdrinier petitioned Parliament for leave to bring in a Bill to revive and extend the term of the patents.[2] The petition was referred to a Select Committee; the ensuing report and the minutes of evidence inevitably form important sources for the historian of this complex story. They are, however, from the historian's viewpoint, tendentious sources. All the witnesses called provided lavish support for the Fourdriniers' case and they were helpfully supplied with leading questions by the chairman of the Committee. The contributions made by Robert, Didot, Gamble, and Donkin were ignored or summarily dismissed. William Harrison, K.C., counsel for Fourdrinier at the time of the application for the 1807 extension of the patent, gave evidence and reported that at that time it had been 'proved distinctly that the invention was brought to perfection entirely by Mr. Fourdrinier'.[3] To an objection, made in the Lords in 1807 by Lord Lauderdale, that the invention was not Fourdrinier's, but had originated in France, it was blandly asserted that 'they could not say that the Frenchman had done anything more than throw out an idea that paper might be manufactured in a different way, but it was distinctly proven that the whole merit of it was Mr. Fourdrinier's'.[4]

---

[1] *Fourdrinier Committee* (1837), pp. 3–5; much of the content of the Fourdrinier Papers is associated with these legal actions. Included amongst them is a solicitor's bill of costs for £432 covering litigation on one action for the period 1816–25.   [2] *C.J.*, vol. xcii, p. 60.

[3] *Fourdrinier Committee* (1837), p. 6. The date of the application for extension of the patent is there incorrectly printed as 1801.

[4] Ibid., p. 6.

Appendix B to the Report comprises a notice sent to the paper manufacturers by the patentees in 1813 giving details of improvements to the machine and of reductions in price. Here alone in the Report, its appendices, and its minutes of evidence, is there any mention of Donkin by name: 'Mr. Donkin the engineer, will engage to furnish machinery' at stated prices; and either the Fourdriniers or 'Mr. Donkin, of Fort-place, Bermondsey, the engineer' will supply any further information that may be required.[1] By 1837 Donkin was a recently elected Fellow of the Royal Society and a distinguished figure in the world of engineering and applied science. But he did not give evidence before the Committee. Mark Brunel appeared, however, said that the machine 'was one of the most splendid inventions of our age', and asserted that the patent specifications were perfectly in order, whatever a learned judge had said about them in the course of litigation.[2] One of the reasons why Donkin did not give evidence is implied between the lines of the following extract, which also provides a good example of the manner in which evidence was taken.[3]

> CHAIRMAN (W. A. Mackinnon): Do you think the paper makers employed the engineers of the patentees to construct the machines, and afterwards refused to pay patent dues for the working of them?
>
> WITNESS (C. J. Bloxam): To my certain knowledge they did.
>
> CHAIRMAN: Taking advantage of their misfortunes?
>
> BLOXAM: Yes.
>
> CHAIRMAN: At what period did the bankruptcy occur?
>
> BLOXAM: On the 8th November, 1810.
>
> CHAIRMAN: The paper makers employed the engineers of the patentees to construct machines, and finding that the

[1] Ibid., pp. 47, 49.
[2] Ibid., pp. 7–9. Lord Tenterden in a case over the patent rights in 1825.
[3] Ibid., pp. 3–4.

patentees were bankrupt, they refused to pay the patent dues?

BLOXAM: Yes.

CHAIRMAN: Were the patentees compelled to institute suits in Chancery or actions at law in consequence?

BLOXAM: They were; I was the solicitor employed by the assignees to institute those suits.

Of the parts played by the Fourdriniers and by Donkin there can be no doubt that it was the latter who was truly responsible for the effective development of the machine. There is no reason whatever to suppose that the Fourdriniers had any knowledge of engineering or that the machine was 'brought to perfection entirely by Mr. Fourdrinier'. Not only is there no reference to Hall and the Bermondsey works or any serious indication of Donkin's role, but the evidence given thirty years earlier to the Committee which considered the application for the extension of patents in 1807 is used in a noticeably selective manner. Donkin gave detailed evidence to that Committee. He showed that in 1802 and 1807 he had done work for the Fourdriniers to the value of £31,667 of which £11,915 was attributable simply to experiments, improvements, and alterations to the machines.[1]

These various omissions are doubtless justifiable on the ground that the 1837 Committee was concerned with the Fourdriniers' legal right to the patents and with the financial responsibilities which they had incurred. But it means that as evidence of their role in developing the machine the Committee's report is misleading.

The other side of the coin of Donkin's achievement was that the Fourdriniers certainly bore the brunt of

---

[1] *Fourdrinier Committee* (1807). See also *A Brief Account of Bryan Donkin . . .*, pp. 12 and 14. This shows that the original drawing of an improved machine patented by Fourdrinier and Gamble in 1807 (Patent No. 3068) was in fact in Bryan Donkin's hand and is in the archives of the Bryan Donkin Co. Ltd.

financing the development of the machine; and it seems likely that much of what they might have expected to reap as rewards of their enterprise found its way, directly or indirectly, into Donkin's pocket. The Fourdriniers were able to prove to the satisfaction of the 1807 Committee that £60,228 was withdrawn from the stationery business to finance the invention; and evidence was given to the 1837 Committee to show a net loss on the machine, taking into account certain sums received by the patentees and their assigns, of £51,685.[1] It was claimed by the petitioners, and accepted by the Committee, that the bankruptcy was directly attributable to the money spent on the machine. In fact, however, it seems probable that there were other contributions to this fate: for example, very lavish expenditure on the St. Neots mill, as well as other financial activities which included investment in a paper-mill in Ireland.[2] Yet it is clear that the bankruptcy was a formidable blow in so far as it hindered the collection of patent dues; moreover the Fourdriniers sustained a further set-back in this as the result of an adverse legal decision made against them on technical grounds.[3]

However inflated the claims made for their achievement, the Fourdriniers do seem to have been unfortunate, financially and legally. The Committee of 1837 was largely a means of drawing attention to their misfortunes. There was never any serious chance of their patents being extended, but the Committee's reports recommended

[1] *Fourdrinier Committee* (1837), pp. iv and 5.

[2] Fourdrinier Papers, Nos. 7, 12, 18–20. The Irish investment involved J. O'B. Sullivan, of Dripsey Mills, Cork, and in 1807 the amount outstanding on that account was £10,815. The Fourdriniers also seem to have advanced money to Edward Russell, paper-maker and hop-grower of Kent, whose failure in the bad hop harvest of 1809 may also have embarrassed them. Donkin's statement of expenditure to the 1807 Committee included £11,276 for the St. Neots mill and drying house.

[3] *Fourdrinier Committee* (1837), pp. 3–4, 6–7.

that they were 'justly entitled to public compensation'.[1] In the end, after sundry delays and not before they had been showered with sympathetic petitions from various parts of the country,[2] the Commons in 1840 resolved in a Committee of Supply that £7,000 should be granted to the Fourdriniers 'in consideration of the great benefit conferred on the public by the introduction of their Machinery for the Improvement of the Manufacture of Paper'.[3] Seven years later, the cause of the surviving brother, Henry Fourdrinier, already an octogenarian, was taken up by *The Times* (17 June 1847) in a leading article. It called for justice, but it contrived to inflate still further the already swollen claims heard in the 1837 Committee. Fourdrinier was put alongside Caxton' . . . the one the father of printing, the other the inventor of a process by which the full benefits of printing have been realised to the civilized world'.[4] Money was raised for a 'Fourdrinier Testimonial'; and Henry Fourdrinier lived on to die just short of his ninetieth year in Staffordshire where he 'spent the last years of his life in humble but cheerful retirement'.[5]

The exaggerated stories about the Fourdriniers[6] moved John Gamble to send to an official of the Patent Office a collection of documents designed to provide support to a different view of the story and also to announce his son's intention of writing the true history of

---

[1] *Fourdrinier Committee* (1837), p. iv.

[2] See *C.J.*, vols. xciii and xciv.   [3] Ibid., 1840, p. 341.

[4] Quoted R. Herring, *Paper and Paper Making* (London, 1856), pp. 47–48.

[5] Ibid., p. 49; *Documents relative to the Introduction of the Paper Machine*; and *D.N.B.*

[6] They have found their way into various garbled versions in secondary authorities; Hunter, p. 349, for instance, states that the Fourdrinier brothers expended about £60,000 on the machine but 'never realized any remuneration'. This is demonstrably untrue even on the evidence given before the 1837 Committee.

the machine.[1] Gamble's account stresses, and reinforces with the original French patent specification, the fact that Robert, whom Gamble had seen at work on the first model in France, was the true inventor. He does not omit mention of the achievement of Donkin, 'an extremely ingenious and clever Mechanist'. Hall's evidence to the 1807 Committee tends to support Gamble, for although he said that the machine as assembled on Gamble's instructions would not make paper, his remarks show clearly that the basic principle of the machine survived all the experiments. Gamble's account inevitably plays down the role of the Fourdriniers and, whilst having its particular axe to grind over the unsuccessful result of their St. Neots venture, quite fails to mention the sum of £16,724 which, according to the Fourdriniers' clerk in 1807, was paid by them to Gamble.[2]

If Gamble should be given his due as a valuable intermediary, Didot demands some brief attention for his similar role. His own claims, set out in 1812,[3] did not stop at anything so meagre. He recited the various Gamble and Fourdrinier patents and also a separate patent taken out by Henry Fourdrinier alone in 1806,[4] and referred to them all as inventions communicated to the patentees 'by a certain Foreigner'. Not only was he that foreigner but he was also more than a mere intermediary:

Leger Didot (son of Pierre François Didot, the younger, of

[1] It is the manuscript of this 'History of the Paper Machine by John Gamble, 1855', which survives in the Patent Office Library. A printed version with some amendments is to be found in the *Journal of the Royal Society of Arts*, vol. v, 1857. Also among the Patent Office collection is a copy of the original specification, in French, of Robert's patent.

[2] *Fourdrinier Committee* (1807).

[3] Patents No. 3568 (June 1812) and 3598 (June 1812).

[4] Patent No. 2951 (July 1806). This it should be emphasized was for a machine of a different type, embodying a number of separate moulds for making laid and wove paper.

Paris, printer) later of Paris, but then residing at Two Waters, in the County of Hertford, the Original Inventor of Certain Machines for making Wove and Laid Paper, such Inventions having been communicated by me to the said John Gamble and Henry Fourdrinier, and who am the Foreigner referred to in the several Patents obtained by them.[1]

Whatever may have been his precise role, it is certain that he was more important than the 1837 inquiry would have one believe. According to the 1807 evidence he had then received £14,879 from the Fourdriniers and had worked with Gamble and Hall at Dartford; it is clear, too, he was still working, on friendly terms, with the Fourdriniers at Two Waters in 1808 and was much concerned with the machine.[2] It is also apparent from a note of Donkin's in June 1809 that Didot was still then experimenting with the Two Waters machine though not, in Donkin's opinion, with either sense or success; Donkin wrote of the 'known perverseness and obstinacy of the man'.[3] However true that may be, his main importance still rests upon his work in seeing the possibilities of Robert's invention and in taking steps to promote its development in England.

Through these diverse channels the Fourdrinier machine came into being and found its way into use in the paper industry. But it was not, in its early stages, without potential rivals. In 1805 another well-known inventor and engineer of the time, Joseph Bramah, took out a patent[4] to cover various improvements in paper manufacture amongst which was a paper-making

---

[1] Patent No. 3568.
[2] Balston MSS.: L. Didot to Balston, 1 Apr. 1808 and H. & S. Fourdrinier to Balston, 2 Apr. 1808; *Fourdrinier Committee* (1807).
[3] Quoted in *A Brief Account of Bryan Donkin . . .*, p. 14.
[4] Patent No. 2840 (Apr. 1805).

machine. Bramah apparently did not develop his invention and it seems to have had little influence on the subsequent technical advance of the industry. Far more important was John Dickinson's paper-making machine, patented in 1809.[1] Although this was the ancestor of the 'cylinder' machine of today,[2] at that time it failed to establish itself, and Dickinson himself eventually installed Fourdrinier machines in his own mills.[3]

The Fourdrinier machine represents a straightforward mechanization of what was formerly done by hand. In this it was entirely analogous to the great innovations in the textile industry which stimulated the spread of factories—machine-spinning and power-loom weaving. Just as, say, the spinning-'mule' mechanized the drawing and twisting processes once performed by hand and with the aid of the distaff or the spinning-wheel, so did the paper-making machine mechanize the actions of the vatman and the coucher. The basic principle of Robert's machine was to form the paper upon an endless belt of woven wire, instead of upon the separate moulds of the hand-made process. This principle remained equally true when the invention was developed by Donkin and the Fourdriniers and remains true of the modern Fourdrinier machines or of the largest newsprint machines turning out newsprint at over 2,000 feet per minute.

[1] Patent No. 3191 (Jan. 1809). On John Dickinson see *infra*, Chap. IX.

[2] The principal element of Dickinson's machine was a hollow brass cylinder perforated with holes; its outer surface was covered with a woven wire cloth. The cylinder rotated above and just in contact with the pulp; by means of air-pumps operating on the air inside the cylinder, suction was created on the surface of the wire, the film of pulp thus adhered to the cylinder and the water was drained off. The paper formed in this manner on the hollow cylinder was then wound off continuously onto other solid cylinders. For the modern cylinder machine see Labarre, p. 67, and Hunter, pp. 368–73.

[3] *Fourdrinier Committee* (1837), p. 49; Joan Evans, *The Endless Web* (London, 1955), p. 23.

Two vital elements in the making process—the 'shake' which the vatman gave to the mould whilst forming the sheet, and the 'couching' of the wet sheets on to a felt— were incorporated in the machine. The former was carried out by imparting a side-to-side motion to the 'wire', the latter by running the newly-formed sheet of paper on to a felt-covered roller. From the comparatively crude device which was Robert's original machine, the paper was taken off in sheets whilst still wet and then hung up to dry. It comprised simply the vital constituents of what would today be called the 'wet end' of a paper machine. It was upon this ingenious but imperfect contrivance that Donkin set to work. And by the 1860's it had become a relatively complex and costly machine.

There is no need to recount here all the various changes which were made in its operation, nor to provide a detailed description of its working. It is important simply to underline the stimulus given by this initial mechanization, coming as it did during the era of the industrial revolution, to a series of cumulative advances not simply in the making process but in all the processes of paper manufacture. Larger and more efficient beating-engines were developed, advances were made in the methods of sizing the paper,[1] and all manner of devices built into the machine itself to improve and speed up production.[2] The drying and finishing processes were mechanized by means of a series of heated cylinders built on to the end of the machine to receive the still moist paper; with this inno-

[1] By the 1830's printing- and writing-paper was normally 'engine sized', i.e. the size was added to the pulp in the engine. See *Fourteenth Report* (1835), p. 105.

[2] The width of the 'wire' and the speed at which it travelled were both increased in the course of the century. In the original machine the width was about 24 inches; by the 1860's machines with 100-inch wires were in use. From 25 to 40 feet per minute was the normal speed in the 1840's but by the 70's as much as 150 feet per minute had been reached.

PLATE III

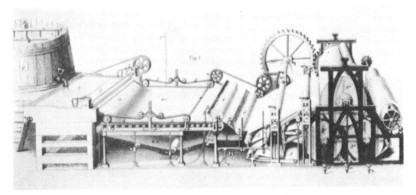

The Fourdrinier Machine, *circa* 1850

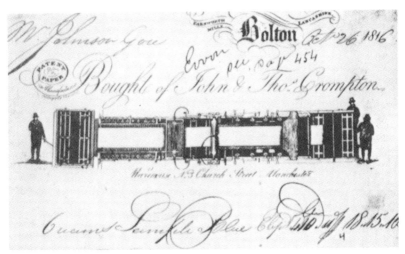

Billhead of Messrs. J. & T. Crompton, 1816, showing the new Fourdrinier Machine
(see p. 238)

vation, the machine thus encompassed the transference of wet pulp at one end into dry paper at the other. Various sorts of cutting-machines were soon developed and came, before the mid-century, to form part of the paper-making machine, thus obviating the earlier practice of winding the paper on to a reel and then removing it for cutting. Finally, there may be mentioned the sundry sorts of rolls designed to impart different finishes or effects to the paper: some have been introduced into the central part of the machine,[1] others at the 'dry end' where sets of hard steel rolls or calenders have gradually made their appearance.[2]

The cumulative improvements in the techniques of machine paper-making were the product of the ingenuity of many men, both engineers and practising paper-makers. Amongst the latter John Dickinson occupies an important place. His various contributions to the techniques of the industry included the patenting of the process of making paper with a continuous thread of cotton, flax, or silk running through it—a type of paper which came to be used as a precaution against counterfeiting in the manufacture of stamps or bank notes. Other patents which he took out covered improvements in the manufacture of paper for copper-plate printing, a paper-cutting machine, and a type of duplex or veneered paper.[3] Another paper-maker who stands

---

[1] For instance, the 'dandy roll' which rides on the upper surface of the paper on the 'wire' and is used to give to the surface of the paper 'laid' or 'wove' marks and also its watermark.

[2] On the early technical development of the machine see Hunter, pp. 345–68; Spicer, pp. 60–66; Strachan, op. cit. in *The Paper Maker* (Suppl.), May 1931; C. Tomlinson (ed.), *Cyclopaedia of Useful Arts and Manufactures* (London, 1854), vol. ii, pp. 357–74.

[3] For Dickinson and his patents see *The Endless Web*, *passim*, and *infra*, pp. 235–7.

high in this list is T. B. Crompton, like Dickinson a highly successful manufacturer, whose name is linked with the method of drying paper by means of heated cylinders, which he patented in 1820; he also made a number of other contributions to technical advance.[1]

Progress also followed from the work of engineers and specialists whose work reflected the increasingly complex technology of the age and its concomitant increase in division of labour. The connexions with the industry of such engineers as Bramah and Hall have already been mentioned, and there is little doubt that the continued association with paper-making on the part of Bryan Donkin and the firm which he built up must have brought successive improvement in the construction and design of the machine. By 1811 he owned the works in Bermondsey; and in addition to the many and various technical matters with which he was concerned[2] he and his firm became for a time the main manufacturers of paper-making machinery in the country.[3] Some forty years after his acquisition of the Bermondsey works the firm had made and erected 191 paper-making machines, 83 of which were in Britain and 89 in various countries of northern Europe.[4] Other engineering firms specializing in paper-making machinery had grown up by the middle of the century, notably the Edinburgh firm of J. Bertram;

[1] Crompton's patents include Nos. 4509 (Nov. 1820) and 8027 (Apr. 1839); see also *infra*, p. 238. Other paper-makers worthy of mention in this context include Richard Ibotson whose pulp strainer was patented in 1830 (No. 5964), Thomas Barratt and Mathew Twogood (see Tomlinson, op. cit., vol. ii, pp. 367–73, and *Abridgement of the Specification relating to the Manufacture of Paper, Pasteboard and Papier-Maché*, pt. i.

[2] They embraced, *inter alia*, lathes, pen-nibs, printing machinery, food-canning, and water-wheels.

[3] As well as the paper-making machine itself they also made other equipment used in the industry, including beating-engines and a spherical rag-boiler developed by Donkin himself (*A Brief Account of Bryan Donkin*, p. 32).   [4] Ibid., pp. 14–15.

the Bryan Donkin Co. later switched its interest to different branches of engineering.[1]

Apart from changes affecting the supply of raw materials in the industry[2] there is one further element in this mechanization which demands some brief attention: the extension of steam-power. The unreliability of water-power became especially tiresome now that the machine had broken the former bottleneck between the preparation and the making processes. A premium was thus put upon a constant power supply. Although during the nineteenth century many of the machine mills continued to use the water-wheel or, from about the mid-century the water-turbine as a source of power, the steam-engine gradually made inroads into the industry. In the earlier years many mills used steam-power to supplement rather than to replace water.[3] The spread of the industry in Lancashire, Yorkshire, Durham, and the central valley of Scotland almost certainly owed much to the ready availability of coal in these regions. Conversely it declined in the remoter areas distant from accessible coal supplies.

It seems likely that mechanization had made no very great impression before the 1830's. The bare record of the number of patents relating to paper-making gives some indication both of the timing of inventive activity and, in general, of the remarkably cumulative effects of applied science in industry. Fig. 6 graphs all those recorded from 1665 to 1860.[4] Although output was rising sharply during the first few decades of the century, it was probably not until the late 1820's and early 30's that the

[1] Ibid. and Strachan, op. cit.
[2] *Infra*, pp. 213–17.
[3] See, for examples in Scotland, *Children's Employment* (1843), pp. k 1–5.
[4] *Abridgements of the Specifications relating to the Manufacture of Paper, Pasteboard and Papier Maché*, pts. i and ii, 1665–1860.

output of hand-made paper began to fall steeply; similarly the effects of mechanization on the number of mills did not begin to make itself felt until about the same time.[1]

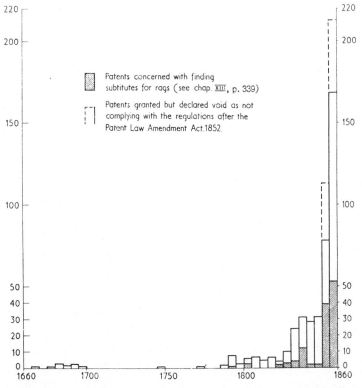

Fig. 6. Paper-making Patents, G.B. 1660–1859 (Totals in 5-yearly periods)

Such records as we have of the number of machines installed seem to tell a similar story. In his evidence to the 1837 Committee Henry Fourdrinier provided a detailed list of the machines that had been erected up to the expiration of the patent in 1882: they totalled 42 (see Table XV).

[1] *Infra*, pp. 205–7, 217–21.

TABLE XV

List of Fourdrinier Machines erected 1807–22[1]

Date of License	To Whom Granted	Where Erected	No. Vats
20 May 1807	Eliz. and James Swan	Evesham, Oxon.	10
4 Nov. ,,	Barn. Sullivan	Cork	3
1 July ,,	Lewis Smith	Aberdeen	10
1 July ,,	J. B. Sullivan	Cork	10
1 July ,,	. . . .	Blarney	3
1 July ,,	John Phipps	Dover	10
1 July ,,	E. Martindale	Cambridge	3
1 July ,,	Bacon Novino	Norwich	4
1 July ,,	Rd. Elliott	Chesham	2
1 July ,,	Wrightons & Co.	Warwick	3
1 July ,,	Wright & Pepper	Marlow	3
1 July ,,	Ibbotson & East	Colnbrook	3
1 July ,,	John Buttenshaw	. . . .	2
			66
14 July 1816	James & John Livesey	Prestoles, nr. Bolton	3
20 July ,,	John Livesey	. . . .	3
25 Jan. 1817	Binning Arnold	Kingsland Rd.	2
28 Aug. ,,	James & Francis Wrigley	Bridge Hall, Bury	2
1 Nov. ,,	Smith & Rhedde	Newcastle-under-Lyne	2
29 Dec. ,,	James Martin	Wood Mills, Leeds	2
3 Jan. 1818	Nelsons	Retford, Notts.	2
20 Feb. ,,	J. &. T. Crompton	Farnworth, nr. Bolton	3
14 Mar. ,,	. . . .	. . . .	2
25 Feb. 1821	. . . .	. . . .	2
25 July 1818	Smith & Ingle	Thoostleness	3
14 Aug. ,,	N. Grace & Co.	Llotwove Mill, Newcastle	3
14 Aug. ,,	Abr. Smith	Langley, nr. Durham	2
16 Nov. ,,	John Ibbotson	White Hall, nr. Manchester	3
3 Nov. 1819	Charles Venables	Hampton Guy, nr. Woodstock	2
11 Nov. ,,	James Pegg	Wooburn, Bucks.	3
5 Nov. ,,	Joseph Wright	Marlow	2
5 Nov. ,,	ditto	ditto	2
30 Nov. ,,	P. J. Fromow	Clapton, nr. Wooburn, Bucks.	2
30 Nov. ,,	J. Allnutt	Chesham, Bucks.	2
5 June 1820	E. Wright	Thorney, Bucks.	2
5 June ,,	Flint & Tregent	Littleton, Evesham	2
15 July ,,	J. C. Radway	Quimmington, Fairford	2
22 Feb. 1821	William Hill	Greenfield, Holywell	3
28 June ,,	Grafton & Co.	Birmingham	2
25 July ,,	W. Tempest	Little Eaton, Derby	2
3 Nov. ,,	William Truer	Coosban, Cornwall	2
16 Feb. 1822	John Pyne	Tovil	2
2 May ,,	George Payne	Cheriton, Dover	2
			66

Source: 1837 *Fourdrinier Committee* (1837).

[1] This list is reproduced as printed. There are a number of mistakes in names. e.g. Thoostleness = Throstle Nest, Hampton Guy = Hampton Gay, Coosban = Coosebeane, Evesham (in the first entry) = Eynsham, and, perhaps the most striking, Llotwove = Scotswood.

Fourdrinier also stated that 279 machines were then (i.e. 1837) at work in the U.K.[1] This figure cannot, however, be taken at its face value, for it was qualified with the phrase, 'each machine doing the work of five vats'. It was customary at the time to reckon the capacity of paper-making machines in terms of the number of vats' work they were estimated to be able to do in a given time: one with a 'wire' 30 inches wide was calculated to be able to do the work of three or four vats, and a 54-inch 'wire' was assumed to be equivalent to twelve vats.[2] Thus what Fourdrinier presumably did to reach the figure of 279 was to express each machine as a five-vat equivalent, thus giving a false impression of the total number of machines of different sizes then at work. Spicer also gives estimates for the number of machines at work:[3] the totals for 1822 roughly agree—38 according to Spicer, 42 according to Fourdrinier—but Spicer's figure of 105 for 1837 bears no relation to Fourdrinier's figure of 279. It must be admitted, moreover, that the sudden leap which Spicer's figures take from 129 in 1839 to 191 in 1840 does not seem to compel confidence in their yearly accuracy for the early decades. Yet another set of figures gives 356 machines as the total at work in the U.K. in 1842.[4]

Obviously these various figures cannot be made to bear the weight of precise deductions. But, assuming that the totals for 1822 are roughly correct and that the total for the 1837–42 period lies somewhere between the two extremes of 105 and 356, the implication is again

---

[1] *Fourdrinier Committee* (1837), p. 37.

[2] This is made quite clear in app. B to *Fourdrinier Committee* (1837), p. 47.

[3] App. vi, pp. 249–51.

[4] Quoted in Royal Commission on the Exhibition of 1851, *Reports of the Juries* (London, 1852) p. 430.

that mechanization did not become truly widespread in the industry until the 1830's and thereafter. On the other hand, of course, it is equally true that enterprising manufacturers in diverse parts of the kingdom, as Table XV shows, had already looked to the future and installed machinery.

VIII

The Period of Expansion, 1800–60

(i)

FIG. 7 presents a sort of graphical sketch of the industry's growth from 1800 to 1860.[1] The general impression which it offers is one of steady, unspectacular but sustained development. In output the rate of growth initiated in the 1730's and 40's was continued, and indeed slightly increased, in the nineteenth century. Between 1800 and 1860 output multiplied about sevenfold in the United Kingdom as a whole, though the contribution made by the Scottish industry advanced at about twice that figure; in 1800 Scotland had provided rather less than 9 per cent. of the total, in 1855 nearly 22 per cent., the corresponding figures for England being 88 per cent. and 74 per cent. respectively. Ireland's contribution remained trifling throughout.[2] Continuous figures for the 140 years from 1715 to 1855 can be obtained only for England and here the advance from approximately 2,500 tons to 78,000 tons gives some indication of the slow but steady expansion.

Imports of paper-making materials rose at a noticeably slower pace than did paper output. The high point of 6,200 tons in 1790 was not reached again until 1818 and thereafter the maximum figure of 16,000 tons was not

---

[1] For the sources from which this was drawn and some notes on its construction and accuracy see App. I.

[2] It should be mentioned here that the Irish figures were notoriously defective, especially before 1837 (see *Fourteenth Report* (1835), pp. 161–71 and 178–86); even were they doubled, however, the Irish contribution would still be insignificant.

attained until the very end of our period. The significance of this discrepancy will be examined later.[1]

Overseas trade in paper showed one outstanding change in this period: an upward trend in imports after many years when they barely existed. Even so, the level which they reached was still insignificant. Net imports averaged only 361 tons per annum in 1858–9 and this accounted for less than 1 per cent. of total home consumption. Although they rose sharply to 1,300 tons in 1860 this was still trifling—for all the protests of home producers[2]—when compared with domestic production of nearly 100,000 tons. Exports, for such years as figures are available, show a vigorous upward trend, though also forming only a small proportion of total output; the average percentage was 4·7 for 1834–8 and 8·9 for 1855–9. They fell off slightly in 1860.[3]

Consumption per head in the United Kingdom was only about 8 lb. in 1860. This still remains, therefore, much nearer to the estimated 2·5 lb. for 1800 or even the 1·5 lb. for 1714–18 than to the levels of modern consumption which the advent of wood-pulp has made possible.[4]

One feature is missing from this picture of industrial change: prices. Fig. 8 goes some way towards remedying this.[5] For the period 1800–60 the average price fall was about 60 per cent. The sharply rising prices of the 1790's

---

[1] *Infra*, p. 214. See also Chap. XIII.

[2] *Select Committee* (1861), *passim*; were the evidence of the paper-makers to be taken at its face value, the impression of an industry almost engulfed by foreign competition would be overwhelming.

[3] Also the subject of woeful comment to the 1861 Committee.

[4] See *supra*, pp. 15, 105.

[5] Based on prices of printing demy bought by Messrs. Longman (see App. I for further details). This was a very widely purchased size and type of printing-paper and it is reasonable to assume that it reflected comparable price changes in other types and sizes.

continued into the first years of the new century. The reduction and simplification of the Excise in 1803 brought temporary respite in the upward movement. But it was not until the second decade of the century that a phase of depression in the economy as a whole[1] combined with the beginning of mechanization to push prices downwards. This trend was further reinforced in 1836 by another reduction in the Excise and perhaps also

FIG. 8. Paper Prices 1797–1860 (logarithmic scale)

strengthened by the gradual lowering of the tariff wall from 1825 onwards.[2]

The results were striking. Quotations by wholesale stationers for a particular grade of writing demy, for example, fell from 52s. per ream in 1808 to 46s. 6d. in 1816—a fall of 11 per cent. The next phase may be illustrated from the fact that the prices of two types of paper bought by the Clarendon Press fell by 27 per cent. and 29 per cent. between 1814 and 1834; the price of tissue papers bought by Staffordshire pottery-makers fell by 40 to 47 per cent. between 1814 and 1833. Thereafter the continuing fall in prices was attested to by the well-known publisher, Charles Knight, who stated that the cost of the paper which he used for his *Penny Cyclopaedia* was reduced from 33s. to 24s. per ream between 1833–7

---

[1] Cf. the temporary flattening of the output curve in Fig. 7.
[2] See Chap. XII.

and 1838–46.[1] Taking the period as a whole, Spicer put the reduction in the average price per lb. as from 1s. 6d. to 10d. between 1800 and 1836 and 10d. to $6\frac{1}{2}d$. between 1836 and 1859.[2] In the late 50's, however, the fall in price was temporarily arrested, for reasons which will be discussed later.[3] It is apparent in Fig. 8 where there is even a slight upward tendency from 1853 to 1860.

(ii)

Because of the changes in the methods of levying the Excise the returns cannot be used to show in what way the composition of paper output changed in this period.[4] But it is clear that, with mechanization, a very much larger range of paper was coming to be manufactured. In 1860 a current paper catalogue listed 681 different kinds, varying by size, weight, colour, finish, intended use, and much more besides.[5] Although the old sizes of hand-made paper were still used—indeed the complexity of sizes was made worse by additions and qualifications— the machine offered new possibilities for particular uses. The roll of paper made its first appearance on the scene; the wallpaper-makers, for example, could now have their fascinatingly named 'long Elephants' in rolls instead of having to join separate pieces together.[6] Quality too, was given both greater variety and improvement.

---

[1] Plant, op. cit., p. 331; also *Fourdrinier Committee* (1837), pp. 20–24, 38–39; Wiggins, Teape MSS.: Johnson Gore Invoice Books.

[2] Spicer, pp. 86–89.

[3] See Chap. XIII.

[4] From 1803 to 1836 the duty was charged by the lb. on two main classes of paper; thereafter one flat rate per lb. covered all types of paper and board. The distinction between class I and class II papers in 1803–36 and the difficulties created thereby are examined in Chap. XII.

[5] R. Herring, *A Practical Guide to the Varieties and Relative Values of Paper* (London, 1860).

[6] *Fourdrinier Committee* (1837), p. 25; Labarre, op. cit., p. 87.

Contrary to a certain sort of romantic notion about handicraft products, the machine product is usually better, as well as being cheaper. This is not, of course, to suggest that all machine-made paper was or is better than all hand-made paper: obviously this is not so. The hand-made sheet of the highest quality linen-rag paper was better than anything the machine could produce and perhaps still is. But for the run of papers in everyday use, wrapping-, printing-, and writing-papers of ordinary standard, the machine—once the early technical difficulties had been overcome—brought a marked improvement in finish, strength, and regularity. Like must be compared with like. Giving evidence before the Fourdrinier Committee in 1837, Edward Wiggins, wholesale stationer of London, put the matter succinctly. Having affirmed that much of the paper then made was better than in the pre-machine days, he was asked 'Cannot Whatman or some of the great paper manufacturers, make paper equally good?' To this he replied: 'That is a totally different article; the machine paper and Whatman's paper are never put into competition.'[1]

The hand-made branch of the industry by no means disappeared in this period, though its output declined as shown in Fig. 9 so that by 1860 it accounted for less than 4 per cent. of total production.[2] Whatever may be the precise accuracy of the figures on which Fig. 9 is based,[3] they tell a plausible tale, for what is known of the extension of machine production would suggest that it was not until the later 1820's that hand-made output would begin to fall sharply. In Ireland a few hand-made

[1] *Fourdrinier Committee* (1837), p. 17.

[2] Spicer, app. ix, pp. 258–60.

[3] Some of the estimates for numbers of vats and machines at different times during the century, on which Spicer's calculations are in part based, seem questionable. See Spicer app. vi, also *supra*, pp. 198–9.

mills making ordinary or coarse paper survived, but the general tendency was for the survival of those vat mills which made the highest grades. It was in this way that

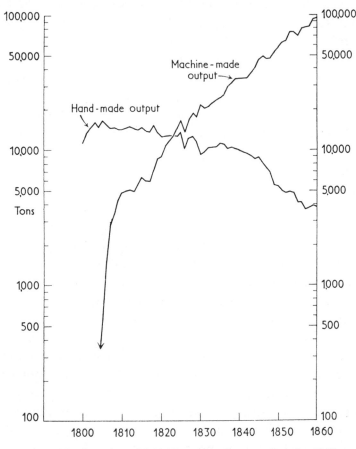

FIG. 9. Hand-made and Machine-made Output, 1800–60, U.K.
(logarithmic scale)

this branch of the industry adjusted itself to the competition of the machine after a period of unhappy struggling in the earlier decades of the century. Some such mills then flourished in this specialized line, acquiring in time prosperity and reputation as producers of the finest quality paper.[1]

Until 1836 it is possible to trace the advance in the output of board separately from that of paper. It rose in the United Kingdom at about the same rate as paper, from an average of 730 tons per annum in 1800–4 to 2,250 tons in 1832–6. 'Board' covered a variety of commodities as it had earlier: pasteboard and cardboard, millboards and glazed paper used by the woollen manufacturers in pressing-cloth, sheathing-paper, and button board.[2]

Finally it is worth noting that the very small amount of imported paper was mainly for writing and printing. France, Holland, and Italy were the main sources in the earlier years after Waterloo; and towards the end of the period more was coming in from Belgium. By the 1850's and 60's increasing imports over lowered tariff walls were bringing in printing-paper for newspapers; *The Times* and *The Scotsman* were said to be using this foreign paper. Foreign manufacturers were regarded as being well behind British makers in the production of the better sorts of printing- and writing-papers.[3]

(iii)

In considering the stimuli to increasing demand, rising population must again take first place. In 1861 the people of the United Kingdom numbered nearly 29

[1] See, e.g., *infra*, pp. 243–5.

[2] For source of figures of board output see App. I; on the different types of board see Labarre, op. cit. *passim*; also C. & E.: Excise-Treasury Letters, 1801–4, ff. 199–200 (Petition of the Card and Pasteboard Makers of the City of London, Dec. 1801).

[3] *Select Committee* (1861), pp. 10, 12, 16–17, 19, 39, 45, app. 3; P.R.O. Customs, 5/5–22.

million, the total having thus almost doubled since 1800.[1] But as population increased, so more and more was it changing in character. We were becoming an urban nation. To this period belong the earliest and most striking phases in the rapid growth of such industrial towns as Glasgow, Liverpool, Leeds, and Birmingham, to name but a few.[2] Along with urban life as a concomitant of the sweeping industrial changes of the age there came new patterns of social intercourse, new problems to discuss, new means and new reasons for securing and disseminating information.

An important element in this process of social change was the early growth of mass communications through new forms of cheap publication—books, tracts, news-papers, encyclopaedias. Two innovations did more than anything else to make this possible: mechanical printing and mechanical paper-making. From the viewpoint of the paper industry increasing literacy and heightened social consciousness in a rapidly expanding population must stand side by side with the cylinder printing press, first developed by Koenig and then improved by Apple-

---

[1] The relevant figures are (approximately):

(millions)

	1801	1861
England and Wales . . .	9	20
Scotland	2	3
Ireland (including what is now Eire) .	5	6
U.K.	16	29

[2] In 1801 London was the only town with over 100,000 inhabitants; it contained nearly 10 per cent. of the total population. Only 7 per cent. of the population then lived in towns of 20,000–100,000 people. Sixty years later London accounted for nearly 14 per cent. of the population, other towns over 100,000 for 11 per cent., and those between 20,000 and 100,000 for over 13 per cent. See W. Ashworth, *The Genesis of Modern British Town Planning* (London, 1954), p. 8.

garth and Cowper, as major stimulants to increased demand.[1]

> Q. To what do you attribute the present great increase in the quantity of paper made?
>
> A. In 1803 I resided in Bristol, and I think at least two-thirds of the people in the country could not read; at the present time, I should say there is not one in 20 but what can read, consequently there are more books sold.
>
> Q. You attribute it, then, very much to the great increase of printing?
>
> A. The great increase of printing, arising from the great increase of education.[2]

These views of a London publisher and printer in 1834 would not of themselves necessarily carry much weight. But recent research has helped to illuminate the extent of literacy in the first half of the nineteenth century—at least to the extent that people were able to read—and to give support to this contention.[3]

Once again, however, a note of warning must be struck. This period saw only the beginnings of mass communication. To informed contemporaries of 1861 there seemed every reason to comment on a great increase in the numbers of cheap newspapers, to see their circulation as 'enormous', and to regard them, rightly, as major items in the demand for paper.[4] The total number of newspapers rose from 563 (of which 17 were dailies) in 1851, to 1,294 (84 dailies) in 1867.[5] But in 1861 *The Times*,

[1] Plant, op. cit., pp. 273 et seq. See also S. H. Steinberg, *Five Hundred Years of Printing* (London, 1955), pp. 189–98.

[2] *Fourteenth Report* (1835), p. 139—evidence of Henry Fisher, publisher, printer, stereotype founder, engraver, steel-plate printer, &c., of London.

[3] See R. K. Webb, *The British Working Class Reader, 1790–1848* (London, 1955), *passim*.

[4] *Select Committee* (1861), p. 81.

[5] A. E. Musson in *The Manchester Guardian*, 28 June, 1955.

then recently reduced in price from 4*d*. to 3*d*., had a daily sale of no more than 65,000 to which it had risen from about 2,000 in the 1790's and about 10,000 in the 1830's.[1] It was still a far cry to the modern popular press with its circulation in millions.

The initial achievements were real enough. Typical of the new era was the appearance in 1832 of such informative periodicals as *The Penny Magazine*, published by Charles Knight for the Society for the Diffusion of Useful Knowledge. It rapidly reached the unheard-of sale of 200,000 weekly. Although it did not maintain this —indeed, it proved to be a comparatively short-lived venture—other publications were in the field to provide a similar fillip to the demand for printing-paper: *The Poor Man's Guardian*, Knight's *Penny Cyclopaedia*, the *Mechanics' Magazine*, the publications of the Chambers brothers and later of Cassell.[2] Though they did not all reach the public they were designed for, such publications, along with the widening range of newspapers, be it *The Times* or *The Northern Star* or the newest local paper, were all helping to usher in a form of communication which the Fourdrinier machine did much to make possible. Prominent printers and publishers of the time agreed on the importance of the machine in so far as it both reduced costs and prices and also permitted larger sheets of paper to be made and printed. As one of them said, the Fourdrinier machine had 'called into existence

[1] *The History of the Times* (London, 1935–52), vol. i, pp. 38–40; vol. ii, p. 299; see also A. P. Wadsworth, *Newspaper Circulation, 1806–1954* (Manchester, 1955), p. 9, and *passim*. Until the 1860's *The Times* has by far the largest circulation of a daily paper but thereafter the new, cheaper papers overtook it, the *Daily Telegraph*'s circulation, for example, rising from 27,000 in 1856 to 141,700 in 1861 and 181,000 in 1871 (ibid., pp. 21, 34).

[2] For details of the founding, the circulation, and the success of these and other publications of this type, see Webb, op. cit., pp. 60–82.

a class of cheap publications which could not otherwise have been produced'.[1]

In addition to these sources of demand there were others arising from the increasing number of uses for paper either created or extended by the continuing course of industrialization. Writing-paper for indefatigable Victorian letter writers, for business or for commerce; printing-paper for government or for industry; wrappings of sundry sorts, tarred paper for roofs, wall-paper for walls;[2] millboard, cardboard, pasteboard for packaging, pressing, or playing-cards—the list is already too long to enumerate. It undoubtedly added up to a formidable proportion of the total demand for the products of the industry.

The contribution made by overseas demand was slight. Britain was said to be the greatest paper exporting country in the world in the middle of the century,[3] a statement which is scarcely surprising as it occupied that position for practically all manufactured goods. We enjoyed an advantage over all our competitors in the lead we had in adopting machinery and we were thus able to compete with the exports of foreign industries operating with much lower wages and raw material costs.[4] But our exports remained small; the bulk of them went to such lands as Australia, India, and Canada as

[1] *Fourdrinier Committee* (1837), p. 24 and *passim*; also *Fourteenth Report* (1835), pp. 16–17.

[2] The machine printing of wallpapers was developed in the 1830's and 1840's (see Labarre, p. 321); on tarred paper see Clow, op. cit., p. 263, and *William Balston—Paper-Maker*, pp. 48–50.

[3] *Select Committee* (1861), pp. 72, 91.

[4] Ibid., pp. 66, 70, 89–90. The first paper machine was set up in France in 1811; by 1827 there were only four and not until after 1830 did they become at all widespread and even then they were mainly made in England. America's first machine dates from 1817 though it was not until 1827 that a Fourdrinier machine was used there: see Hunter, pp. 536–8, 544; and C. Ballot, op. cit., p. 561.

well as the U.S.A. They mainly consisted of the better
sorts of writing- and printing-paper.[1]

(iv)

Outstanding amongst the forces influencing supply
conditions were those which flowed from mechanization.
The extent to which costs were reduced and productivity increased cannot be measured with precision; it
varied from mill to mill according to types of paper, and
it changed over the years. The claims initially made for
the machine were perhaps not always realized but they
may serve as a guide to hopes and achievements.

In the statement put out by the patentees in 1806 it
was claimed that the cost per annum for a machine which
would do the work of seven vats was £734, while the cost
of working seven vats would be £2,604. The machine
thus yielded a saving of about 72 per cent.; it could be
worked with nine persons instead of forty-one.[2] A reduction in cost per cwt. of paper made was claimed as from
16s. by hand to 3s. 9d. by machine—a similar percentage.[3]
The patentees did not rest their claims simply on these
direct savings. They pointed to the increased demand
which would result from reduced prices and the resulting
greater profit to the manufacturers; in another statement,
put out in 1813, they stressed that machinery allowed
advantage to be taken of the power supply which formerly could be used only for the preparation process and
not for making the paper.[4] In both statements the merits
of the machine in allowing the manufacturers to be free
from the power of skilled and organized labour were
heavily underlined. It did not require workmen 'edu-

---

[1] *Select Committee* (1861), pp. 10, 19, and 72.
[2] *Fourdrinier Committee* (1837), app. A, p. 43.
[3] Ibid., p. 44.   [4] Ibid., p. 45, and app. B, p. 48.

cated to the trade'; the manufacturer would be 'effectually relieved from the perplexing difficulties and loss consequent upon the perpetual combinations for the increase of wages'.[1]

In one way or another these claims impressed manufacturers and persuaded them to mechanize. And in varying measure the claims were realized. Output rose, the productivity of mills increased, prices fell, the power of the workers' combinations was severely weakened, industry and enterprise were rewarded by substantial profits.[2] As improvements were made the cumulative effects of mechanization left their mark. Spicer calculated that the speed, the width, and the number of machines contributed in that order to increasing machine output; whereas an early machine might produce 300 tons in a year, by 1860 a faster-running and bigger machine would have an output of 1,000 tons per year.[3] Even by 1835 it was said, without undue exaggeration, that the same quantity of paper could then be completed in as many minutes as formerly it took weeks.[4]

In a later chapter the ever-increasing problem of rag shortages, and the efforts made to solve it during this period, will be examined.[5] Meanwhile the positive contribution made to expanding output by improved raw material supplies demands some attention.

At the beginning of the century the interruptions of

---

[1] Ibid., pp. 44 and 48. These sentiments were echoed by paper-makers giving evidence before the *Fourdrinier Committee* (1807).

[2] See Chaps. IX and X.   [3] Spicer, p. 69.

[4] *Fourteenth Report* (1835), p. 10. Because of the different size of machines and of the different types and sizes of paper it is impossible to give a precise indication of the effect of mechanization in increasing output. At Chartham Mill mechanization is said to have increased output fivefold, from 1 ton to 5 tons per week (Spicer, p. 184); at a mill in E. Kilpatrick the new methods brought a threefold increase (*New Statistical Account*, vol. viii, p. 27).   [5] Chap. XIII.

war made foreign rags scarce; although home supplies were increasing, prices were very high. Fine quality rags which were already 52s. and 58s. per cwt. in 1803–4 had soared to 74s. in 1810 and 76s. in 1812. Thereafter and until the 1850's prices fell. The same quality of rags were fetching only 32s. in 1844; lower qualities fell in price from 50s. to 60s. in 1810 to 23s., to 25s. in 1844.[1]

As Fig. 7 shows, during this period a declining proportion of total output was dependent on imported rags. In 1830 it was calculated that 24 per cent. of paper output was made from imported rags. Thereafter the position is summed up in the following estimates:[2]

Five-year Period	Average percentage of total production which could be made from imported rags
1830–4	20·6
1835–9	18·2
1840–4	11·0
1845–9	10·2
1850–4	9·2
1855–9	9·2

This increased home production arose from various sources. The spread of improved methods of cleaning and bleaching continued the effects already started by the introduction of chlorine, i.e. to render rags useful which would formerly have been rejected. Rising population and rising levels of linen and cotton consumption made more suitable rags available. The greatly expanded cotton and linen industries of the kingdom helped directly by producing various sorts of waste, cuttings, and mill sweepings. But the larger home supplies were not always of materials suitable for making the finer grades of paper, and for many of these foreign supplies were still necessary[3]. The bulk of these came from Ger-

[1] Balston MSS.
[2] *Select Committee* (1861), p. 71, and app. 3, p. 110.
[3] *Fourteenth Report* (1835), p. 155.

many where Hamburg had a rag market of international importance.

TABLE XVI

Sources of Imports of Rags (G.B.)

Annual averages in five-year periods	Germany		Italy		Russia		Others		Total
	tons	%	tons	%	tons	%	tons	%	
1800–4 .	2,138	62	542	16	27	1	760	21	3,467
1820–4 .	4,066	58	1,391	20	846	12	657	10	6,960
1830–4 .	4,436	51	2,306	26	1,104	13	667	21	8,715

Source: P.R.O. Customs 17/22–26; 5/9–13, 19–23.

For the last five years of the period, 1856–60, Germany's share of the total imports, then averaging nearly 13,000 tons annually, was 57 per cent. and Russia's 16 per cent.[1]

Although rags formed the main item in raw material costs, other constituents had their place, and here too falling prices contributed to expansion both in output and in profits of the industry.

China clay or kaolin had come into use in British paper-making, possibly about the turn of the eighteenth century; it was added in very small quantities to the pulp as a 'loading' in order to give body and weight to the finished sheet. It was, and still is, mined principally in Devon and Cornwall, and the scale and output of these workings grew markedly in the later eighteenth century. The paper industry drew upon these, though not heavily whilst paper was still almost entirely made from rags. Still, it was an item in production costs and its fall in price from about £10 per ton in 1820 to £4 in 1850 helped the paper-maker accordingly.[2]

The techniques of rag-bleaching by means of chlorine advanced appreciably with the discovery of chloride of

[1] *Select Committee* (1861), app. 3; also Spicer, pp. 25–32.
[2] Spicer, pp. 72–76.

lime (bleaching-powder) in 1799. Its production on a large scale was developed first by Charles Tennant at the St. Rollox chemical works near Glasgow. Output rose and prices fell: in 1805 the works produced 147 tons at a price of £112 per ton; in 1870 over 9,000 tons at £8. 10s. per ton.[1] The use of bleaching-powder so spread that it was claimed in 1815 that the majority of paper-makers used it; the older process of using chlorine still persisted, however, in some mills.[2] In the earlier years of the century manufacturers regularly made their own bleaching agent, be it powder or gas, and in this context a conflict developed between the Excise authorities and the industry over the salt duty, salt being needed in the process of making the bleaching agent. The Board of Excise refused to permit the paper-makers to have duty-free salt, though certain others who wanted it for bleaching purposes were allowed this right. Between 1815 and 1817 the usual battle of words took place, in the course of which John Dickinson fired a particularly vigorous broadside. The paper-makers were granted the desired privilege, at least in so far as the making of chloride of lime was concerned.[3]

To the advantages accruing from the removal of restrictions of this sort were added those which flowed from the final removal of the salt duty in 1823 and the falling prices of salt, coal, soda, alum, dyes, and other necessary, though comparatively minor, items in the paper-makers' expenditure.[4] The output of soda, for example, which

[1] Clow, op. cit., pp. 192–3.

[2] C. & E.: Excise-Treasury Letters, 1812–16, ff. 3–6; Spicer, p. 77.

[3] For the dispute over duty-free salt see C. & E.: Excise-Treasury Letters, 1812–16, ff. 3–6, 1812–18, ff. 415 et seq., 1813–18, f. 438, &c. The Acts regulating the position were 55 Geo. III, c. 66, and 56 Geo. III, c. 94.

[4] Dickinson summed up many of the reasons for falling paper prices in 1835 by noting, *inter alia*, the reduction in the cost of machinery and buildings and in the prices of 'coals, soap, salt, manganese, and other things

was commonly used in the boiling and cleaning of the rags, was greatly increased by the invention of the Leblanc process and the consequential growth, especially from about the 1820's onwards, of an alkali industry. Soda prices followed a course very similar to those of paper and indeed of many other commodities during this period. Rising from about £45 per ton in 1800 to over £60 in 1810, they fell thereafter to £35 in 1820, £10 in 1840, and about £7 in 1860.[1] The price of alum fell from about £25 per ton at the turn of the century to under £10 by 1846.[2]

(v)

The expansion of the industry brought changes in the number, location, and size of mills. Fig. 10 graphs the number of licences issued to paper-makers and pasteboard-makers.[3] It thereby provides some indication of the course of change in numbers of mills. The number of such licences is obviously not the same as the number of paper-mills; and as it stands the graph almost certainly exaggerates both the rate of growth in the number of mills before the peak of 1829 and the decline thereafter.[4]

essential to the manufacture' (*Fourteenth Report* (1835), p. 111). See also Spicer, pp. 78 et seq.; Clow, op. cit., *passim*.

[1] Ibid., pp. 108-12.

[2] Ibid., pp. 240-1.

[3] *First Inland Revenue Report* (1857), app. 30.

[4] There are four main reasons for these qualifications. First, not every licence was translated into a functioning mill. Second, pasteboard-makers were not specified in the Act 24 Geo. III, c. 41 imposing the licence duty in 1784 but were in 43 Geo. III, c. 69. This presumably accounts for the major part of the increase in numbers in 1803-4. Third, after 1836 it was no longer necessary for pasteboard-makers to take out licences (6 & 7 Wm. IV, c. 52). Fourth, after 1839 it was allowed that if two or more mills belonging to one person or partnership were not more than one mile apart, they could be worked under one licence (2 & 3 Vic., c. 23). For these reasons the true curve of numbers of mills should be flatter than that in Fig. 10.

Some idea of the relationships between numbers of licences, paper-

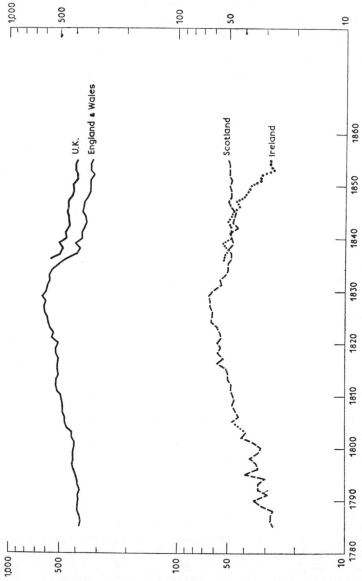

FIG. 10. Number of Licences issued to Paper-makers and Pasteboard-makers, 1785–1855 (logarithmic scale)

The following figures, from Dr. Shorter's detailed work on the number and location of mills, probably provide a more accurate guide to the rate of change in England after 1800:[1]

Decade	Paper-mills in existence	Began work	Ceased work
1801–10	434	42	17
1811–20	502	85	36
1821–30	516	49	67
1831–40	491	42	98
1841–50	432	39	87
1851–60	377	29	92

Whichever way it is presented, the significance of these changes is clear enough: in the paper industry, as in other industries, the Industrial Revolution brought a fall in the number of producing units as a concomitant of an increasing output; and that change became apparent in the third decade of the century. Until the machine had proved itself, the establishment of new units of the old type continued to be an economic way of helping to meet the rising demand for paper; but so soon as the economies of scale opened up by the larger mills began to tell, so did small vat mills disappear. This reduction in numbers did not, of course, proceed uniformly. Changes in the numbers of licences issued reflect the entry of capital and enterprise into the industry; and the flattening of the curve in Fig. 10 in the later 1790's and between 1812 and

makers, and pasteboard-makers may be gauged from the following figures which refer to England and Wales only:

	Paper-mills at work	Pasteboard-makers	Licences
1816	467	38	522
	Paper-makers		
1835	442	56	521

(C. & E.: General Letter 1816; *Fourteenth Report* (1835), p. 73).

[1] Shorter, *Historical Geography*, pp. 132 and 138.

1820 mirrors those troubled and depressed periods when economic expectations were unpromising.[1]

These changes in numbers are clearly linked with changes in location, for it was mainly the mills in the remoter areas which disappeared. Comparison of Figs. 11 and 12 reveals the notable contraction in the geographical spread of mills in England between 1816 and 1851.[2] By the latter date such counties as Cornwall, Somerset, Monmouthshire, Herefordshire, Shropshire, and Sussex, had lost much of their representation in the industry; even in counties which remained important, such as Devon, Buckinghamshire, and Hertfordshire, some of the smaller and obscurer mills were eliminated. In Scotland, where total numbers were much smaller and where, as Fig. 10 showed, the proportional increase in numbers up to 1829 was much the same as in England, the decrease was markedly smaller; indeed, after 1842 the total numbers rose slightly, the mills being concentrated in broadly the same areas as they had been earlier. For Ireland reliable comparative figures for the earlier years are hard to come by, though it is possible that here, too, total numbers were increasing up to the 1830's, and thereafter it is certain that the mills which disappeared were those in the remoter valleys.[3] To sum up the evidence of

[1] Other aspects of the decline in numbers are considered in Chap. IX, see in particular pp. 227–34.

[2] See App. I, *infra*, pp. 348–9.

[3] The figures for paper-makers' licences in Ireland as printed in the *First Inland Revenue Report* (1857), app. 30, are wholly misleading in so far as they include paper-stainers' licences from 1815, when the series starts, to 1823. In 1823–4 the totals fall from 115 to 79. From 1824 to 1835 they obviously include pasteboard-makers. In 1835–6 the totals fall from 94 to 53. This last figure is the first to be truly related to the number of paper-mills. In *Eighth Report* (1824) the Inspector of Paper Duties in Ireland stated that there were 54 mills there and that the number was slightly decreasing; elsewhere in the same report the Commissioner of Excise in Ireland informed the Treasury that there were 47 licensed paper-mills in Ireland (app. 33, p. 136 and app. 37, p. 148.

worked up with cheap labour. The comment voiced in 1824 by a leading Irish paper manufacturer about Ireland could well have applied, *mutatis mutandis*, to England two or three centuries earlier, as compared then with France or Italy: 'The poverty of the country requires the coarse paper and the materials of the country are fit for that coarse article.'[1]

Scotland, by contrast, enjoyed a reputation for the manufacture of medium- and good-quality printing-papers. It made some, though very little, writing-paper and a certain amount of wrapping and board. The absence of a multitude of old mills in remote areas, the early and effective concentration in areas admirably adjacent to coal supplies, port facilities, and large towns, the rapid industrialization and the important growth of both linen and chemical works in the Glasgow area—these were some of the factors which conduced to the speedy expansion of the Scottish industry. Foreign rags for making printing-papers were regularly imported in substantial quantities and formed an increasing share of the British total. Scottish rag imports averaged 9·8 per cent. of total British rag imports in 1826–7 and 19·2 per cent. in 1836–7.[2] Within Scotland Midlothian predominated amongst the counties producing mainly printing-papers, and, as might be expected, the mills of the more remote Aberdeenshire tended to make relatively more brown and other wrapping-papers.[3]

[1] *Eighth Report* (1824), app. 35, p. 143 and *passim*; *Fourteenth Report* (1835), pp. 161–71.

The Excise also encouraged a concentration on the lower qualities of paper and contributed to the decline of the industry in Ireland (see *infra*, p. 320 & n. 4.).   [2] P.R.O. Customs 5/15, 16, 25, 26.

[3] Alexander Irvine, for instance, of the Peterculter Mills, near Aberdeen, was making paper in both the Excise classes in the 1830's but 'nothing finer than cartridge; no printing papers' (*Fourteenth Report* (1835), p. 149; also, in general, pp. 140–61).

Out of the great range of types made in the many English and the very few Welsh mills,[1] a few obvious localized concentrations may be noted. The demands of industry, notably textile manufacture, for wrapping-paper and board, joined with the sorts of factors already mentioned to bring about some degree of specialization in Lancashire, Northumberland, and other northern counties upon these types. 'Manchester packing papers' or 'Manchester papers' were recognized trade terms of the time.[2] The continuing importance of Devon in this line of business has already been noted, and the output of many of the smaller mills in the remoter paper-making regions from Cornwall to East Anglia also contained a large proportion of brown paper. Although the northern counties also made printing-papers of various sorts, and although Scottish paper found its way southwards, the three counties of Kent, Buckinghamshire, and Hertfordshire undoubtedly remained the great suppliers of the immense and varied London demand for the better sorts of paper, be it the finest Whatman writing- and drawing-papers, high quality printing for books and ledgers, or ordinary paper for ordinary purposes.

[1] On the industry in North Wales see A. H. Dodd, *The Industrial Revolution in North Wales* (Cardiff, 2nd ed. 1956), pp. 26, 247, 316–17, &c.

[2] Labarre, op. cit., p. 154; see also *Children's Employment* (1834) and *Select Committee* (1861), *passim*, for various comments on local specialization.

IX

Organization and Finance

(i)

In 1813 one paper-maker, in a letter to another, remarked that the ultimate effect of various recent changes would be 'to place the manufacture in larger hands'.[1] Nearly fifty years later the contention that the paper manufacture of this country was passing into the hands of the larger makers was a platitude of the trade.[2] The following table offers apparent confirmation:

TABLE XVIII

Output by Firms, 1849–59 (U.K.)

Output of manufacturers	Number of firms	
	1849	*1859*
Not more than 100,000 lb.	151	90
100,001–500,000	172	160
500,001–1,000,000	62	66
1,000,001–1,500,000	17	34
1,500,001–2,000,000	6	17
2,000,001–2,500,000	3	4
2,500,001–3,000,000	..	2
3,000,001–3,500,000	1	1
3,500,001–4,000,000	..	2
4,000,001–4,500,000	..	1
4,500,001–5,000,000	..	1
Total number of manufacturers . . .	412	378
,, ,, paper-mills at work . .	436	385
Output, U.K. (tons)	58,988	97,250

Source: *Select Committee* (1861), p. 90.

[1] Balston MSS.: R. M. Bacon to W. Balston, 5 Aug. 1813.
[2] *Select Committee* (1861), pp. 25, 27, 41, 96.

There are two elements in this: increases in the size and output of mills and increases in the capacity controlled by individual manufacturers. Something has already been said[1] of the former in the context of the industry as a whole, though not in terms of output, layout, and control of particular mills. It now demands attention in its relation to concentration of ownership.

The contrast between 1849 and 1859 in Table XVIII certainly points to an increase in the proportion of total capacity controlled by the larger makers. In this it represents a development which is part of the logic of change apparent from about 1830 onwards in the disappearance of the smaller mills. But how far it represents a position significantly different in terms of ownership and control from the final pre-machine period is quite another matter. Examples both of large mills and of the operating of several mills by one maker can be found in the later eighteenth century.[2] The Excise list of mills in 1816[3] also provides many instances of the latter. Unfortunately no figures are available which would permit an accurate comparison with those in Table XVIII. It is probable, however, that contemporary comment was correct. For the impression one has of the heyday of the vat mills is of many small men with small mills and of a great gap between them and a few outstanding figures, of whom Whatman was the most prominent. By 1859 it is evident that the gap is slowly being filled up: as those at the bottom drop out, so are those at the top joined by others who are at least in a position to be able to rival the leaders.

When put in relation to such accepted economic patterns as those of competition, monopoly, or oligopoly,

---

[1] *Supra*, pp. 217–23.   [2] *Supra*, pp. 151–61.
[3] C. & E.: General Letter (1816).

there is little doubt that in the mid-century the industry was substantially competitive. No single producer or controlling group was responsible for any large proportion of total output; moreover within the market for particular types of paper there was usually a competitive situation.[1] Of the makers in 1859 93 per cent. came within the four lowest categories in Table XVIII (i.e. up to 1,500,000 lb.) and were responsible for approximately two-thirds of total output. The trend towards concentration was not yet very strong. But it was there: the remaining 7 per cent. were responsible for perhaps as much as one-third of the country's output. This was a signpost to the future rather than a link with the past.

In 1820 Thomas Creswick could boast, rightly or wrongly, that in paying £1,600 per annum in Excise duty he was paying 'a greater Sum than any other two-vat Paper Mills in the Kingdom';[2] from his three-vat mill John Gater paid £1,700 duty in 1835 (with a lower rate of duty).[3] In contrast to such sums as these were the £12,000 per annum which Dickinson's machine mills were contributing to the Excise as early as 1817[4] or the £20,000 coming in from Crompton's works in Lancashire in the 1850's (again with a lower rate of duty).[5] Against the small vat mills of 1800 must be put the much bigger mills coming into operation in the middle decades of the century. Many had several steam-engines, two or three machines, and sometimes a veritable battery of beating-engines.

---

[1] This seems to follow from various observations made by manufacturers when giving evidence before such bodies as the Commissioners of Excise Enquiry or the Select Committee of 1861. On price-fixing earlier in the century, however, see *infra*, pp. 274 et seq.

[2] C. & E.: Excise-Treasury Letters, 1814–22, f. 422.

[3] *Fourteenth Report* (1835), p. 124.

[4] C. & E.: Excise-Treasury Letters, 1812–18, f. 415.

[5] *Reports of the Juries*, p. 428.

Among the constituent items in the capital costs of enterprise on this scale the Fourdrinier machine was only one and not of itself especially costly. More important was the range of expenditure to which machine production gave rise and which had to be incurred if a mill was to survive in a competitive, expanding, and changing industry. To the initial cost of building and plant must be added, as the century progressed, capital expenditure on such items as drying, cutting, sizing, or glazing machinery, new and better and more expensive presses, beaters, or boilers. If water-power continued in use it often entailed deepening work on the river or the installation of a turbine; steam-power meant the cost of engines, of maintenance, and of fuel.

Careful thought had to be given by paper-makers to such problems as these. Good mill sites were not unlimited and they often owed their value more to a constant supply of clear water for manufacture than to any excellence in available water for power. Little or nothing could be done about the rivers which froze in the winter or lost their flow in dry summers.[1] Nor were natural facilities independent of man's attention:

Falls of Water, that is Embankments upon streams, may . . . be considered as a species of real security, but no more are they indestructible than the steam engine itself. Both are liable to constant attention and repeated repairs, and in my opinion in this respect the latter has the advantage, so long at least as a supply of fuel can be obtained at a reasonable price. For there are no Falls of water that I have seen but have been erected at great expense, require constant reparations in all instances, and

[1] This was a common enough phenomenon; see *Fourteenth Report* (1835), p. 169, and Excise-Treasury Letters, 1814–18, f. 138, for examples. In the latter instance a Durham paper-maker complained that his mill, 'from the frequent want of water is only calculated to make a small quantity of Paper and that he has frequently been obliged to purchase Paper from the Paper Mills in the Neighbourhood in order to supply his Customers'.

in some most heavy expenses, with additional risk of the attached property in winter seasons from heavy floods.[1]

The likely expenses for the maintenance of a large water-powered mill may perhaps be imagined from a description of Peterculter Mill, near Aberdeen, in this period. In the 1840's it was a fair-sized mill with two machines driven by two large water-wheels fed from an artificial reservoir half a mile long and 20 feet deep; the water was conducted from this in a wooden aqueduct 700 feet long, 7 feet wide, and 2 feet deep, supported by pillars of both stone and wood.[2] Even when such spectacular arrangements as this were not necessary, there was still the problem that sites which were favourable from the point of view of water-power might well be inaccessible or at least only poorly placed for the transport of raw materials or the finished product. Similarly they might well also present the problems both of finding workers and of providing accommodation for them.[3]

It was with arguments of this sort that Balston in about 1813 justified his investment some six years previously in a 36 h.p. Watt engine, one of the earliest steam-engines to be installed in a paper-mill. Its basic cost, without any of the additions and alterations later made to it, was about £1,700; it remained in use for ninety years.[4] A paper-maker installing a Fourdrinier machine in the early years would have had to pay £1,000 or thereabouts for the machine, together with a rental of £150 or more per annum under the terms of the patents.[5]

[1] Balston MSS.: Balston to (?) Capt. Agnew (undated, probably 1813).
[2] *New Statistical Account*, vol. xii, p. 111.
[3] Balston MSS.: Balston to (?) Agnew, *c.* 1813.
[4] *William Balston—Paper-Maker*, pp. 39–41.
[5] *Fourdrinier Committee* (1837), app. A, p. 45, and app. B, p. 47–48. In 1806 the patentees charged £1,250 for a machine and an annual premium ranging from £150 for a machine which would do two vats' work to £500

Agreements between the Fourdriniers and makers who installed machines in 1808 show, however, that payment both of the capital sum and the annual fees was done by instalments, thus easing the burden of the initial outlay.[1]

These figures do not give an adequate impression of the capital needed to launch into paper-making, on any substantial scale, in the changing conditions of the time. It was estimated in 1860 that to erect a paper-mill using water-power would cost £4,000 to £5,000 and using steam-power £10,000 to £11,000.[2] In fact Balston, building what was then, at the beginning of the century, the largest paper-mill in the country, spent £47,000 in the first seven years. Of this, some £35,000 was spent on the land, the erection of the mill, and a house and the plant.[3] This was then an exceptional sum for an exceptional mill, at a time of greatly inflated prices. Equally exceptional for the beginning though not for the end of the period were the large sums which the Fourdriniers spent on their pioneer machine mills.[4] Still uncommon was the £13,000 asked for a fair-sized mill near Balston's at Maidstone in 1805; more usual the £7,000 offered for another at about the same time, or the £4,000 which Chartham Mill fetched in 1817;[5] and the many tiny one- or two-vat mills, making coarse paper in the remoter

for one doing five vats' work. In 1813 the price of the machine varied from £715 to £1,040 and the premium for a machine equivalent to five vats was £380.

[1] Fourdrinier Papers, Nos. 38–42. Ibbotson & East of Colnbrook Mill, for example, contracted to pay £1,250 in four instalments, for which they gave bills at 3, 6, 9, and 12 months; and an annual fee of £100 for 14 years, in four annual instalments of £25.

[2] *Hansard*, series 3, vol. clvii (1860), p. 363.

[3] *William Balston—Paper-Maker*, p. 96.

[4] e.g. the £11,276 on St. Neots. See *supra*, p. 187, n. 2.

[5] Balston MSS.: John Wise to Balston, Mar. 1805, offering his mill for £13,000; draft by Balston, *c.* 1804–5, mentioning offer of £7,000 for Loose Mill; Wiggins, Teape MSS.: Chartham Deeds.

counties, no doubt changed hands for still lower figures. But the magnitude of Balston's spending was typical of future developments. By 1861 it was estimated that the total capital invested in the industry was between £7,000,000 and £10,000,000, which means that the average per mill was something between £18,000 and £26,000.[1] This suggests that the £20,000 for which Chartham Mill was sold in 1862[2] represents, approximately, an average figure for fixed capital investment per mill at the end of our period, just as the £4,000 in 1817 fits readily into a similar picture for the earlier years of the century.

If steam-power and mechanization demanded that production should be concentrated in larger units and the tendency of later technical development was to make them still larger, so at the time the problems of control which were posed when one manufacturer tried to run a number of small units also tended to be answered in terms of larger mills. This is another force in the disappearance of the small mill. Of the several mills which Whatman controlled, only Turkey was of any great size; his successors at Turkey, the Hollingworth brothers, controlled five mills in the Maidstone area in 1816; by 1851 three of those small mills had ceased to work. In the 1816 list the Hereford Excise collection provides many instances of multi-mill operation by one maker: five by Joseph Lloyd, four by John Reece, three by Thomas Botfield, and a number of examples of makers with two mills. Most of these mills, in the counties of Monmouthshire, Hereford, and Shropshire, were almost certainly tiny affairs and most had disappeared by the mid-century.[3]

---

[1] *Select Committee* (1861), pp. 60 and 62.

[2] Wiggins, Teape MSS.: Chartham Deeds.

[3] For 1816, C. & E.: General Letter (1816); for 1851, *B.P.P.* 1852, vol. li, pp. 554–5, and A. H. Shorter, 'The Distribution of British Paper Mills in 1851', *The Paper Maker*, June 1951.

The disadvantages of dispersal seemed evident to Balston:

. . . if ten vats are placed in separate mills at considerable distances from each other, and used by the same proprietor, . . . nothing can be so evident as that the impossibility of the Proprietor's giving his constant and personal attention must operate greatly to the injury of the concern or, admitting it could be procured, the expense of others to effect the same must be greater. And I am certain you will agree with me that the great object of all manufacturing concerns is to produce the greatest possible return at the least expense, and consequently that in the erection of several separate mills to produce the effect of a single one, a much larger portion of expense must necessarily be incurred in the Embankment (Falls of Water), Buildings and consequent machinery.[1]

He was presumably not alone in these opinions amongst those contemplating manufacture on a large scale. And the general trend of change was certainly towards the enterprise which controlled one comparatively large mill; where such enterprises expanded into the running of more than one mill, the mills were normally in close proximity to each other and were sometimes worked as one unit.

If the solutions to these various problems called for the bigger unit and thus put a premium upon the man who could command capital resources, at one and the same time they called for the vigour and enterprise which would put the capital to efficient uses. Who, then, were the entrepreneurs who built up the industry in its first half century or so of mechanization and what sort of things did they build?

[1] Balston MSS.: Balston to (?) Agnew, c. 1813.

(ii)

Outstanding among the paper manufacturers of this period was John Dickinson.[1] In the first fifty or so years of the nineteenth century he built up a firm which is today one of the largest in the English industry. John Dickinson came from a middle-class family of moderate prosperity and with some association with the world of printing, publishing, and literature. These associations sprang largely from the friendship of Dickinson's mother, who was of Huguenot origin, with the Strahan family. It was on the advice of Andrew Strahan, perhaps the biggest printer of his day, that in 1797 John Dickinson was apprenticed to a London stationer, and it was later with the assistance of money advanced by Strahan that he built up his business.[2] On the completion of his apprenticeship he set up as a wholesale stationer in the City; in 1806 he was selling paper not only to Strahan but to such important customers as the East India Company. But to energy and enterprise Dickinson added mechanical ingenuity. He was then 24 and a young man in a hurry. In three years he had invented and patented both his cylinder machine and a new type of cartridge paper and had started up as a paper-maker, in partnership with George Longman of the publishing family, by purchasing Apsley Mill on the River Gade in Hertfordshire. Apsley, already a paper-mill and close to the Fourdriniers' mills, was well served both with water and also with canal and road transport to and from London. So the choice had sound economic reasons. Moreover, Dickinson's sister was married to the Rev. J. S. Grover,

[1] Unless otherwise stated, the following account of John Dickinson is derived variously from *The Firm of John Dickinson & Co. Ltd.* (London, 1896), Joan Evans, *Time and Chance* (London, 1943) and *The Endless Web, passim.*

[2] *Infra,* p. 246.

Vice-Provost of Eton, whose brother H. Grover was the leading solicitor and banker in the adjoining town of Hemel Hempstead. In 1810 Dickinson very sensibly married one of the banker's daughters.

From this useful beginning Dickinson forged ahead rapidly in the industry. The adjoining Nash Mill, about half a mile downstream, was bought in 1811; machinery and steam-power were installed. As early as 1815 he was already being classed by the Excise Commissioners among those makers who had 'Manufactories of great magnitude'.[1] From his memorandum to the Excise authorities two years later, on the subject of the salt duties,[2] it is evident that Dickinson regarded his words as carrying weight in the industry; from a photograph of him in later life it is equally plain that he had seen to it that they did. He was apparently a man of great vigour and even greater temper. Dr. Joan Evans records that someone who knew him had observed that when in a temper 'he kicked like a serpent and threw his legs about like a 90-gun ship'.[3] He knew how he wanted things done and brooked no interference. He built cottages for his workmen, and let them at 2s. 6d. per week, but rather than pay union rates[4] he trained up his own men with such assiduity that it came to be said that 'John Dickinson could make a paper maker out of a hedge'.[5]

In 1818 he took over the neighbouring Batchworth Mill simply to prepare pulp for his other mills; in 1825–6 he built Home Park Mill, a mile downstream from Nash Mill; five years later he built Croxley Mill, near Watford; finally in 1835–7 he built another mill at Manchester to be used for pulping cotton-mill sweepings. By 1838 the

[1] C. & E.: Excise-Treasury Letters, 1812–16, f. 9.
[2] Ibid.: Excise-Treasury Letters, 1812–18, f. 415.
[3] *The Endless Web*, p. 17.   [4] See *infra*, pp. 285–7, 303.
[5] *The Endless Web*, p. 29.

enterprise was producing the then large total of 41 tons of paper per week, representing perhaps 4 per cent. or 5 per cent. of the total British output. He continued to enlarge and improve his works. It is some indication of the scale and size of his works compared with those of his neighbours in the same county that in 1851 his four mills contained forty-six beating-engines and the remaining six mills in Hertfordshire had only thirty between them.[1] Throughout his active business life he frequently experimented with various mechanical improvements; he took out thirteen patents between 1807 and 1855, some covering important advances in paper-making technology.

Dickinson retired from the business in 1857 and died in 1869. His partners had meanwhile carried on a similar policy of expansion, so that shortly after his death, the firm owned or operated seven mills in Hertfordshire; two were used simply for preparing pulp and in the remaining five there were fourteen paper-making machines. In addition there was the pulping-mill at Manchester, a share in a mill at Sunderland as well as offices and warehouses in London and other towns. Various special lines were pursued quite early in the firm's development, notably cards, envelopes, and other branches of the stationery trade, in addition to printing- and writing-paper. Dickinson's thus came to have a wide range of interests, some far afield and including, for instance, a box-making business in Belfast. Not until the 1880's was a process of concentration followed; so for our period John Dickinson's enterprise remains a remarkable example of one of the leading firms in the industry possessing a number of what were, by the standards of the time, large units.

[1] Apsley 10, Croxley 11 and 2 silent, Home Park 12, and Nash 11 (*B.P.P.* 1852, vol. li, pp. 554–5).

In 1861 John Evans (later Sir John Evans)[1] senior partner in Dickinsons, referred to the firm as 'one of the oldest of the paper houses'.[2] Fifty-two years is no great claim to antiquity in the paper industry. By contrast, another of the major firms of that period, Crompton's of Lancashire, could trace the family name back through several generations in paper-making. In the early years of the nineteenth century first Joseph and Adam Crompton and then John and Thomas B. Crompton represented the family mainly at the mills which they built up at Farnworth.[3] They were amongst the earlier investors in machine manufacture (see Table XV) and they were soon proudly displaying a picture of their new machine on their bill heads.[4] (See Plate III, *supra*, p. 192). Other members of the family, which also had textile interests, operated paper-mills in this period at Kearsley nearby and at Collyhurst.[5] Thomas Crompton's technical contribution to the industry rests mainly on his 1820 patent for his drying-cylinders; in addition he patented in 1839 an improvement to the operation of the Fourdrinier machine.[6] His Farnworth mills grew into an extensive works (with thirty-six beating-engines in 1851), specializing in ordinary printing-paper, particularly for newspapers which he supplied both in the north and in London.

[1] K.C.B. 1892. For a study of Sir John Evans and his activities outside the world of paper-making see Joan Evans, *Time and Chance*.

[2] *Select Committee* (1861), p. 1.

[3] At various times in the eighteenth century the names of Robert, Adam, Ellis, and James Crompton figured in local records as paper-makers at Farnworth, Great Lever, Little Lever, Collyhurst, and Darley in the area around Bolton and Manchester (*V.C.H. Lancashire*, vol. ii, pp. 406–7, and vol. v, p. 34).   [4] Wiggins, Teape MSS.: Gore invoice books.

[5] E. Baines, *History, Directory and Gazetteer of the County Palatine of Lancaster* (1824); J. Pigot, *National Commercial Directory* (1834); and I. Slater, *Directory of Manchester and Salford and their Vicinities* (1850).

[6] Patent No. 8027 (Apr. 1839); for his drying-cylinders patent see *supra*, p. 194.

In the mid-century his mills were paying an annual average of £15,000 in Excise duty and before his death in 1858 the figure reached £20,000. This meant, in the words of the jurors of the 1851 Exhibition, 'the enormous weight per annum of 1,400 tons'.[1] This was very probably less than the output of the Dickinson mills by that date; but it was nearly 2 per cent. of the total national production. Contemporaries were duly impressed.

Amongst the Scottish makers of the time the outstanding was a member of a family which, like the Dickinsons and the Cromptons, has its names perpetuated in the industry today—Cowan, of Edinburgh. The three adjacent mills which the firm already controlled at Penicuik at the beginning of the century[2] were worked as a unit; machines were installed and steam-power used to supplement water; in 1851, with twenty-one beating-engines at work, the Cowan mills were the biggest in Scotland. The Cowans specialized in the better sorts of printing- and writing-papers, some of which they showed at the 1851 Exhibition; they carried on business both as makers and as stationers at Edinburgh. Charles Cowan, who became a M.P. and a leading figure in the commerce and politics of Edinburgh, was the leader of a deputation of Scottish makers to the Excise authorities in 1833; he took out patents for certain improvements in manufacturing in 1840 and 1846. The family business continued to expand: it employed rather over 200 persons in the 1840's and, as Alexander Cowan & Sons, 500 in the 1860's.[3]

---

[1] *Reports of the Juries*, p. 428.

[2] *Supra*, pp. 158–9, for the earlier years of this enterprise.

[3] W. H. Marwick, *Economic Developments in Victorian Scotland* (London, 1936), *passim; Fourteenth Report* (1835), app. 57, p. 143; *Children's Employment* (1843), app., pt. ii, k 1; *Children's Employment* (1865), p. 178; *B.P.P.* 1852, vol. li; *Reports of the Juries*, p. 431; patents Nos. 8334 (Jan. 1840), and

The large number of makers and mills precludes much more than a mention of several of even the bigger manufacturers. In the Newcastle and Durham area large-scale enterprise in the industry was represented by the substantial Scotswood and Shotley Bridge Mills respectively.[1] South-west across the Pennines other large enterprises grew up to rival that of the Cromptons. At Darwen Messrs. Hilton's mills were already employing over 300 people in the 1840's; the nucleus of the modern wall-paper-making industry was expanding.[2] The Bridge Hall Mills, near Bury, boasting thirty-four beating-engines in 1851, embodied the enterprise of the Wrigley family; James and Francis Wrigley operated them in 1816; James Wrigley and Sons were the proprietors in 1865 when they employed some 470 persons. Thomas Wrigley was a leading figure in the industry during the middle decades of the century; he patented improvements to paper-making machinery; played an active part first with Crompton and then Evans in the disputes over the Excise and Custom duties; and was a major witness before the 1861 Committee.[3] Across the Irish Sea the most important name in paper-making was probably that of the M'Donnel family, associated with the Saggard Mills near Dublin. Machinery was installed in the 1840's, and it became one of the few Irish firms which developed to any appreciable extent the making of the better sorts of paper. In the 1851 list the Saggard Mills

11,063 (Jan. 1846). Figures given in *Select Committee* (1861), app. 2, p. 109, show that rag imports for Cowan's Valleyfield mills for the year ending September 1860 were 812 tons or about 5 per cent. of total British rag imports.

[1] *Children's Employment* (1843), p. L 32; Shorter, *Historical Geography*, pp. 114–15.   [2] *Children's Employment* (1843), p. M 66.

[3] C. & E.: General Letter (1816); *B.P.P.* 1852, vol. li; *Children's Employment* (1865), p. 172; Patents Nos. 6437 (June 1833) and 9513 (Nov. 1842); *Select Committee* (1861), pp. 33–46 and 102–4; and *infra*, pp. 330, 337, 340, 342.

were by far the largest in Ireland, in terms of number of beating-engines, with fifteen; and it would seem that in 1861 James M'Donnel was regarded as quite an important figure in the industry.[1]

In the Home Counties were a number of family firms which illustrate the connexion between stationers and paper-makers. The introduction of paper-making to the Berkshire village of Cookham in the mid-eighteenth century has been credited to William Venables. Subsequent generations of the family developed this business as well as that of the stationer in London.[2] Very close to the Venables' mills, early in the nineteenth century, were those of the Spicers, who, as mentioned earlier, had long been connected with this area. Later, however, they developed interests elsewhere, and it is an interesting pointer to the future of the business that Messrs. Spicer exhibited at the Exhibition of 1851 not as paper-makers but as wholesale stationers of London.[3] Also in Buckinghamshire at one time were the three mills operated by Messrs. Magnay & Pickering, who were London wholesale stationers in the late eighteenth century and certainly

[1] *Eighth Report* (1824), app. 34 and 35, pp. 141–4; *Children's Employment* (1843), pt. ii, pp. G 25–27; *Fourteenth Report* (1835), app. 69 and 70, pp. 168–71; Spicer, p. 211; *B.P.P.* 1852, vol. li; *Select Committee* (1861), p. 47.

[2] In the 1840's Charles and George Venables operated four mills on the Bucks.–Berks. border, at Cookham, Cliveden, Taplow, and Bourne End; one of these, Cliveden, had 11 engines in 1851. William Venables, a stationer, who died in 1840, was elected an alderman of the City of London in 1821 and at the 1851 Exhibition Charles and George exhibited papers from their own mills, and Venables, Wilson, and Tyler exhibited as stationers (*V.C.H. Berkshire*, vol. i, p. 382; *Report from the Select Committee on Import Duties* (*B.P.P.* 1840, vol. v), p. 14; *Children's Employment* (1843), p. A 7; *B.P.P.* 1852, vol. li; A. Beaven, *The Aldermen of the City of London* (London, 1908), p. 195; *Reports of the Juries*, p. 431; Spicer, pp. 192–5).

[3] In the 1840's they operated three mills on the Wye stream, though none seem to have been particularly large. In the 1860's Spicer Bros. operated a mill, employing about 100 persons, near Alton, Hampshire (*Children's Employment* (1843), pp. a 27, a 30; *Children's Employment* (1865), p. 168; *Reports of the Juries*, p. 431; Spicer, p. 193).

by 1809, if not earlier, also paper-makers. Christopher Magnay was an alderman of the City of London from 1809 to his death in 1826 and William, who apparently succeeded him in the business, was made an alderman in 1838 and blossomed into Sir William Magnay, Bt., in 1844. Christopher Magnay & Co. had three mills in Buckinghamshire in 1816, but by the 1840's the firm's mills were in Surrey, near Guildford, where the main mill had two machines making printing- and writing-papers. Sir William Magnay, who seems to have been an important figure in the trade, was not alone in the family business: James Magnay was concerned with the Surrey mills, another William Magnay was a partner in the Dripsey paper-mills near Cork, and in the 1860's Frederick Magnay was a partner in the firm of Delane, Magnay & Co. of Taverham Mills, near Norwich; the firm, as might be imagined from the name of the first partner, was connected with the Delanes of *The Times* to which it supplied paper.[1]

Finally, returning to Kent, the cradle of the industry, we may take note of two very different enterprises: Balston's at Springfield Mill, Maidstone, and William Joynson's at St. Mary Cray.

Joynson was much admired by contemporaries. A major exhibitor at the 1851 Exhibition, his papers were held by the Jurors to be 'all of high qualities, fully maintaining Mr Joynson's reputation as a first-rate manufacturer'.[2] His machine-made writing-papers were the

---

[1] C. & E.: General Letter (1816); Wiggins, Teape MSS.; Balston MSS. and *William Balston Paper-Maker*, pp. 111–12; Beaven, op. cit., p. 214; *Children's Employment* (1843), pp. r 8–9; *Eighth Report* (1824), app. 36, p. 145; *Fourteenth Report* (1835), app. 41 and p. 157; *B.P.P.* 1852, vol. li; *Select Committee* (1861), pp. 12–15; *V.C.H. Surrey*, vol. ii, pp. 418–20; *The History of the Times* (London, 1935–52).

[2] *Reports of the Juries*, p. 431.

best of their kind. Even to John Dickinson such a mill appeared as a formidable competitor; confident in his ability to cope with the Scottish makers by sheer superiority in product, Dickinson observed in the 1850's that 'Joynson's paper is a different thing, and we are far from his secret, whatever it may be'.[1] But admiration was not built simply on quality of product. William Joynson had helped himself. 'Undoubtedly the most enterprising and successful paper manufacturer of his day . . . who by individual effort succeeded in working his upward way from a poor and uneducated journeyman, in a humble paper-mill, to the level of the most respected, and probably the most wealthy of paper manufacturers.'[2] Migrating from the High Wycombe area, he took over the St. Mary Cray mills from Thomas Barratt, and working with Barratt mechanized them in 1828. Both Barratt and Joynson patented various improvements in paper-making by machine, and it is not clear just how much of the acclaim accorded to Joynson may have been due to Barratt. It was Joynson, however, who built up the enterprise. In 1842 it had 120 hands; in 1851 his mill, with eleven engines and two machines, was turning out 25 tons of fine quality writing-paper per week; by 1865 William Joynson & Son employed some 630 persons and was possibly the largest single paper-mill of the time.[3]

Balston's enterprise was a striking contrast.[4] It was in many ways an eccentric venture. In deliberately eschew-

[1] Evans, *The Endless Web*, p. 98.

[2] A. Ure, *Dictionary of Arts, Manufactures and Mines* (7th ed. edited R. Hunt, London, 1878), vol. iii, p. 498.

[3] Spicer, pp. 187–8; *Arbitration on Wages . . .*, p. 57; Patents Nos. 5987 (Aug. 1830), 7977 (Feb. 1839), and 8715 (Nov. 1840); *Children's Employment* (1843), pp. r 11–12; *Children's Employment* (1865), p. 151; *B.P.P.* 1852, vol. li.

[4] This section is derived entirely from Balston MSS. and *William Balston—Paper-Maker*, *passim*.

ing the machine it ran contrary to the prevailing trend;
in being a large steam-operated mill it swam with the
current. Balston had been apprenticed to Whatman and
when the latter sold his mills to the Hollingworth brothers
in 1794, Balston, with a loan of £5,000 from Whatman,
became a partner in the new firm of Hollingworth &
Balston. Prospering here, he took an active part in the
trade, becoming chairman of an association of employers.[1] In 1805, at the age of 46, he withdrew from the
firm and set about the construction of a new ten-vat,
steam-powered mill on the Medway, downstream from
Maidstone. General economic depression, over-capitali-
zation and inadequate resources, the competition of
machine-made paper, and his own lack of talent as a
business man combined to bring the enterprise to a near
bankruptcy. He was rescued by the creation in 1814 of
a partnership—the firm of Balston, Gaussen & Bosanquet. Not until the 1820's did the business begin to
prosper to any appreciable extent; thereafter, by con-
centrating on those sorts of writing- and drawing-papers
which can be produced only with the best raw materials,
fine craftsmanship, and the use of the vat instead of the
machine, the firm moved into the front rank of the hand-
made producers. But in terms of size, value, and output
it was less remarkable. In 1860 the mill with its eight
engines, ten vats, and a staff of over 350 was valued at
about £18,000. This was probably less than an average-
sized machine mill at that time, such as Chartham, and
very different from the £35,000 spent on its construction.
Balston himself died in 1849 having in his lifetime built
up from relatively humble beginnings a solid, though
moderate, prosperity, produced a large family, and sent
one of them, Edward, to Eton with the imperishably

[1] See *infra*, pp. 270 et seq.

English words: 'Always remember, Edward, that you are not a gentleman.' In 1862 the headmaster of Eton was Dr. Edward Balston.[1]

(iii)

The foregoing examples have provided a small, though not perhaps unrepresentative, sample of the paper-making enterprise of the time. The pattern has not been uniform throughout. New men came in alongside the old-established families; but innovation was no prerogative of such men. A wider or different sample might perhaps have revealed a stronger hold of conservatism amongst the old paper-making families. Certainly in some branches of the industry's life some of the leaders of the vat trade showed a regard for entrenched habits which would hardly have been compatible with the competitive needs of the new machine industry.[2] On the other hand, the older firms were not necessarily the slowest to mechanize.

Whatever the truth here, there is one thread which runs through the pattern: the strongly personal nature of the business scene. Maybe this was more striking in paper-making than in some of the newer industries growing to power in these years. But in reality it is no more than a part of the general picture of the eighteenth- and nineteenth-century business world with its family concerns and close personal ties. The public limited liability company had no place in the paper industry of the day. The partnership reigned. If organization is linked to techniques, so does control within that organization hinge upon the manner in which long-term finance is provided. And throughout this period of the nineteenth

[1] Thomas Balston, *Dr. Balston at Eton* (London, 1952), p. 8.
[2] See *infra*, Chap. X, *passim*.

century the well-tried methods of the previous age remained: the partnership, the mortgage, the loan on bond.
Expansion was financed by these methods as well as
through the channel of profits ploughed back into the
business. As capital requirements rose, so sometimes did
the weaknesses and difficulties of these devices become
more evident. But they sufficed, and many a paper-
making firm did not adopt the limited liability joint-
stock company form until well after the legislation of
1856.

One point of difference from earlier practices was the
almost certain decline in the leasing of mills from landlords. It was no longer possible to compete in the industry simply by following the old routine of renting a
former corn- or fulling-mill and converting it to hand-
made paper manufacture. In the changing conditions of
the industry neither the site nor the building itself was
necessarily useful for the new machine mill. Though
many a mill continued to be leased, more were being
built and owned by the manufacturers who operated
them.

Through the complex network of loans and leases, of
mortgages, purchases, and partnerships, there came into
the world of paper-making many who might otherwise
have remained either on its fringe or indeed quite un-
acquainted with it. The entrée was their possession of
money which they were willing to invest and the personal
tie which brought that money in a particular direction.
It was with a substantial loan from Andrew Strahan that
John Dickinson was enabled to buy Apsley Mill in 1809;
and it was another £12,500 borrowed later from Strahan
that financed much of the expansion of his business in
the 1820's. Not that Strahan was his only financier: in
1841 Dickinson paid off £7,000 to another mortgagee of

the business.[1] It was perhaps not surprising that a friend in the world of printing should have helped to finance the paper-making venture or that George and later Charles Longman from the world of publishing should have been partners.[2] But that John Evans and Frederick Pratt Barlow should later have become partners in the firm was largely a product of those family interconnexions by which such sons-in-law do thus find their way into particular enterprises.[3] When Balston set up his Springfield Mill, the purchase of the land, the building of the mill, and all that went with it was financed partly out of his own £15,000 capital, much of which was presumably accumulated during the partnership with the Hollingworths, and partly from various loans, mainly from Mrs. Whatman, the widow of his one-time master, James Whatman. By 1810 the mill was mortgaged to her for some £13,000. When the new firm was created in 1814 to ward off financial collapse, the money came from Mrs. Whatman's brother, Jacob Bosanquet, director and sometime chairman of the East India Company; and the new partners were his nominees—William Gaussen his nephew, and Richard Bosanquet one of his sons.[4]

If eminent printers and rich merchant financiers can be readily identified among the contributors to the industry's growth, there are many in the records whose precise role lies concealed beneath that amiable suffix 'gent'. The financial arrangements of a mill in Somerset in the first decade of the century, for instance, involved a

[1] Evans, *Time and Chance*, p. 61, and *The Endless Web*, pp. 13 & n., 26 & n., 45, 54.

[2] Until 1825 the firm was known as Longman & Dickinson. Although George Longman died in 1822, there were close contacts between the firms (and the families) for many years thereafter (*The Endless Web*, *passim*).

[3] Ibid. For John Evans there was a double connexion in that John Dickinson was also his great-uncle.

[4] *William Balston—Paper-Maker*, pp. 14–18, 27–28, 53–54, 70–117.

partnership between one Edward Nicholls, paper-maker, and Thomas Hyde, gentleman, both of Cheddar and a loan of £800 from Hyde to Nicholls, secured on a mortgage of the mill.[1]

A particularly rich and varied array of persons and provisions entered into the finances of Chartham Mill in the century of its growth from, roughly, 1770 to 1870. Its financial history is given below in some detail as an illustration of the practices of the time.[2]

Until 1869 the freehold of the property was owned by Canterbury Cathedral and a rent of £3. 6s. 8d. was paid annually to the Dean and Chapter; the leasehold meanwhile changed hands many times. In the 1770's the lease was held by one Sarah Pearson, widow of William Pearson, paper-maker, of Horton, Buckinghamshire. After bankruptcy and death had taken their toll in the Pearson family, the lease found its way to a certain David Ogilvy, gentleman, of Datchett, father-in-law of James Pearson who was one of William Pearson's sons. In 1792 this Buckinghamshire interest in a Kentish mill ended with the sale of the leasehold to Edward Paine of Chartham, paper-maker, for £1,625. It was then a small, two-vat mill. Paine then borrowed £1,300 at 4½ per cent. on bond from a firm of Canterbury bankers[3] and in 1796 raised a further sum of £1,666. 13s. 4d. by selling two-thirds of the property to two other paper-makers, the brothers G. & D. R. Pike, also of Chartham; at the same time the Pike brothers lent £670 at 5 per cent. to Paine on the security of a mortgage of his remaining one-third of the mill. In 1799 Paine sold his remaining third share to the Pikes for £1,199. The Pikes, however, were themselves anxious to turn fixed assets into cash and in the same year

---

[1] Wiggins, Teape MSS. [2] Ibid.: Chartham Deeds.
[3] Messrs. Baker, Denne, Kingsford, Wigzell, and Kingsford.

they sold one-half of the mill to Samuel Durrant, Esq., of Sussex, for £1,457. George Pike then acquired his brother's quarter of the mill, but in 1806 he mortgaged his half to Durrant, raising thereby £2,000 at 5 per cent. Pike continued to run the mill under these arrangements until 1817 when he sold his share to Durrant.

There is no evidence that Durrant was a practical paper-maker; he sold the mill in 1818 for £4,000, though retaining £2,000 of the purchase price on mortgage. The purchasers were William Weatherley, paper-maker of Dartford, and John Lane of Dartford, inn-holder.[1] A period of successful development, after the vicissitudes of the war years, then followed; Lane sold his half of the mill to Weatherley in 1822 and by 1839 the £2,000 on mortgage to Durrant had been paid off. Machinery was installed,[2] and this was presumably financed out of accumulated profits, for it was not until 1841 that Weatherley began to borrow money for the stated purpose of 'further building or re-building'. In 1841 he borrowed £1,400 on mortgage from a Canterbury linen-draper; during the next eight years further sums totalling £2,100 came from the same source. In 1851 the mill was seriously damaged by fire, and to finance rebuilding Weatherley borrowed £7,500 on a bond at 5 per cent. from Charles West, a Berkshire paper-maker, to whom the mill was also mortgaged as a further security. An additional £3,500 came from West shortly afterwards. By this time the mill had grown to include three steam-engines, four beating-engines, and one Fourdrinier machine.

On the death of Weatherley the mill passed to his nephew, the younger William Weatherley. After some early troubles which need not detain us, he continued to

[1] In 1816 Weatherley & Lane ran a mill on the River Darenth (C. & E.: General Letter (1816)).   [2] See also Spicer, pp. 184–5.

run the mill and paid off part of the mortgage to West. Then in 1853, £2,500 was borrowed on a further mortgage, this time from Robert and Herbert Sankey of Canterbury.[1] During the next seven years a settlement was effected with West, the Sankeys became the main mortgagees (to the sum of £8,500), and the freehold was bought from the Dean and Chapter of Canterbury Cathedral. Further expansion was undertaken, and in 1859 a second mortgage was taken out by Weatherley for 'sums due or to become due for work done, materials supplied', &c. The mortgagees were S. G. Drury and W. Biggleston, partners and iron-founders of Canterbury. By 1862 the mortgages outstanding were £13,650 plus interest; of this sum £5,000 was due to Drury and Biggleston and £8,500 to R. & H. T. Sankey. At this stage recourse was had to the newly accessible joint-stock limited liability company. The Chartham Paper Mills Co. Ltd. was formed, two of the directors of which were Drury and H. T. Sankey, and the mill was sold to the Company for £20,000. Finally, in 1874 it passed, for £28,750, to William Howard and thus began its connexion with the present firm of William Howard & Sons Ltd., itself now part of Wiggins, Teape & Co. Ltd.

Here, then, in the history of one mill are most of the important elements in the industry's long-term finance during this period. Two big gaps remain in our picture of the organization and financial structure of the industry: the role of the stationer and the provision of short-term credit. The two are themselves inter-connected just as is the provision of long-term funds for the installation of fixed capital entwined with that of working capital or short-term accommodation.

It will be convenient to begin by considering the nexus

---

[1] According to Pigot's *Directory*, Robert Sankey was an attorney.

of payments and credit transactions which were part and parcel of ordinary business operations.

(iv)

The inland bill of exchange was a normal means of commercial payment in the eighteenth century and continued to be used in the early nineteenth century, though less frequently as the cheque became more common. Examples of transactions in the paper industry carried out through the medium of the bill can be found, for instance in Whatman's ledger of the 1780's.[1] In a typical transaction he would draw a bill on a stationer to whom he had sold paper, payable to a rag merchant from whom he had obtained his rags. A large collection of bills and cheques[2] dating from the first two decades of the nineteenth century, drawn on or by the London wholesale stationers, Jones & Leventhorp, reveals the continuation of these and similar arrangements. Many of the bills drawn on them by paper-makers from places ranging from Aberdeen to Somerset—though mostly from southeastern England—are of the type 'pay to ourselves or order', though some involve third parties; an example of the latter, in which the third party is not a rag merchant, is a bill drawn in 1816, by E. Wildman, a paper-maker of Woburn, Buckinghamshire, on Jones & Leventhorp and payable to Messrs. Tennant, the Scottish chemical firm, who had doubtless supplied Wildman with his bleaching materials. The use of the cheque in conjunction with the bill may be illustrated from the following example: a three-month bill for £152. 18s. was drawn on Jones & Leventhorp by a firm of Midlothian paper-makers on 29 March 1816; it passed through various hands, including

[1] Balston MSS. See also *The Paper Maker*, Aug. 1955, pp. 130–40.
[2] Wiggins, Teape MSS.

those of a firm of London bankers, and was finally paid
on maturity by a cheque dated 3 July 1816, drawn by
Jones & Leventhorp on their bankers, Messrs. Sikes,
Snaith & Co. of Mansion House Street.

It was through these mundane channels that there also
passed the links of short-term credit. Between paper-
makers and stationers the credit allowed was normally
three months, sometimes two; shorter credit meant a
lower price.[1] Terms between rag merchant and paper-
maker were much the same. The majority of bills drawn
on Jones & Leventhorp were at three months, though
there were also one-, two-, and four-month bills. A
manufacturer who was short of ready cash could anti-
cipate the proceeds of sales by discounting bills drawn
upon the stationers with whom he normally dealt, or he
might in effect reverse the flow of credit by the use of
accommodation bills. This depended, of course, on the
willingness of the stationers to accept such bills. Whilst
trade was good, whilst stationers and makers, both
operating in a protected and expanding market, could
normally sell all that could be made, then it seems
likely that stationers often gave credit in such ways to
makers whom they knew and whose credit-worthiness
they respected. Certainly Balston received credit advances on these lines, during his early days at Springfield, from the London stationers to whom he sold his
paper. Certainly, too, it was the changing state of the
market bringing in its turn the contraction of this
dangerous form of credit that helped to bring him into
financial difficulties.[2] Another example of a similar sort

[1] Balston MSS.: Balston to (?) Agnew, c. 1813; *Fourteenth Report* (1835),
app. 39, p. 101.

[2] *William Balston—Paper-Maker*, pp. 29, 53–55, 66–69, 80–81. Also
Balston MSS.: Balston to (?) Agnew, c. 1813. In the letter he makes it clear
that he expected to be able to solve the problem of obtaining floating capital

of arrangement was that entered into by a Devonshire maker, T. B. Pim, with Magnay & Pickering in January 1809. They agreed to take his papers on commission and to accept his bills in anticipation of the proceeds; as security he assigned them the leases of his mills. At the time of his applying to them for this the balance in their favour in his account with them was £276; by the end of 1809 it was £4,250. They were thus financing his operations to an appreciable extent.[1]

A different and rather curious source of credit was provided by the Excise duties themselves, at least until 1836. This arose from the time lag between receiving payment for paper made and paying the duty, a time lag which had been extended by the shortening of the manufacturing period consequent upon the introduction of the machine and of the drying cylinders. As a result the twelve weeks' grace which the makers were given for paying the duty, whilst appropriate to the older methods of manufacture, now simply provided free credit. It was said to offer a temptation to small men to set up with inadequate capital and then, in effect, to trade on public money; if they failed, as not infrequently happened, they would leave large amounts of duty owing and there would be nothing with which to pay them.[2]

In 1836 at the same time as the rate of duty was cut, the period of grace for payment was reduced to six weeks.[3] Evidence was given before the 1861 Committee to sug-

by such means. That he should have hoped to succeed may be a testimony to his lack of business foresight, but it may also be an indication of the general market conditions in which the industry had long operated. When contraction came, during the second decade of the nineteenth century, the stationers not unnaturally took up a very different attitude, sometimes being willing to act merely as selling agents.

[1] Wiggins, Teape MSS.
[2] *Fourteenth Report* (1835), pp. 26–27, 121–2, 156, 161.
[3] See *infra*, p. 334.

gest that this had been one of the reasons for the disappearance of the smaller mills.[1] How much weight
should be put on this it is hard to know; at least it seems
possible that this gratuitous credit provision and its
curtailment acted as a stimulant to the rapidity with
which new mills appeared in the 1820's and disappeared
in the 30's and 40's.

It was the banks, however, which formed the other
main source of credit. Just as his father-in-law's bank
assisted Dickinson, so did the local Maidstone bank
advance credit to Balston. In the summer of 1810 his
overdraft with his Maidstone bankers (Sir William
Bishop, Larking, Hughes & Co.) was between £2,000
and £3,000; at about the same time his London bankers,
Forster, Lubbock & Co. were asking him to put his
account with them 'in a more respectable state and not
call upon us for such a large advance'. This suggests that
comparatively small, short-term credit was regarded as
normal. Later in the same year he owed his Maidstone
bankers £17,000. On what terms this debt was allowed
to rise to such a sum is not clear but it is clear that it was
regarded as exceptional. After much negotiation it was
later supported, up to £10,000, by Jacob Bosanquet.[2]
A similar state of affairs, though on a smaller scale and
resolved in a different manner, occurred when Messrs.
Wise, also paper-makers of the Maidstone area, had
overdrawn their account with another firm of local
bankers, by rather over £4,800.[3] They then gave security
for this and further sums (the total overdraft not to exceed
£5,000) by a bond to the bankers, binding themselves as
was normal in double the amount, i.e. in £10,000—just as

---

[1] *Select Committee* (1861), pp. 25 and 96.
[2] *William Balston—Paper-Maker*, pp. 74–75, 96–98, 103–4, 106.
[3] Law Reports: E.R. 105, p. 1232.

Edward Paine of Chartham had given a bond of £2,600 for his loan of £1,300 from the Canterbury bankers in 1792.[1]

It is possible that such advances as these contributed to the provision of fixed capital in the industry, though it is more likely that they were normally destined for working capital. As mills grew bigger, larger outlays on raw materials, wages, and maintenance all made demands on liquid resources which could be met only by provisions of this type. A leading Scottish maker estimated at the end of this period that £5,000 was needed simply as working capital in the setting-up of a one-machine mill.[2] At the same time Dickinson stated that 'independent of the mills and machinery, the value of which was very great indeed, we had embarked in our trade £160,000; but then we had six mills'.[3] A large part of Balston's heavy indebtedness in his early years at Springfield was incurred by the need to make big outlays for wages, raw materials, and the varied running costs of a large new mill.

As the big new machine mills began to make their mark, the old relationship with the stationers slowly changed. Larger mills linked by the new railways to the towns, able to command credit from the expanding and improving banking system or to draw upon the reserves of large profits, made redundant those long and tedious journeys by stationers or their representatives to a multitude of remote and tiny mills; and at the same time they weakened the potentialities and the importance of the credit links between maker and stationer. Not only would the ultimate effect of these changes be to 'place

[1] Wiggins, Teape MSS.: Chartham Deeds.
[2] *Select Committee* (1861), p. 33.
[3] Ibid., p. 58.

the manufacture in larger hands' but also, to continue the remarks quoted at the beginning of this chapter,

cither to render the stationer what he formerly was—the holder of stock—or to convert the maker into something resembling the stationer. At present the stationer has contrived to throw the burden of what idle stock there is upon the maker. He buys sparingly and not infrequently sells before he buys. The necessity, therefore, to which he reduces the manufacture by this mode of purchase we look upon to be the most efficient agent of evil. . . .[1]

This was in 1813, during a period of strain and change; and it was remarkably prophetic. The new trends in the relative positions of paper-makers and stationers can be broadly summarized under three headlines. The paper merchants tended to replace the older type of wholesale stationer; some of the bigger makers developed their own selling outlets and thus moved forward into the merchanting end of the business, just as in earlier centuries the stationers had moved into making; some makers also became manufacturing stationers. These trends gathered force only towards the end of this period; and they stand to some extent on the periphery of our subject. It may suffice to illustrate them by noting the stationery trade of the Spicers, the move by Dickinsons into the manufacture of envelopes, cards, and stationery, or the growth of the modern firm of E. S. & A. Robinson Ltd., based on the venture in the 1840's by Elisha Robinson away from his father's paper-mill at Overbury, Worcestershire, and into the paper-bag business at Bristol.[2] Even by the 1830's the bigger makers had their offices and warehouses in the neighbouring towns and cities and were far from dependent on the visits of the stationer: Cromptons in

---

[1] Balston MSS.: R. M. Bacon to Balston, 7 Aug. 1813.
[2] B. Darwin, *Robinsons of Bristol* (Bristol, 1945), pp. 2, 3, and 13.

Manchester, Cowans in Edinburgh, Dickinsons not only in London but also with branches in more distant towns such as Nottingham in order to push the sale of special lines locally in demand.[1] The export trade remained largely in the stationers' hands;[2] but it was a sign of the times that a Scottish stationer in 1835, in voicing his objections to a proposal by some local paper-makers in regard to the Excise regulations covering exports, should have attacked the proposal on the ground that

This might give them advantages in exporting that would be injurious to what we term the stationery trade, as the manufacturer would then be the merchant also; and it might give facilities that I do not think they are entitled to over the stationer, who is the merchant; it would drive that class of traders out of the market, and throw the monopoly into the hands of a few wealthy paper makers, who might have sufficient capital to command that trade.[3]

The stationers also gradually lost the association which many of them had with the supply of rags. As their commanding position in relation to the maker was weakened, so did the trade pass more and more into the hands of specialized rag merchants. The stationer-cum-rag dealer of the earlier years of the century gradually disappears.

But all these new developments appeared comparatively slowly. In 1861 most makers still sold their paper to merchants and stationers; and the latter still largely controlled the export trade.[4] The survival of many smaller mills thus had its counterpart in the continuance of these older arrangements alongside the new.

---

[1] Pigot, op. cit., and Slater, op. cit.; C. & E.: Excise-Treasury Letters, 1811–15, ff. 68–72; *Fourteenth Report* (1835), pp. 143 et seq.; *The Endless Web*, pp. 67 and *passim*.

[2] *Fourteenth Report*, p. 121.

[3] Ibid., p. 159.

[4] *Select Committee* (1861), p. 30

X

Trade Unions and Trade Associations

(i)

Q. You were formerly a good deal at the mercy of your men?

A. Those that adopted the old system were very much at the mercy of the men, because they had a very powerful club, and were in fact the masters, and not the proprietors of the mills; but we always protested against it, and never employed men connected with the club, on that account.

Q. Then this Fourdrinier's machine has in a great measure done away with the means of combination?

A. Yes, in the machine mills it has done away with it; but the old system still exists in the other mills.[1]

THIS is a tendentious set of observations from a tendentious report but it contains the essence of a widely expressed and basically true statement. Confirmatory remarks can be drawn from various sources. When the minister of the parish of Denny, Stirlingshire, drew up an account of his parish in the 1840's, he observed apropos of the older of the two paper-mills there that when the paper had been made by hand, 'combinations among operative paper-makers were, at that time, a frequent cause of great annoyance to masters and of misery to many innocent families'. But machinery had been installed and therefore 'the improvements put an end to combinations among paper-makers'.[2]

Although it would be dangerous to assume, *post hoc ergo propter hoc*, that labour troubles were the cause of the

---

[1] *Fourdrinier Committee* (1837), p. 12; see also pp. 10 and 14–15.

[2] *New Statistical Account*, vol. viii, p. 129.

introduction of the machine, there can be little doubt
that they played a very important part in securing the
interests of the masters in its development and in per-
suading them to adopt it as soon as it became a practical
device.[1] For it is certain that the skilled workers in the
hand-made industry possessed a powerful trade union
and used the strike to enforce their demands. At a time
when relations between master and servant were very
different from today such a situation readily brought to
the lips of employers those expressions of righteous indignation, of virtue outraged, which help to load these
problems with emotional overtones. But fundamentally
the situation arose from those skilled techniques of production sketched in Chapter II; it is not surprising
therefore that the history of combinations of workers in
the industry should stretch back a long way into the past.

Special skills can be a rich mine of labour troubles. It
was the desire to guard the secrets enshrined in paper-
making that provided the basis of a dispute at Strömer's
mill at Nuremberg as early as 1390.[2] The encouragement
given to foreign paper-makers to bring their skills to
England in the sixteenth and seventeenth centuries was
not, as we have seen, greeted with unalloyed enthusiasm
by native workers here.[3] And it was because of their
particular skills that journeymen paper-workers were
able to develop powerful organizations in France in the
seventeenth and eighteenth centuries and in England in
the eighteenth.

The French *compagnonnages* merit some brief attention

---

[1] See *Fourdrinier Committee* (1807), evidence of various paper-makers.
They spoke of the trade being inconvenienced by combinations of workers;
James Swan, an Oxfordshire paper-maker, who stated that one of his mills
was then idle as a result of a combination amongst the men, thought that
the machine would get rid of this.

[2] Hunter, pp. 231–5.   [3] *Supra*, pp. 69, 74–5.

for two reasons. First, because it seems likely that the
later English union may have owed something to their
example; second, because of the relevance of their
activities to the initial experiments of Robert and the
final emergence of the Fourdrinier machine.

Certainly by the later seventeenth century, if not
earlier, powerful associations of journeymen paper-
makers had come into being in all the more important
paper-making areas of France.[1] In spite of action taken
against them, whether by local employers or by royal
decree they continued more vigorously than comparable
organizations in other industries, and even to the extent
of achieving that degree of unity which permitted, in the
eighteenth century, nation-wide strikes. In 1698 there
was a large-scale strike, lasting about a month and
involving some 300 or 400 employees in Auvergne. An
inquiry was followed by the appearance of a *règlement*
which attempted to control many of the relations between masters and men. The *règlement* dealt with such
questions as the amount of work to be done in a day or
the terms on which workers could be discharged or
apprentices taken; it laid down that masters should be
free to take as many apprentices as they thought fit. It
was on matters of this sort that the English employers and
the English journeymen's association were quarrelling
a hundred years later.

As the eighteenth century progressed, there were more
strikes and more *règlements*. The men struck over such
matters as working hours; the masters complained about
various workers' customs which interfered with work
and restricted production. They were able to maintain

---

[1] The following account of capital–labour relations in the French industry
is largely based on Briquet, op. cit.; also G. Martin, *La Grande Industrie sous
le règne de Louis XIV* (Paris, 1899), Sée, op. cit., and Ballot, op. cit.

these customs[1] because of the extreme dependence of the ordinary small master upon the skilled labour of his journeymen. Moreover as strikes spread it became clear that the unity of the worker's organization was such as to secure collective or sympathetic action in different provinces. Strikes, disputes, and imprisonments continued through the period of the Revolution and in various parts of France. The association of paper-workers became perhaps the most powerful and unruly of such bodies in the country. Political changes made no difference: 'l'indiscipline des ouvriers avait survécu à la Royauté, à la République, à l'Empire'.[2] Only the coming of the machine brought change to these relationships. And it is said that it was because of the troublesomeness of the workers that Robert first conceived the idea, at Didot's mill, of inventing a paper-making machine.[3]

In England, as might be expected, there is no indication of such workers' organizations or of such disputes at so early a date as in France. The English industry never came within the specific ambit of the Statute of Artificers of 1563, for the good reason that it did not then exist; nor is there any evidence that it was ever the subject of formal guild control. The comparatively late development in this country of the more skilled branch of the industry, white-paper making, makes it improbable that a workers' organization could have grown up until well after the turn of the seventeenth century.

---

[1] Some of these customs, such as those known as *lever la rente* and *le droit de gueulage*, were very evidently designed to relieve the tedium of work by finding pretexts for drinking wine at such times and in such quantities as to make agreeably irregular work which the masters naturally wanted to be regular.

[2] This was said of the workers in the Dauphiné (quoted Briquet, p. 188).

[3] Ballot, p. 559.

The journeyman's union which did emerge became known as The Original Society of Paper Makers. It is not clear when it acquired that title[1] nor when it started as a recognizable entity. One writer dates its foundation from 1735,[2] another from 1800;[3] neither provides any evidence for these statements. A spokesman of the Society stated in 1874: 'We are an old trade society and . . . I suppose the history of our Society will go back 100 years.'[4] Whatever the truth may be, it is clear that it was the situation created by the steeply rising prices of the later years of the eighteenth century that first brought the paper-makers and their doings into the limelight of official disapproval. In 1788 a combination of journeymen paper-makers was noted in or near Manchester and in 1790 some workers in the industry in Hertfordshire were indicted for conspiring to compel their employer to increase their wages.[5] Two years later there was news from the paper-mills of the Edinburgh area of a 'Confederacy of workmen employed at six of the principal manufactories in this neighbourhood, for increase of wages from the highest to the lowest'.[6] In 1796 the strained relations between the two sides in the industry were brought to a head when the employers petitioned the House of Commons for leave to bring in

[1] It seems quite likely that the full title and particularly the word 'Original' is an invention of the later nineteenth century, designed to distinguish the Society from other unions in the industry. On the other hand the emblem and motto of the organization (incorporating clasped hands and the words 'united to support but not combined to injure') certainly derives from the early years of the century (see the verses quoted *infra*, p. 267, n. 1).

[2] R. M. Rayner, *The Story of Trade Unionism* (London, 1929), p. 75.

[3] Spicer, p. 150.

[4] *Arbitration on Wages* (1874), pp. 9–10.

[5] Lipson, op. cit., vol. iii, p. 409; Shorter, *Historical Geography*, p. 82.

[6] Balston MSS.: R. E. Philips (Whatman's brother-in-law, in Edinburgh) to Whatman, Dec. 1792.

a Bill to prohibit combinations of workers in the paper industry.

The evidence[1] presented to the Commons came, as was the way of the times, from the employers only; it was asserted that combinations of workmen had been in existence since 1789. This particular year may have been put forward in the hope that its political significance might conjure up appropriate visions of revolution, though the reported combinations of 1788 and 1790 seem to provide a rough confirmation of the date. The masters stated that they had often been obliged to submit to the men's demands and that an increase in wages had recently been given. A further 5s. per week per man had now been sought and refusal to grant this had provoked a strike among the men who were supported, it was said, from a general fund. The men took action against 'blacklegs' and refused to allow the importation of cheaper labour from outside. William Phipps, paper-maker of Dover, stated that journeymen had consistently refused between 1789 and 1796 to work in mills where Scottish or Irish workers were employed.[2]

The trouble had started at a Kentish mill. It spread from there to all the main paper-making counties of the south-east.[3] It was answered by the lock-out and the 'document' which became so well known in the later

---

[1] *C.J.*, vol. li, pp. 595–6.

[2] Kentish paper-making wages were higher than elsewhere in England and English wages were higher than Scottish and Irish (see Chap. XI). That some masters were attempting to fill vacancies arising from the strike by importing Scottish workers is confirmed in a letter from a Scottish firm to 'The Journeymen Paper Makers at the Coach and Horses, Maidstone' of Apr. 1796 (Balston MSS.). The letter, which was in reply to a letter from the journeymen, gave the terms of employment in Scotland and asked if any of the Kentish workers would go there; it pointed out that though wages were lower, so was the cost of living.

[3] *C.J.*, vol. li, pp. 595–6. The counties were Kent, Surrey, Buckinghamshire, Hampshire, Berkshire, and Hertfordshire.

history of trade unions.[1] A meeting of the master paper-makers of Buckinghamshire at High Wycombe in 1796 resolved that their journeymen should be given a fort-night's notice; at the end of that period their mills were to remain closed down 'until Mr. John Taylor's or any other Mills that have been or may be laid still on Account of Wages, shall be set to Work again'.[2] Similar meetings were held and similar resolutions passed in other counties. On 13 April 1796 William Phipps wrote to another paper-maker to say that several of his men 'have signed the Agreement not to assist any Club neither give any assistance to any Journeymen'. He added: 'however, I have not yet employed those that have large families in consequence of their receiving considerably from the Club'. He reported that there were only three or four who would not sign and 'them I do not suffer to get employ in this Neighbourhood'.[3] Eight days later he was telling the Commons Committee how he and other masters had been obliged to stop their mills. In May the Bill passed into law.[4]

The passage of this Act marked the onset of a period of strife in the industry. It no more crushed the journey-men's organization than it checked the rising prices which fanned the flames of conflict. And it is clear that in that conflict the workers deployed a highly organized trade union. Some letters written in 1801 by journeymen

[1] See S. & B. Webb, *The History of Trade Unionism* (London, 1926), *passim*.

[2] Balston MSS.: printed resolutions of meetings of Buckinghamshire masters, 4 Feb. 1796.

[3] Ibid.: Phipps to Hollingworth and Balston, 13 Apr. 1796.

[4] 36 Geo. III, c. 111: it was called 'An Act to prevent unlawful Com-binations of Workmen employed in the Paper Manufactory'. It prohibited combination of workmen for the purpose of increasing wages and conferred on the Justices the power to commit to the House of Correction any journey-men paper-makers entering into such contracts, as well as various rights of summary jurisdiction.

paper-makers, and which fell into the hands of authority, give some indication of the nature of this body. It seems that these letters were brought from Sickle Mill, near Haslemere, to Iping Mill, near Midhurst, Sussex; their receipt was immediately followed by the workmen striking for an extra 3s. per week. The letters were as follows:[1]

To Mr. Mullard, Iping Mill

Gents—The enclosed was sent to Guildford, and forwarded to Haslemere, and thence to Iping.

Health and Fraternity
Sickle Mill
2ⁿ September 1801

The enclosed letter ran:

Neckinger, 28 August 1801

Sir,—This is to acquaint you that we have now made our fifth subscription of 2s. 6d. each, which makes 12s. 6d. per man. Now our request is that your division will come forward now, as money is much wanted. We also desire you will forward this to the other divisions of Haslemere and Iping, etc., without delay. I have many things to acquaint you of, but for want of time I must defer till another opportunity. I shall mention to you that I have been to Maidstone by appointment, where I was met by a very respectable body of our trade, 44 in number where I produced the sick, and secret articles of our trade, which were generally and universally approved and signed, and are to be printed; also the cards of freedom. Everything bears a favourable aspect, and I hope will have a favourable issue. It would be a pity, after spending so many hundreds, to lose the cause at last for want of support. Manchester and Wells approve of our plan, and they say that they will establish it in every mill from Berwick to the Lands End.

[1] Quoted in A. Aspinall, *The Early English Trade Unions* (London, 1949), pp. 36–37, from Home Office records. As printed the names of the mills appear as Sping and as Seikee. For the location of these two mills see Shorter, *Historical Geography*, pp. 265, 266, 388, 393.

This letter suggests very strongly that there existed at that time something similar to the organization described before the Committee of 1825 on the Repeal of the Combination Laws.[1] The nature of the trade union then is apparent partly from the verbal evidence there given and partly from the 'Rules and Articles to be observed by the Journeymen Paper Makers throughout England', produced to the Committee.

The rules mentioned five 'Grand Divisions': No. 1, Maidstone; No. 2, Carshalton; No. 3, Wells; No. 4, Leeds; No. 5, Manchester.[2] The divisions acted as regional centres for the collection of money; headquarters were at Maidstone whither, according to Spicer, it had moved in 1815 from St. Pauls Cray.[3] The Rules and Articles go into considerable detail; they appear, moreover, to have the widest geographical application of all such sets of union rules submitted to the Committee. They cover various matters concerning the administration and organization of the union; they lay down that apprenticeship shall be for seven years, at the end of which time admission to the Society costs 10s. for the son of a paper-maker and £2 for the son of a non-paper-maker; they limit the number of apprentices to one per vat, but grant certain privileges here in respect of the sons of paper-makers; they state that apprentices taken against the wishes of the journeymen after 1 July 1803 shall not be acceptable to the Society; they provide for payment to those who, with the support of the Society, 'leave for wages or customs'; and finally they seal the whole thirty-one rules with three four-lined stanzas

[1] *Report from the Select Committee on Combination Laws* (1825), in *B.P.P.* 1825, vol. iv.

[2] Ibid., app., p. 56. To each of these divisions surrounding counties were attached.

[3] Spicer, p. 150.

which express sentiments of peaceful, co-operative, and conservative rectitude.[1]

Evidence given to the Committee by Thomas Gardner, paper-maker of St. Pauls Cray, offered confirmation that the journeymen's society to which he belonged had existed along similar lines and since well before 1825. He did not know when it had been established as a society; it was 'before my memory'. Its membership he thought to be about a thousand in Kent and probably another two thousand elsewhere. He stated that if an unemployed journeyman were to call at a mill and not receive work, he would receive a ticket on the fund of the Society for a sum to support him until he arrived at the next town in search of work; this practice was regularly followed throughout England, Scotland, and Ireland. He recalled that during the preceding eight or nine years relief had been given to men who had struck to foil attempts by employers to reduce wages. Some of his remarks seemed to suggest, however, that the national organization was not so closely knit as the elaborate Rules and Articles would imply; that both in strength and practices, local

> May masters with their men unite,
> Each other ne'er oppress;
> And their assistance freely give
> When men are in distress.
>
> We covet not our master's wealth,
> Nor crave for nothing more,
> But to support our families
> As our fathers have before.
>
> Then may the God that rules above
> Look on our mean endeavour,
> And masters with their men unite
> In hand and hand for ever.

(*Report from the Select Committee on Combination Laws*, app., p. 59.) In connexion with the last line of these verses, it is interesting to note that the emblem of clasped hands was used later both by the Original Society and by the National Union of Paper-Mill Workers in the 1890's.

clubs or bodies in the trade varied considerably; and that what held for Kent did not necessarily hold for all other counties.[1] The industry, it must be remembered, was widely dispersed, and the creation of an effective union, in the conditions of the time, would not have been easy even had it been legal. In fact it seems to have existed before, after, and throughout the period of the Combination Laws, to have been successful in action, and at the same time to have contended with a body of employers organized on similar lines into a trade association.

(ii)

On the masters' side a combination of employers was hammered into being by the force of three problems: taxation, rising rag prices, and the wage demands of workers in the face of mounting costs of living.

It is natural that in an industry subject to such complicated taxation and protection as was paper-making there should arise co-operative action by the manufacturers designed to influence the government. The menace of free trade, as represented by the negotiations for the Eden Treaty of 1787, stimulated the papermakers to opposition. But this threat to the tariff wall was not severe in the eighteenth century; when free trade did come in the next century, the situation had been changed by the advent of machinery. In the 1780's the paper manufacturers were amongst those opposed to the proposals, emanating from the cotton, iron, and pottery trades, for reciprocal tariff reductions.[2] The events of the time, however, diminished the hopes of less restricted

---

[1] Ibid., Minutes of Evidence, pp. 26–32.

[2] Witt Bowden, *Industrial Society in England towards the end of the Eighteenth Century* (New York, 1925), pp. 164 et seq., p. 185.

commerce and so the paper-makers' protective wall remained unbreached.

The problems posed by the Excise and by rising rag prices and wages were all much stiffer. How far the 'Committee appointed by a General Meeting of the Paper Makers of Great Britain', which petitioned on Excise matters in 1765,[1] represented a continuing association of employers it is impossible to say. What is clear, however, is that such an association did exist in the 1780's, that its members were concerned with the new duties of 1781, and that the simplification of the duties in 1794 almost certainly owed something to representations by this body of employers.[2] In the meetings and correspondence of the trade at this time, James Whatman, John Portal, William Lepard, and Messrs. Fourdrinier were amongst those who played important parts. Lepard seems to have been responsible for drawing up a plan for the simplification of the duties, though disagreements on its merits induced Whatman in February 1792 to indicate his unwillingness to support an approach to Pitt on this subject whilst there were still divided counsels in the trade. Indeed Whatman seems to have followed a line of his own, and in December 1792 he wrote of the 'many reasons that made me think it necessary to withdraw myself from the meetings of the Trade'.

Those meetings were held in London, usually at the George and Vulture Tavern, Cornhill. In the 1790's the association described itself as 'The Committee of Master

---

[1] *Supra*, pp. 131–2.

[2] The following account of the employers' association is largely based on letters, drafts, minutes, and resolutions of meetings, &c., in the Balston MSS. All references and quotations in this section are drawn therefrom unless otherwise stated. Some rather more detailed references will be found in my article 'Combinations of Capital and of Labour in the English Paper Industry, 1789–1825', *Economica*, Feb. 1954.

Paper-Makers'. Reports of meetings were printed and circulated to members. This central committee seems to have been dominated by the paper-makers and wholesale stationers of London and the Home Counties. Corresponding to the central committee were regional groups which likewise held their meetings at local inns.[1] The chairman of the Master Paper Makers from about 1798 to 1816 was William Balston, who also presided over a local committee of Kent and Surrey employers. The main body met sufficiently frequently and carried on such an amount of business as to make it worth while to employ a regular solicitor. From 1789, if not earlier, this was Nathaniel Davies of Lothbury; thirty-six years later at a meeting at the 'George and Vulture' it was noted that there was 'an outstanding account due to the late Mr. Davies, whose well-known attention to the interests of the trade entitle his executors and family to every mark of attention'.[2] They might indeed: for twenty-five of those years the body which he had served so faithfully had been an illegal combination and some of its activities were notably 'in restraint of trade'. He did not, as we shall see, fail to warn members of this.[3]

The efforts of the masters' association to control rag prices shed some light on the economic ideas and practices of the paper manufacturers at the turn of the century; they also give a further indication of the obstacles in the path of unanimity in such an association. In January 1799, after a meeting of the Master Paper Makers and the rag merchants, it was resolved by the

[1] Those of the Wycombe district sometimes met at the 'Three Tuns', High Wycombe, those of Hertfordshire at the Swan Inn, Rickmansworth, and the makers of Kent patronized the 'Star' at Maidstone.

[2] *Report from the Select Committee on Combination Laws*, Minutes of Evidence, p. 30.

[3] *Infra*, p. 281.

former that no one of the forty-four signatories there present should pay more than 48*s*. per cwt. for a certain grade of rags: and that the stoppage of all mills for a month would be the most effective way of forcing down rag prices. At a meeting of a special committee one month later, however, it was made clear that only a minority of the trade accepted this idea. A compromise plan, apparently devised by Balston and followed previously by the Kentish employers, was recommended.[1]

Schemes of a restrictive nature are sometimes easier to devise than to operate. And in this instance operation was made particularly difficult by the wide dispersion of the paper industry and the inadequacies of eighteenth-century communications. Moreover, the Master Paper Makers Committee was essentially the mouthpiece of the southern manufacturers, especially those of Kent. In March 1799 it was complained from the West of England that many counties had failed to send deputations to local meetings. Headquarters circularized the deputies of twenty-one counties,[2] asking them to call meetings to discuss the proposals. But by May temporary failure had to be admitted, and with a rather naïve surprise it was ascribed to 'the unexpected opposition which the measures adopted by the Trade have met from the Importers of Foreign Rags; who rather than submit to the Prices agreed upon, have actually housed them and are now withholding the necessary supplies'. In spite of this setback, similar attempts continued, though again with little success. The blame for the failure to secure a general

---

[1] Some details are given in *Economica*, Feb. 1954, pp. 39–40. An interesting comment on the economics of rag supply is contained in the remark by the Kentish employers that they recognized that the 'present high price has not in the least operated to increase the collection of rags . . . and that the advance has arisen from a competition amongst ourselves'.

[2] See *Economica*, Feb. 1954, p. 40 n., for details.

suspension in June 1799 was laid upon the defections of the masters in Hampshire and Berkshire.

The most vigorous stimulus to effective combination by the masters came with the intensification of the workers' demands. On the outbreak of the strike of 1796 meetings both local and central were held with the express purpose of discussing the action to be taken. The speed with which results were secured is impressive. Resolutions were passed, correspondence flowed between the interested parties, for instance between Nathaniel Davies and Sir Edward Knatchbull, one of the M.P.s for Kent. The trouble had started in January and the Bill to prohibit combinations in the industry had passed into law by May.

But neither the law nor the concerted action of the masters—or, at least, an important group of them—was adequate to prevent the journeymen's union from continuing in being and from securing a further rise in wages. This they did in 1801 when the general level of prices had soared to its first big peak in its upward movement.[1] At this time there was much activity on both sides of the industry, and in April 1801 twenty-three employers of Kent and Surrey[2] resolved to constitute themselves into 'The Society of Master Paper-Makers of the Counties of Kent and Surrey, associated for the Purpose of resisting the illegal Combinations amongst the Journeymen Paper-Makers'. They thundered against the formation of clubs; the raising of subscriptions; the 'adoption of a *regular system of constant encroachment* on the *fair* and *established* customs and usages of the trade'; and the existence

[1] On prices see A. D. Gayer, A. J. Schwartz, and W. W. Rostow, op. cit., vol. i, pp. 471–2.

[2] The names of these employers are given in a reproduction of part of the original document which will be found in my article 'Masters and Men in the Paper Industry during the Industrial Revolution', *The Paper Maker*, Nov. and Dec. 1954, p. 464.

of unrest amongst the journeymen in Hertfordshire and Buckinghamshire. They declared themselves as determined to resist 'wanton unnecessary and *extortionate demands*', and resolved to raise a fund by subscription for the purpose of meeting expenses arising from the prosecution of workmen illegally combining.[1]

After the local meeting came the wider organization. At a general meeting of the Master Paper Makers at the 'George and Vulture' in June 1803 it was unanimously resolved that it was 'highly expedient the Whole of the Trade should be formed into one general Society, under the Denomination of, The United Society of Master Paper-Makers of Great Britain, associated solely for the purpose of resisting the illegal Combinations existing amongst their journeymen'. The resolutions included the establishment of a permanent central committee in London; the determination not to employ journeymen belonging to the club; agreement to employ those refusing to join or withdrawing from it, for terms of three, five, or seven years; and the intention to take on such apprentices and new men as the employers thought proper.

In spite of the impressive and resounding title of this organization there was no truly national coverage, any more than there had been earlier: a contrast, apparently, to the range of the workers' society. The resolutions were signed by 24 deputies representing 120 masters who claimed, in turn, to represent 400 vats. This meant approximately two-thirds of the English industry in terms of capacity and about one-third in terms of firms. In spite of the 'Great Britain' of the title, Scotland does not seem to have been included. Although the organiza-

---

[1] The fund was to be of £1,500–£2,000. The leading firm, Hollingworth & Balston, contributed £200.

tion included employers of importance and influence such as Hollingworth & Balston, the Spicers, Portal & Bridges, and the Fourdriniers, there was no representation from the Lancashire area and in fact nearly half of the 120 masters were from Kent and Buckinghamshire.[1] And again it was to prove evident that it was by no means easy to secure unanimity even amongst those who were members.

(iii)

Thus, by the turn of the century, both sides of the industry had regular, organized associations, the men to fight for wages, conditions of work, and the right to restrict entry into the trade; the employers to resist the men's demands and also to take concerted action on such matters as the Excise duties, the price of rags, and the undesirability of excessive competition.

Price-fixing was evidently one of the functions of the Master Paper Makers. In June 1799 at the same time as the committee had had to admit defeat in the attempts to force down rag prices, a new scale of agreed higher prices for ten sorts of writing- and five sorts of printing-papers was sent out by Balston, as chairman, along with the printed resolutions of the latest meeting. The prices agreed at the meetings of the makers did not always concur with the views of the stationers; the latter held their own meetings but those stationers who were also makers attended those of the Master Paper Makers as well. A month after Balston had sent out the new scale of agreed prices in 1799, he was obliged to qualify it by the following printed circular which suggests a nice

[1] A reproduction of the original printed resolutions of this meeting of 3 June, giving the names, by counties, of all the masters who signed, will be found in *The Paper Maker*, Dec. 1954, pp. 466–7.

discrimination between competition, compulsion, and discretion:

Sir,

A Re-consideration of the advanced Price lately fixed on Thin-Post, at the George and Vulture, having been requested by some of the principal Stationery Houses in London, a Special Meeting of the Trade of this County was held, this Day, at Maidstone,

When it was Resolved,

That the Advance upon Medium and Thin-Post not appearing to bear a fair Proportion with the other Papers, that the same be altered as follows, viz.

Thin-Post to be advanced 1s. per Ream instead of 1s. 6d. and Medium 2s. 6d. per Ream instead of 2s. 0d.

And that our Brethren, in other Districts, be recommended to adopt the same Alteration.

Signed by Order.

William Balston, Chairman

Maidstone, July 17,

1799

Stationers made no pretence of concealing the manner in which prices were agreed upon. In 1815 and 1816, for example, lists of prices for writing-, drawing-, and fine printing-papers were sent out to retailers by Hollingworth & Lyon of Watling St., London. This was the stationery end of the Hollingworth business which controlled Turkey Mill and others in Kent. At the head of their list they announced that this was a 'List of the Prices of Fine Papers as agreed upon at the last Meeting of the principal Wholesale Stationers of London'. They then described themselves as 'Manufacturers of Whatman's Papers'.[1]

On the Excise front the doubling of the rate of duty

---

[1] Wiggins, Teape MSS.: Johnson Gore Invoice Books.

in April 1801[1] precipitated a battle in which the paper-makers were in alliance with the stationers, printers, and booksellers. Parliament was petitioned and a Committee reported in March 1802. Of those who gave evidence before the Committee the three paper manufacturers were members of the Master Paper Makers; and two of the wholesale stationers were men with whom Balston had frequent business dealings. It was duly demonstrated that the rise in duty, by weight, as it fell especially heavily upon printing-papers, was injurious to the trade; evidence was brought forward to show that the recent steep rise in price was largely ascribable to the increase in duty, and that stocks of paper lay upon the makers' or stationers' hands.[2] Recourse was again had to Sir Edward Knatchbull, Balston addressing to him a petition on behalf of the paper-makers of Kent in which he bewailed the declining manufacture, falling demand, mounting stocks, and the like. In 1803 the duty was reduced.[3]

The attempts to reduce rag prices by restricting output were continued in later years. But if the aims of paper-makers were sometimes frustrated, they could at least make their sentiments known; those of one paper-maker in June 1804 were doubtless shared by many of his friends and competitors: 'The Rag merchants, I consider (between ourselves) d—d deep, low, cunning, and cheating Chaps, who don't care who is ruin'd, if they get £5 by an advance.' In 1812, when depression was accompanied by falling paper prices but still rising rag prices, Balston proposed a new suspension of work with a view to sustaining the one set of prices and reducing the other.

[1] 41 Geo. III, c. 8.

[2] *Report from the Committee on the Booksellers and Printers Petitions* (1802), *B.P.P.* 1801–2, vol. ii. Amongst those who gave evidence were William Cobbett and Luke Hansard.   [3] 43 Geo. III, c. 108.

The spokesmen of some areas, including Devon and Somerset, agreed to such proposals in the summer of that year. In 1813, too, there was a further reduction of work. At a general meeting at the 'George and Vulture' in April 1814 the high price of raw materials was again set down as a subject of discussion for a further meeting to be called in July. At the same time the meeting expressed itself as being confident that 'as the object of reducing the present glut of Paper in the market has been obtained by the unanimity in the Trade, that equal success will attend their efforts in reducing the price of Raw Materials to their proper standard [*sic*], or at least in preventing any encrease in the present prices'. This suggests that the restrictive activities of the makers had been blessed with some success or, at any rate, that it had so appeared to them.

The fight against the men's 'encroachments' continued. To the 'document' and the intention to take as many apprentices and new men as possible there was added the attempted establishment by the employers of relief funds. This was recommended in Kent and apparently put into practice by Portal in Hampshire.[1] But in other ways Portal was less willing to agree with Kent. Whilst some Hampshire paper-makers were agreeing with the Central Committee's policy of a lock-out against a demand in 1803 for higher wages, Portal & Bridges were accused of paying their men a higher rate. In a letter of

---

[1] The Kentish employers recommended, on 26 June 1803, the setting up at each mill of a fund for the relief of workmen suffering from sickness or misfortune or for the relief of journeymen on tramp. To it the masters were willing to contribute at the rate of one guinea per vat per annum, but the control was to remain in their hands, it being stipulated that each master should be treasurer. From Hampshire it was reported that Portal's men had 'totally relinquished the Club and have delivered over the Money subscribed to Mr. P. who has made a handsome addition to it for the establishment of a Clubb for the relief of their sick'.

August 1803, to Balston, denying this charge, and laying the blame on an advance made in Kent earlier that year, they affirmed their willingness to reduce their wages in proportion as soon as the Kent masters succeeded in effecting the reduction then being tried. At the same time they took strong exception to making changes in the rules, customs, and wages 'to support the fancy and whim of individuals', and having received a 'most unwarrantable letter' from their district chairman, declared their intention in future of avoiding 'all meetings whatsoever thinking it the surest Mode of being on the best of terms with the trade'.

By the autumn of that year rising rag prices and further troubles with the men produced the familiar woes and the familiar remedies: '. . . the only means that I think are left is a universal suspension of the Manufactory. . . . Do not let us be the dupes of the Men which I am persuaded we at present are. . . . Nor let the private Interests of any prevail over the general good'. In Kent, in face of concerted labour action against attempts to reduce wages, appeals were made for unity. The necessity of introducing new men into the mills was stressed; lists of men leaving or discharged were circulated to employers. But again the masters' unity wavered. Though Devon supported the employers fighting on the Kentish front, claiming that many new hands were introduced and that 'clubs are drop't all thro' Devonshire', from another source an approach to Manchester was urged. In December 1803 and January 1804 deputations were sent to various parts of the country to seek support for the Kent masters in their protracted lock-out, but the show of unanimity from the north was not impressive. The Manchester manufacturers were willing enough to agree in theory to a projected nation-wide suspension of work, but expressed great doubt whether their neighbours and rivals at Bolton would agree.[1] The Somerset employers were willing to suspend operations if three-quarters of the trade in England would do likewise. From Hampshire John Portal treated Balston to a fine specimen of sarcasm and unco-operative letter writing.[2] But in the end the Kentish masters had at least a temporary success, the men returning to work on the masters' terms.

That this should have occurred was almost certainly due to the greater financial resources of the employers. The following letter offers some insight into the men's viewpoint in this conflict:[3]

Brothers,

I take the opurtunity to acquaint you that I sent you 25 Cards and 26 Certifycates and Every Card is 2[d] and Every Cert. 1[d] which make the sum of 6[s] 4[d] & I thank you if you would send it as I must give an account to the Stewards. Likewise I am sory to inform you that all the Brown Mills in this County is still for wages some time & and the Masters talk of laying the white Mills still we are at this time under very great Expence to suport the fameileys. It amounts to very Near £20 per week. I should sent the Cards before but I heard that you got the advance which I was very glad of when you write Direct for Jospeh Purcell Papermaker Maids[tone] to Be left at the White Lion Stone Street Maidstone

So I remain your Brother in Tread

Joseph Purcell

It seems unlikely that the resources of the workers' union would long be able to sustain expenditure at this rate.

---

[1] They also wanted a guarantee that in the event of their carrying it out and their men demanding an advance of wages on returning to work, the Kentish masters would, in turn, agree to close down their mills.

[2] Quoted in *Economica*, Feb. 1954, pp. 48–49.

[3] The letter, which is among the Balston MSS., is dated 20 May 1803, and is addressed to Mr. William Gill, paper-maker, originally sent to Whitchurch, Hampshire, and re-addressed to Downton, near Salisbury.

But the masters' success left its mark in the restrictive clauses of the 'Rules and Articles';[1] and it was also soon apparent that the journeymen were loath to accept the idea of a relief fund out of their own control. Before the inflation of these years had run its course, the men had contrived to raise their wages again.[2] And if the evidence of Thomas Gardner can be accepted as a confirmation of the sentiments quoted at the beginning of this chapter, they were able to maintain a considerable power in labour–capital relations. In connexion with the rule that there should be only one apprentice per vat, Gardiner agreed that 'the men have made the regulation and required that the masters agreed to it'. He admitted, too, that although there were more apprentices than this in some mills, journeymen sometimes refused to work because there were too many apprentices in a mill.[3]

These combinations of employers and of employees existed and led active lives irrespective of the Combination Laws. The general Acts of 1799 and 1800[4] apparently had no more effect on either side than had the special Act of 1796. Both sides were aware of the law. There may be some truth in the evidence offered to the 1825 Committee to the effect that the journeymen paper-makers knew little about the existence of the Combination Laws.[5] But certainly some of the trade did in 1804. An anonymous letter addressed to the 'Master Paper Makers, George and Vulture Tavern, Cornhill', in March of that year, referred to the current battle in Kent. Announcing

---

[1] It will be remembered that the clause concerning unacceptable apprentices was specifically dated from July 1803.

[2] See *infra*, p. 301.

[3] *Report from the Select Committee on Combination Laws*, Minutes of Evidence, p. 28.

[4] 39 Geo. III, c. 81, and 39 & 40 Geo. III, c. 106.

[5] *Report from the Select Committee on Combination Laws*, Minutes of Evidence, p. 31.

the journeymen's 'unalterable determination . . . not to submit by any means to your Arbitrary and Unjustifiable Articles and Resolutions', and intimating that they were ready 'at your Notice to serve upon the same Wages and Customs which they enjoyed before you discharged them', it adds with a flourish that 'the Amendment to the Combination Act expresses that Masters shall not combine to reduce Wages or lengthen the time of labour'.

The masters, for their part, were more than once reminded by their solicitor of the illegality of their activities. A letter written by Nathaniel Davies in March 1799 provides both a fitting comment on Adam Smith's observation that 'whoever imagines . . . that masters rarely combine is as ignorant of this world as of the subject' and an example of nice legal discretion:

. . . When I first had the Honour to be concerned for the Trade it struck me that the Meetings for the purpose of reducing the price of Rags and laying the Mills still (which had often been practised) were illegal and therefore took the opinion of Counsel on that point who concurring that such proceedings were illegal I submitted that opinion to a very numerous meeting of the Trade in the Yr. 1789 and to various subsequent meetings in that and the following year when they determined nevertheless to persevere in the usual mode of effecting a reduction, under the Idea, that as nobody would be injured by those measures that (they) could not conceive that any person would indict them and were therefore determined to run that risque. . . .

. . . Should it so happen from any extraordinary orders that the Market should not be sufficiently supplied with Paper (of which, however, I presume there is no fear) perhaps Government might take it up or as the Excise must evidently know (from the returns made to them) of the stoppage of the Mills and they thereby receiving a Temporary diminution (tho' I

admit in the end it would not be prejudiced) do you not think the Commissions of the Excise would take up the affair?
... Ps. ... I need not hint to you the Mischief which might arise from the resolutions getting into the hands of persons who are not well wishers to the Trade.

(iv)

The introduction of machinery brought to the masters a ready-made answer to the problem of labour relations. At the same time, by undermining the effectiveness of both societies, it brought an end to the war within the industry. It was not a sudden peace nor were both armies instantly disbanded. Change came at a rate commensurate with the spread of mechanization.

In 1812 John Bates of the Wycombe Marsh Mill, Buckinghamshire, writing to Balston about the high price of rags, remarked that he did not see what measures could be adopted to reduce them as 'it will be quite impracticable to suspend our works as we have formerly done on account of the great extension of the trade by machinery and the many new works which are daily carried on, the several proprietors of which we cannot expect will accede to such a measure'.[1]

This was a particularly pertinent summing-up of the position and a true pointer to the future. The masters' society lost the comprehensiveness—albeit limited—which it had enjoyed. It continued what was probably an increasingly tenuous existence for many years as an employers' association for the producers of hand-made paper.[2] A 'general and very numerous Meeting of the Master Paper Makers' was held at the 'George and Vul-

[1] Balston MSS.
[2] See *Reports of Meetings on Wages* (1873), and *Arbitration on Wages* (1874), *passim*.

ture' in March 1825.[1] The chairman then was James Smith, grandson of William Lepard and his successor at Hamper Mill, Watford, which was still then a vat mill.[2] The meeting related to prices and wages, and it is apparent that the resolutions passed referred to the vat trade only. There was to be a further meeting in May to which 'the attendance of the whole Trade is invited'. It seems improbable that the whole trade ever accepted the invitation.

The body of makers which met six years later had a rather different air about it. It described itself as 'A Meeting of the Manufacturers of Paper and Pasteboard in England and Wales held at the London Coffee House, on the 18th August 1831, John Dickinson, Esq. in the Chair.'[3] Its purpose was nothing less than to secure the repeal of the Excise duty, a desire which it reinforced with much reference to the woes of falling paper prices and the facts of a passing economic depression. It is hard to say how much continuity there was between this meeting and the earlier society. Certainly there were some links. Not only was James Smith one of those appointed to a committee for carrying out the purposes of the meeting, but the forty-nine names appended to the resolutions show once again a very marked concentration of manufacturers from the south-east. It was also noted that communications had been received from several manufacturers from distant parts of the kingdom approving of the objects of the meeting.

The reduction of the duties in 1836 marked at least a partial success for the makers, and thereafter what was probably a temporary organization faded away. With

[1] *Report from the Select Committee on Combination Laws*, Minutes of Evidence, p. 30.   [2] Lepard & Smith MSS.
[3] *Fourteenth Report* (1835), app. 73, pp. 180–1.

raw material prices falling, machine production expanding, and labour problems solved there was little or no
reason for a trade association. Competition prevailed
because economic conditions happened to favour it. The
interval of bliss was brief. In the 1850's rag prices began
to rise again, competition from overseas sharpened, the
ancient spectre of free trade had reappeared. If the tariff
walls were to be lowered, should not the Excise duties go
too? It was in such new circumstances that a fresh
impetus was given to the establishment of an employers'
association. Just as the problems of the later eighteenth
century had brought the Master Paper Makers into being
so did their closely related successors of the 1850's and
60's bring into being the Paper Makers Association,
which continues in existence today.

The movement to secure unanimity amongst the paper
manufacturers and to fashion a powerful lobby in the
matter of free trade, the Excise, and the foreign duties on
rags[1] was actively promoted by John Evans, the senior
partner in Dickinsons. At the end of our period he was
instrumental in founding the Paper Makers Association,
and was the first president both of it and of the Paper
Makers Club.[2] This movement, it has been said, 'did
much to remove that isolation among paper makers that
previously had been the rule'. If this statement, made by
Lewis Evans in 1896,[3] can be taken at its face value it

[1] See *infra*, Chap. XII.

[2] *The Endless Web*, pp. 103 and 117; *Firm of John Dickinson & Co. Ltd.*,
p. 20.

[3] It appears on p. 20 of *Firm of John Dickinson & Co. Ltd.*, which was in
fact written by Lewis Evans (see *Time and Chance*, p. 60 n.), son of Sir John
Evans.

It should perhaps be mentioned that a Stationers and Paper Makers
Provident Society had been started in 1840. The officers of this body and
main contributors to it included many eminent names in the industry, but
there is no reason to suppose that it represented anything in the way of an
active trade association (Wiggins, Teape MSS.).

offers a striking confirmation of the uncontrolled and competitive situation from roughly the 1820's to the 1850's and an equally striking contrast to the combinations and restrictions of the decades around the late eighteenth and early nineteenth centuries.

On the men's side the Original Society continued in being as an independent body up to very recent years.[1] It survived to exercise its jurisdiction, to enforce its rules and practices, and to provide its benefits to the employees in the hand-made mills. In this branch of the industry meetings to discuss wages and conditions continued to be held periodically between representatives of the Society and of the employers. The workers' success in getting a series of wage increases in the course of the century[2] in a slowly declining branch of the industry is a tribute to the effectiveness of the body. Spicer regards it as having reached the zenith of its power in the 1840's.[3] To judge by the employers' observation quoted at the beginning of this chapter it would seem probable, however, that its power was on the wane by the 1820's and 30's. The advent of machinery meant that in many mills it was no longer necessary to employ 'carded' labour, i.e. members of the Society who had 'Cards of Freedom' given to them after their seven-year apprenticeship. From 3,000 or so members in 1825 membership had fallen to 1,045 in 1847; in 1874 it had dropped to about 700, of which 420 worked in the nineteen vat mills which then remained in the country.[4]

The progress of trade unions in the machine branch

[1] It has now been absorbed by the National Union of Printing, Bookbinding, and Paper Workers.

[2] *Infra*, pp. 299–302.

[3] Spicer, p. 151. It has also been said that 'for a period of Twenty years after its foundation it wielded a power that was both feared and dreaded by the employers' (quoted Spicer, p. 157).

[4] *Report from the Select Committee on Combination Laws*, Minutes of Evidence, p. 26; Spicer, p. 156; *Arbitration on Wages* (1874), pp. 53–55.

of the industry seems to have been very slight before the later decades of the nineteenth century. The Original Society was essentially a craft union; it had few interests in common with the machine workers; and it does not seem to have made very effective attempts to include them. In 1853 a section of the Society split off to form a union for machine workers, calling themselves the United Brotherhood. This apparently enjoyed some limited success in increasing wages though its influence was, in general, slight, and by the later 1860's a further split in its membership had occurred.[1] It was not until the establishment of the National Union of Paper-Mill Workers in 1890 that a comprehensive union for the machine branch of the industry was launched.[2]

Meanwhile the power which machinery put into the hands of the employers combined with the essential restrictiveness of the Original Society to weaken such hold as the Society had ever had in the machine mills. As early as 1816 the journeymen paper-makers of Maidstone had petitioned the House of Commons, alleging distress amongst their ranks and laying the blame at the door of 'Fourdriniers Patent Machinery which requires but few hands to work it and those of little experience'. They asked for its suppression.[3] Some branches of the Society may also have ventured on to the dangerous paths of machine wrecking. There are records of riots at Two Waters in the early days[4] and of a foray in 1831 against the newly installed machinery of a Buckinghamshire mill; the ensuing battle ended in victory for the

---

[1] Spicer, pp. 157–60.

[2] Ibid.; also reports, accounts, &c., relating to this union, in the *Webb Trade Union Collection*, part B, vol. 73 (British Library of Political and Economic Science).

[3] *C.J.*, 1816, p. 130.

[4] Strachan, op. cit., in *The Paper Maker* (supplement), May 1931.

defenders and imprisonment for the attackers.[1] Quite apart from such drastic futility the efforts by the Original Society to force their rules in machine mills brought odium upon their members; and not unnaturally employers refused to employ Society men at higher wages when they could get the work done quite adequately at lower rates.

By 1874 a mere six of the 350 or so machine mills in the kingdom employed Society men at Society wages; these mills were all in Kent and they accounted for eighty out of the 280 members of the Society who worked in machine mills. The remaining 200, working outside Kent in 'mixed' mills, i.e. with both union and non-union men, accepted whatever rate of pay was current at the mill where they worked. At the six Kentish mills the Society secured the payment of wages appreciably higher than elsewhere and also enforced a closed shop. That there were only six such mills is hardly surprising; at one time twenty-two machine mills in the county had employed Society men.[2] It is perhaps more of a tribute to the employers' conservatism than to the power of the Society that those six mills should still have existed in 1874.

Kent was the home of the Original Society and it was there that it retained such control as it had over the machine mills. Elsewhere, though harried for a time by the power of this once formidable body, the machine industry was built up substantially with non-union labour. Throughout the central decades of the century there was indeed something like free competition on both sides of the industry, at least in that growing section of it which had been created by the Industrial Revolution.

[1] Spicer, p. 192.
[2] *Arbitration on Wages* (1874), pp. 53–55.

XI

Work and Wages

How many people worked in the industry? What did they earn? In what conditions did they work? To these simple but important questions it is difficult to find adequate answers for the first three centuries of the industry's existence in this country. Only with the appearance of the innumerable inquiries, committees, and commissions of the nineteenth century do such answers begin to be available. And even then they are not always as comprehensive or as continuous as could be wished. These shortcomings are apparent as soon as one seeks to answer the first of the questions.

(i)

The report on paper-mills submitted in 1865 to the Children's Employment Commission starts with an admission of failure: the author of the report had been unable to obtain an accurate estimate of the total numbers engaged in the industry.[1] He stated that the census of 1861 gave a figure of some 16,000 persons for England and Wales;[2] a firm of paper manufacturers had suggested 100,000 in the U.K.; a calculation by the author of the report, based on a trade directory and average employment in twenty-five of the mills which he had visited, produced a total of 63,000 in England and Wales. Four years earlier two other paper manufacturers had put total employment in the industry at 80,000 to

[1] *Children's Employment* (1865), p. 142.
[2] This is not strictly accurate; see *infra*, p. 289.

100,000; a third, John Dickinson, had been more
cautious and reckoned that in England alone, the total
was about 50,000, though included in this was 'the necessary employment the manufacture creates for artisans,
bricklayers, carpenters, smiths, millwrights, turners, wire
weavers, felt makers and engineers'.[1]
This would make Dickinson's estimate the nearest to
the census totals. There can be little doubt that the dis-
crepancies between the latter and other estimates based
on the total numbers employed at individual mills is
substantially accounted for by the work of the sorts of
persons that Dickinson mentions. They were not included
under paper manufacture in the census but under their
particular trades.

The three censuses of 1841, 1851, and 1861, give the
following totals:

TABLE XIX

*Total Employment in Paper Manufacture according to the Census
returns, 1841, 1851, and 1861 (U.K.)*

	1841	*1851*	*1861*
England and Wales . .	5,842	10,831	13,248
Scotland	1,466	3,424	4,421
G.B.	7,308	14,255	17,669
Ireland	713	751	402
U.K.	8,021	15,006	18,071

Source: The relevant census figures are derived as follows: 1841: *B.P.P.* 1843,
vol. xxiv; 1844, vol. xxvii, pts. 1 and 2; 1851: *B.P.P.* 1852–3, vol. lxxxviii, pts. 1
and 2; 1861: *B.P.P.* 1863, vols. liii, lx; 1864, vol. li.

It is not feasible to set earlier data against these figures:
the 1831 occupational census was not taken on a comparable basis; still earlier estimates[2] are little more than

---

[1] *Select Committee* (1861), pp. 58, 60, 62.
[2] For instance that in Chap. III, *supra*, p. 88.

guesswork. Within the decades covered by these figures the rate of expansion, assuming reasonable comparability between the censuses, was considerable; the English industry more than doubled its numbers, the Scottish multiplied over threefold.

What these figures do not show is the total employment which paper manufacture provided. Nor can they be used to calculate the average labour force of paper-mills. In 1845 seventeen Scottish mills employed an average of sixty-five persons each;[1] but in 1841 there were forty-eight mills in Scotland[2] and if this is divided into the figure for Scotland given in Table XIX, the result is only thirty per mill. Or, to take another example, the average number per mill at twenty-five English mills in 1865 was 180;[3] but dividing the 1861 census figure by the number of mills in England in 1861[4] produces the very different figure of forty-three per mill. Where between these extremes the truth lay it is not easy to say. Certainly the seventeen Scottish mills in 1845 and the twenty-five English in 1865 were biased towards the larger establishments.[5] Of the English mills eleven were in Kent and employed an average of 230 per mill; in 1861, however, the average for that county, working from the census data, would be about ninety-six per mill. It is perhaps worth noting that in this Kentish example of 1861–5 and the Scottish example of 1841–5 the ratio between average numbers per mill according to the sample and according to the census is about the same: 2·4 in Kent

---

[1] Calculated from figures given in the *New Statistical Account*, vol. i, pp. 44–45, 334, 609; vol. ii/2, p. 271; vol. vii/1, p. 442; vol. viii, pp. 27, 58, 127–8; vol. ix, pp. 672–3; vol. xii, p. 239.

[2] *B.P.P.* 1861, vol. lviii.

[3] *Children's Employment* (1865), *passim.*   [4] *B.P.P.* 1861, vol. lviii.

[5] The range of numbers of employees in the 25 English mills was from 42 to 631; for the Scottish, which accounted for a much larger proportion of the total number of Scottish mills, it was 25 to 150.

and 2·2 in Scotland. As a very rough approximation, then, it may be suggested that total employment offered by paper-mills was in the neighbourhood of twice that given by the census figures. This would bring employment in the United Kingdom in 1861 to 36,000; this is still well below Dickinson's estimate of 50,000 for England alone in that year, but it may at least suggest an extent to which the gap may reasonably be narrowed.

Neither the census figures nor Dickinson's estimate takes any account of a different range of occupations also dependent on the paper industry the numbers in which undoubtedly increased during these years. They may be broadly classed under three headings: those concerned with the collection and sale of rags, those processing paper in some way, for instance, making envelopes, boxes, or bags, and those dealing in paper, such as stationers, paper merchants, or even waste-paper dealers. In 1861 these together added another 17,000 for England and Wales. Doubling the census figure, to allow for all those, skilled and unskilled, who were in some way engaged in helping to produce paper but were otherwise recorded, and adding this 17,000, we are still left with only 43,000 for England and Wales in 1861 as in some way concerned with paper. Compared with the much larger number to which the textile and metal industries gave employment, this is small stuff.[1] But the paper industry is not and never has been a great employer of labour and its importance in the economy cannot be thus measured.

Although the occupational censuses are not very reliable indices of total numbers employed in the paper-

---

[1] In 1871 436,000 were employed in the cotton industry, 233,000 in the woollen and worsted industries, and 166,000 in iron-making (J. Clapham, *Economic History of Modern Britain* (Cambridge, 1932), vol. ii, p. 117).

mills of the country, they are of some value in revealing the ages and sexes of those whom they do record:[1]

TABLE XX

Employment by Age and Sex in Paper Manufacture (G.B.), 1841, 1851, 1861

	1841				1851				1861			
	Eng. & Wales		Scotland		Eng. & Wales		Scotland		Eng. & Wales		Scotland	
	Totals	%	Totals	%	Totals	%	Totals	%	Totals	%	Totals	%
Males, all ages .	4,533	77	728	50	6,143	57	1,265	37	7,638	58	1,648	37
Females, all ages .	1,309	23	738	50	4,688	43	2,159	63	5,610	42	2,773	63
TOTAL . .	5,842	100	1,466	100	10,831	100	3,424	100	13,248	100	4,421	100
of which:												
Males, under 20 .	618	10	126	9	2,155	20	493	14	3,002	23	456	10
Females ,, 20 .	389	7	252	18	2,493	23	1,395	40	3,105	23	1,148	26
TOTAL ,, 20 .	1,007	17	378	27	4,648	43	1,888	54	6,107	46	1,604	36

Source: The relevant census figures are derived as follows: 1841: *B.P.P.* 1843, vol. xxiv; 1844, vol. xxvii, pts. 1 and 2; 1851: *B.P.P.* 1852–3, vol. lxxxviii, pts. 1 and 2; 1861: *B.P.P.* 1863, vols. liii, lx; 1864, vol. li.

In general these figures tell the tale which one has learned to expect. The extension of mechanized manufacture brought increasing proportions of women and young persons into the factory. The relatively more extensive adoption of machinery in Scotland is revealed in the comparison of the English and Scottish figures in 1841. Both countries show a striking increase in the next decade; as the total numbers in the industry roughly doubled, so did the percentage of women and young persons, especially girls. So far so good. Thereafter the picture is less clear. Between 1851 and 1861 the proportion of males and females of all ages remained virtually the same. In England and Wales the percentage of boys and young men increased by some 3 per cent., that of

[1] Ireland has been omitted partly because comparable figures are not available and partly because the very small and declining numbers tend to confuse the general picture.

young women remaining the same. But in Scotland there was a decrease of 14 per cent. in the proportion of girls employed and 4 per cent. in that of males under 20 years of age.

The explanation of this apparent anomaly is in part a matter of numbers. The very much smaller total of mills and workers in Scotland meant that the actions of a few large employers could influence the general pattern far more readily than in England. Why, therefore, should the employers have acted in this way? It seems possible that this may have been due to the extremely rapid and extensive mechanization of the Scottish industry with the result that, in the first flush of enthusiasm, the proportion of children and young persons employed was too high to be compatible with efficiency. Humanitarian motives also played a part, notably in the actions of Messrs. Cowan & Co. Although it was not until 1868 that the industry came within the purview of the Factory Acts, Cowan had already decided not to employ children under 13 years of age as well as otherwise to restrict the employment of women and children.[1] As the largest paper-makers in Scotland their action would certainly have been influential in affecting the aggregate figures.

Within the general scene there were notable regional variations. Paper-mills in those counties with few other opportunities for industrial work, such as Devon or Kent, tended to have a comparatively high proportion of girls. Lancashire, by contrast, with the powerful magnet of the cotton-mills, had a much lower ratio. Or again, mills making high-grade paper had more use for young persons in the finishing process than did those making ordinary

[1] See *infra*, p. 313; the industry came within the Factory Acts through 30 & 31 Vic., c. 103. See B. L. Hutchins and A. Harrison, *A History of Factory Legislation* (London, 1926), p. 168.

printing- or wrapping-papers.[1] The numbers at particular ages also varied appreciably. As an example of the
distribution by age, sex, and job throughout a big
machine mill making writing-paper, the following
analysis may be taken as fairly representative for the end
of the period:

TABLE XXI

*Age, Sex, and Employment of the Staff of William Joynson's
Mill, St. Mary Cray, 1865*

Occupations	Ages			Totals
	Under 13	13–18	Over 18	
Males:				
Paper-making . .	9	18	77	
Finishing . . .	—	5	28	
Engineers, Carpenters,				
&c. . . .	—	1	15	
Glazing . . .	48	34	12	
Rag Store. . .	3	—	5	
Overlooker . .	—	—	1	
TOTAL MALES . .	60	58	138	= 256
Females:				
Glazing . . .	29	51	72	
Rag Cutting . .	6	33	184	
TOTAL FEMALES .	35	84	256	= 375
GRAND TOTALS . .	95	142	394	= 631

Source: Children's Employment (1865), p. 151.

In counties which had many mills and where many
were still turning over to machine production, the percentage of girls employed was continuing to rise through-

[1] Thomas Wrigley, of Bridge Hall Mills, Bury, put the matter thus in
1865:
'If the proportion of younger hands is less here than in the south, the only
reason is that they have a greater supply of young ones there; the factories
here take them as soon as they are able to work. . . . It may also be that more
children are required for folding in the south; we don't make fine writing
paper here' (*Children's Employment* (1865), p. 173).

out the 1850's and 60's. In Kent, for example, the numbers of females under 20 years in paper-mills rose from 21 per cent. to 31 per cent. between 1851 and 1861, in Buckinghamshire from 13 per cent. to 20 per cent., in the West Riding of Yorkshire from 18 per cent. to 21 per cent. In other areas, with fewer mills but comparatively extensive mechanization, it tended to decrease as in Scotland; in Northumberland, for instance, the proportions fell from 26 per cent. to 17 per cent. between 1851 and 1861, in Durham from 22 per cent. to 18 per cent.[1]

Some idea of the impact of this new source of work for young persons in mainly agricultural areas may be gauged from the following figures:

TABLE XXII

Employment in Paper-making, Somerset and Devon,
1841 and 1861

	(1) Total employed according to the Census returns	(2) Males and Females under 20 years	Percentage of (2) to (1)
Somerset			
(8 paper-mills in 1851) { 1841	131	14	11
1861	296	155	52
Devon			
(21 paper-mills in 1851) { 1841	334	44	13
1861	815	349	43

Source: The relevant census figures are derived as follows: 1841: *B.P.P.* 1843, vol. xxiv; 1844, vol. xxvii, pts. 1 and 2; 1861: *B.P.P.* 1863, vol. xliii, lx; 1864, vol. li. For number of mills in 1851: *B.P.P.* 1852, vol. li.

At a time when the already high proportion of young persons in the population was growing still higher, the introduction of such opportunities for employment was looked upon with general approval. Rising numbers in

---

[1] All figures calculated from Census returns.

the under-employed population of rural parishes were a portent, during the years of the Industrial Revolution, of still further increases in the already high poor rates. The answer to such a problem could only be migration or the appearance of new work on the spot. Paper-making was one of the trades which offered the latter opportunity, for much of its expansion was still in rural areas. As early as 1793 the minister of the parish of Currie, near Edinburgh, writing of the desirability of encouraging manufactures which employed both the young and the old, commented favourably on the paper-mills in his parish because they gave employment to both those categories of persons; it was particularly good that paper-making could give some employment to children between 10 and 12 years for this was '. . . a period when they can do nothing very laborious, and when their morals, from idleness and neglect, are very apt to be corrupted'.[1] Had the minister been alive a few decades later, he would perhaps have been overjoyed to see the far greater extent to which the new machine mills were able to put such children to work.

(ii)

Wages in the industry can be divided for present purposes into three main categories. First, the wages of the various skilled and semi-skilled men who were concerned with the main production processes; second, those of the women engaged in rag-cutting and sorting; third, the wages of the children and young persons doing sundry jobs about the mill.[2] The first of these categories has

[1] *Old Statistical Account*, vol. v, p. 323.

[2] These categories exclude any consideration of the wages paid to such persons as millwrights, blacksmiths, carpenters, labourers, and others employed about the mills but not directly concerned with production.

further to be divided into the wages of men in vat mills
and in machine mills. Comparison between the two is not
easy to make because of the complex wage structure in
the hand-made industry and the quite different tasks and
methods of payment in the machine industry. Certain
rather arbitrary assumptions have therefore to be made
in order to secure any sort of comparison of the changing
remuneration afforded to workers as the Industrial
Revolution left its mark.

Wages in vat mills cannot be examined in any detail
before the turn of the eighteenth century.[1] In 1792 James
Whatman was paying his vatmen 13s. 6d. per week for
a 12-hour day, together with 6d. per week beer money
and periodic gratuities of one or two guineas, made up
at Christmas to as much as seven guineas for a few
specially favoured men.[2] Taking these payments as
roughly equivalent to a weekly wage of about 15s. this
would put paper-makers' wages on a level similar to those
of other skilled craftsmen of the time.[3] But the weekly
wage is not a very suitable term in which to express the
pay of paper-makers, owing to the bases on which their
remuneration was calculated. They were paid by the
'day' of a conventional number of hours in which they
were to make agreed or conventional quantities of paper,
varying by type and weight. Moreover, by the 1790's,
if not earlier, they were certainly paid for overtime, so
that their effective earnings might regularly be appreciably greater than their nominal wages. The Kentish
maker, Clement Taylor, for example, was said at that
time to be paying his vatmen such rates for 'all over work

[1] Until sufficiently full wage statistics are discovered, such isolated figures
as I have found are inadequate for this purpose.
[2] Balston MSS.: Whatman to R. E. Philips, Dec. 1792.
[3] See E. W. Gilboy, *Wages in Eighteenth Century England* (Cambridge,
Mass., 1934).

made' that his vatmen were receiving anything from 18*s.*
to 30*s.* per week.[1]

The earliest statement, so far discovered, of the intri-
cate wage arrangements of the English industry dates
from 1803. In that year it was resolved by a meeting of
Kentish masters, held at the Bell Inn, Rochester, that
whatever 'Wages, Customs and Usages' then existed
should be abolished and that new rates should be adopted.
How far these new arrangements were put into operation
is not clear, but it is clear that a very similar wage structure did exist later, and it is probable that this differed
from whatever had existed before 1803 only in rates paid
and in small matters of detail. It may, then, be reasonably taken as representative of the wage arrangements
for skilled men in the vat trade. The rates were as follows:

	Class I	Class II	Class III
Vatman . . .	4*s.* 1*d.* per day	3*s.* 8*d.* per day	3*s.* 7*d.* per day
Coucher . . .	3*s.* 11*d.* ,, ,,	3*s.* 6*d.* ,, ,,	3*s.* 5*d.* ,, ,,
Layer and dry-worker	3*s.* 2*d.* ,, ,,	3*s.* 2*d.* ,, ,,	3*s.* 2*d.* ,, ,,

The classes referred to different types and sizes of paper.
For each sort of paper the amount to be made per 'day'
was set out; the day was to be not less than 10 hours,
exclusive of meals. The masters agreed to find work for
their men for six days per week and 'when short of water
to find them other employment equivalent thereto'—
a significant testimony to the vagaries of water-power.
Beer was provided or 1*s.* per week allowed instead; in
lieu of holidays each man was to be paid 5*s.* at Whitsun,
5*s.* 6*d.* at Easter, and 7*s.* 6*d.* at Christmas. Overtime was
to be paid at full rates.[2]

---

[1] Balston MSS.

[2] Ibid. The resolutions are printed in full in *William Balston—Paper-
Maker*, app. iii, pp. 159–63.

The increases on these rates which were secured in the course of our period were striking. The following refer to Kent only:

TABLE XXIII

Vatmen's Daily Wages in Kent, 1792–1865

	Class I	Average classes I & III	Beer money per week	Hours per 'day'	Extras
1792	(2s. 3d.)		6d.	(12)	Money gratuities.
1803	4s. 1d.	3s. 10d.	1s.	10	..
1824	4s. 6d.	4s. 1d.	..	..	..
1840	4s. 7d.	4s. 4d.	2s.	7½	Some alterations in day's
1853	4s. 11d.	4s. 8d.	2s.	8	work; all rates brought into class I; certain in-
1865	5s. 3d.		2s.	8½	creased allowances.

Sources: 1792 (Whatman's mill only): Balston MSS.; 1803: Rochester resolutions, Balston MSS.; 1824: *Select Committee on Combination Laws*, Minutes of Evidence, pp. 26–32; 1840, 1853, and 1865: *Report of Meetings on Wages* (1873), pp. 17 et seq. and *Arbitration on Wages* (1874), p. 33.

Rates in other parts of the country were appreciably lower. In Scotland a daily wage of 1s. 10d. rose to 2s. 2d. in 1796; in North Wales a mill foreman's wages were only 24s. per week in 1843. Weekly wages in English counties other than Kent were said to be 5s. to 7s. less than those in Kent in 1825; certainly in 1851 a vatman in class I outside Kent received only 3s. 11d. per day, with no beer allowance, as compared with the Kentish 4s. 7d. and beer allowance. After 1853, however, the Kentish wages were extended to other areas.[1]

Before further considering the circumstances attending these increases, a word must be said about earnings as distinct from wages. Overtime was normal. By the middle

[1] Balston MSS.; *Selected Committee on Combination Laws* (1825), Minutes of Evidence, pp. 29 and 31; *Children's Employment* (1843), p. t 5; *Reports of Meetings on Wages* (1873), pp. 16–18.

of the century it was apparently usual to work an '8-day' week, i.e. about 68 hours per week.[1] For a vatman on class I, in Kent, this would mean weekly earnings, including beer money, of 38s. 8d. in 1840 and 44s. in 1865. At about the same time, in 1867, the average agricultural earnings in the neighbouring county of Sussex were about 16s. 6d. per week.[2]

English urban wages are estimated to have increased by 61 per cent. between 1790 and 1860, London artisans' wages by 62 per cent. between 1782 and 1865.[3] By contrast Kentish vatmen's wages rose by 133 per cent. between 1792 and 1865. If, however, the wages in 1803 and 1865 are compared, then the rise is 37 per cent.[4] for the paper-makers and 38 per cent. for the London artisans. This emphasis upon the increase secured at the beginning of the period is a pointer to the twin foundations upon which was built the course of wage increases in the hand-made branch of the industry. It rested, first, upon the power of the men's Union during that crucial decade of rising prices in the Napoleonic war period; and, second, upon the subsequent gradual and successful adaptation of the vat trade to the new situation created by the advent of machinery, the vat trade moving into a specialized position in the industry as a whole. The other side of this medal of the high wages which the Original Society was able to secure was the Society's dwindling

---

[1] *Report of Meetings on Wages* (1873), p. 17, and *Arbitration on Wages* (1874), p. 33.

[2] A. L. Bowley, *Wages in the United Kingdom in the Nineteenth Century* (Cambridge, 1900), p. 43.

[3] G. H. Wood, 'The Course of Average Wages between 1790 and 1860', *Economic Journal*, vol. ix (1899), and R. S. Tucker, 'Real Wages of Artisans in London, 1729–1935', *Journal of the American Statistical Association*, vol. xxxi (1936).

[4] Taking the average of class I and class III; 29 per cent. taking class I only.

membership; a few hundred men only were earning these wages and they were in an industry which was becoming economically separated from its mechanized relative.

During the period of its ascendancy the men's organization was successful in securing wage increases when the cost of living was rising and sometimes in frustrating attempts by the employers to reduce wages at times of depression. According to Spicer the workers had succeeded in the second of these tasks in 1784 and 1797. In evidence given before the Commons in 1796 one of the employers stated that he had to give an increase in pay to the extent of 3s. to 4s. in 1795; it was a demand for a further increase which precipitated the strike and the Combination Act of that year. A further advance was secured in March 1801. During the next few years the rate of increase in general prices slackened and the employers succeeded in reducing wages. The rates given in the 1803 Rochester resolutions formed part of the masters' attempt to deal with the men's power, so they may well represent a reduction in the rates then prevailing; Spicer states that a slight reduction was effected in 1806. A further sharp increase in prices up to the end of the war brought another strike and the replacement of the wage cut. A sharp temporary increase in prices in 1825 brought a further rise in wages. Thereafter pay stayed at the same level until 1853 and 1865 when small increases were negotiated between the Original Society and the employers.[1]

Thus did the renumeration of this powerful, though

[1] *C.J.*, vol. li, 1795–6, pp. 585–6, 595; *Report from the Committee on the Booksellers' and Printers' Petition* (*B.P.P.* 1801–2, vol. ii), pp. 97–98; Spicer, pp. 150–1; Balston MSS.; *Select Committee on the Combination Laws* (1825), Minutes of Evidence, pp. 28–29; *Report of Meetings on Wages* (1873), pp. 17 et seq.

contracting group of skilled artisans, remain at a high level during these years. They were undoubtedly amongst the best-paid workers of the time, being roughly on a level with those of engineers, millwrights, and mechanics. Their skill, their union, and the adaptation of their branch of manufacture to the changing circumstances of the time combined to prevent them sinking into poverty and destitution as did the hand-loom weavers or similar wretched survivors of an earlier form of industry.

The workers in the new machine mills derived an initial advantage from the high existing wages of the vat mills. When it came to be decided what pay to offer workmen in the first machine mills, it was probably thought that it should be such as to attract them from the vat mills. Paper was paper however it was made; technical problems arose to which the skilled paper-maker might be thought to know the answers; however different the hand and machine processes were later seen to be, it is unlikely that the employers in the first machine mills would have gone entirely outside the existing industry for the recruitment of their staff. In the statement about the machine issued by the patentees in 1806,[1] men's wages are put at a level similar to those paid in the vat mills, even slightly higher. Vatmen are put at 3s. 3d. per day[2] and journeymen in machine mills at 3s. 6d.; the range in men's weekly wages ran from 15s. to 21s. In the 1820's men's wages in machine mills in Northumberland and Durham ranged from 14s. to 30s. per week, and in Lancashire from 21s. to 30s. per week.[3] Just after the end of the period with which we are concerned, in the 1870's, the wages of machine men in the great majority of mills

---

[1] *Fourdrinier Committee* (1837), app. A, p. 43.
[2] Cf. the comparable Kent wages given in Table XXIII.
[3] *Children's Employment* (1843), p. l 33.

which did not employ union labour averaged about 5*d*.
per hour or 25*s*. per week assuming a 60-hour week or
30*s*. on a 72-hour week.[1]

A very approximate comparison can be made between
these wages and those paid in the hand-made branch of
the industry. The non-Kent vatmen's wage of 23*s*. 6*d*.
per week in 1851 or the general Society rate for vatmen
in 1865 of 33*s*. 6*d*. and in 1872 of 36*s*. 6*d*.[2] all seem to
compare favourably with the machine men's wages. The
very small number of men in machine mills at the end of
the period who were being paid union rates were getting
7*d*. per hour as machine men;[3] and this figure, as might
be expected, meant a weekly wage roughly equivalent
to that of the vatmen. Thus, although not normally so
high as in the vat mills, the wages paid to men in the
machine mills were not very far behind, a state of affairs
which evidently owed much to the situation inherited
from the heyday of the Original Society. In spite of the
fact that many employers refused to hire union labour
and that such major figures in the industry as John
Dickinson and William Joynson resolved to train up their
own men,[4] it is clear that the machine mills needed many
skilled men who had to be paid at rates above the general
level of industrial wages of the time. Moreover, in spite
of a reduction in wages made some time before 1835,[5] the
non-unionized machine men succeeded in raising their

---

[1] *Arbitration on Wages* (1874), p. 55.

[2] These weekly wages are calculated on the basis of 6 days at 3*s*. 11*d*.,
6 days at 5*s*. 3*d*.+2*s*. beer money, and 6 days at 5*s*. 9*d*.+2*s*. beer money
respectively. The weekly earnings were normally greater than this, as an
'8-day' week was worked (*Report of Meetings on Wages* (1873), p. 18).

[3] *Arbitration on Wages* (1874), p. 55.

[4] See *supra*, p. 236. In 1865 Joynson stated that all those in his employment were 'of his own breeding' (*Children's Employment* (1865), p. 152; see
also *Arbitration on Wages* (1874), pp. 46 and 57).

[5] *Fourteenth Report* (1835), p. 111.

wages in the late decades of our period, roughly to the same extent as did the Society men in the vat mills.

Evidence on this last point is not readily available for England, but the following figures for Scotland may serve to illustrate change over time. They also indicate the marked regional difference in the general level of wages as between the two countries and especially as between Scotland and Kent:

TABLE XXIV

Wages of Men in Machine Mills, Scotland 1840–66

Date	Range	Crude averages	
		per week	*per day*
1840–2 . . .	10 to 18s.	14s.	2s. 4d.
1845 . . .	9 to 22s.	15s. 6d.	2s. 7d.
1850 . . .	13 to 18s.	15s. 6d.	2s. 7d.
1855–7 . . .	14 to 19s.	16s. 6d.	2s. 9d.
1858–60 . .	15 to 20s.	17s. 6d.	2s. 4d.
1861–6 . . .	12 to 22s.	17s.	2s. 10d.

Source: Calculated from figures in *New Statistical Account*, vol. i, pp. 44–45; vol. ii/2, p. 271; vol. vii/1, p. 442; vol. viii, pp. 27, 127–8; vol. ix, pp. 672–3; Spicer, app. x. The figures almost all relate to mills in the Edinburgh area.

Although the samples at each date are not homogeneous and comparison cannot be pushed to strict limits, these figures suggest an increase of roughly 20 per cent. between the 1840's and 60's. This is approximately the same as in the indices of English urban wages and London artisans' wages mentioned earlier; it is also approximately the same as the increase achieved by the Society at that time.[1]

Between the wages paid to these men, all skilled in varying degrees, and those earned by women, young persons, and children there was a substantial gap.

[1] Although the Society men did also achieve certain other advantages (see Table XXIII).

In vat and machine mills alike the wages earned by the women and girls who did most of the rag-sorting, dusting, and cutting varied from 4*s*. 6*d*. to 7*s*. per week, according to area and to age of worker. The job was normally paid on piece-rates. In the 1840's, for example, Scottish mills were paying piece-rates by which women earned from 9*d*. to 1*s*. 3*d*. per day as rag-cutters; girls of about 16 years of age at the Scotswood mill, Northumberland, were being paid at 1*s*. to 1*s*. 6*d*. per cwt. which amounted to about the same earnings; in North Wales, however, a girl of 17 was only making 3*s*. 6*d*. to 4*s*. per week at rag-cutting; similarly lower rates held for mills in Ireland. Kentish wages were rather higher than those of other areas, though the difference was not so marked as in the wages of skilled men. Nor, similarly, was there so marked a rise in these wages in the course of time: Scottish rag-cutting wages rose from about 7*s*. to almost 8*s*. per week between the 1840's and the 1860's.[1]

Youths were also employed in both vat and machine mills either as apprentices or as assistants to the 'beatermen' who tended the beating-engines. Wages here varied according to age and ability, as well as regionally. They ranged from 5*s*. to 13*s*. near London, less elsewhere.[2]

A few children of both sexes were sometimes employed in vat mills. In John Gater's mill in Hampshire in 1843, for instance, three girls assisted by two boys about 14 years old were working at the hot-pressing of hand-made papers. The girls were paid by the piece, the boys by the day—a nice distinction. Their earnings were respectively about 6*d*. and 8*d*. per day.[3]

[1] On women's wages see *New Statistical Account*, vol. i, pp. 44–45; vol. ii/2, p. 271; vol. vii/1, p. 442; vol. viii, pp. 27, 127–8; vol. ix, pp. 672–3; *Children's Employment* (1843), pp. a 1–19, G 24–25, k 195, l 32–35, t 4; Spicer, app. x.
[2] *Children's Employment* (1843), p. A 5.
[3] Ibid., p. r 9–10.

The much greater number of children employed in the machine mills worked not only at the glazing and cutting machinery but also at sorting paper and assisting men in tending the Fourdrinier machines. Table XXI showed something of the distribution of children in a mill making writing-paper in the 1860's. In the 1840's a different sort of mill, Hilton's at Over Darwen, Lancashire, employed about 300 persons in making paper from cotton-mill sweepings; it had 45 of the 52 children and young persons distributed thus:[1]

	Males		Females	
	No.	*Range in age*	*No.*	*Range in age*
Initial preparation of raw materials	4	9–15 years	3	11–13 years
Machinery used in further preparation and pulping . . .	6	10–17 ,,	1	17 ,,
Paper-making machine . .	9	15–17 ,,		—
Paper-cutting machine . .	6	9–14 ,,	1	13 ,,
Sorting paper		—	15	10–17 ,,
	25	9–17 ,,	20	11–17 ,,

For this work wages were then about 2s. 6d. to 3s. per week for children (12 and under) and 4s. to 7s. for young persons (13–18 years), although as shown already among the latter youths sometimes earned more according to age and ability as apprentices or the like.[2] By the 1860's wages had risen; children earned about 3s. to 5s., young persons 7s. to 9s. per week, apprentices from 6s. to 15s.[3] With the exception of apprentices the wages were almost always paid as piece-rates. In general they seemed to be about the same as comparable earnings in other industries, rather higher than those in such sweated trades as the metal industry of the Black Country. In 1843 a

[1] *Children's Employment* (1843), pp. M 66–67.
[2] Ibid., pp. M 66–67, also pp. G 59–61; rather higher rates prevailed near London.   [3] Ibid. (1865), p. 142 and *passim*.

14-year-old rag-cutter in Midlothian, remarking that her father was a weaver, added: 'I can weave, but not earn so much as I can by rag-work.'[1] She made about 1s. per day. Her views may well have been shared by many another child of a poor weaver.

Family earnings are often more deserving of our attention than individual wages. Just as the industry had often been almost a hereditary business in the past, so it became not at all uncommon to find whole families working in the mill. The advent of machinery widened the scope already existing. Gater stated, for example, that all the children employed at his vat mill were of the families of men working in the concern; at the Killeen Mills, near Dublin, a 15-year-old rag-cutter had her father and mother as well as a brother and sister all working in the mill; the Dickinson mills provide several examples of similar arrangements and of the growth of virtual dynasties of workers. Married women and their daughters regularly worked together in the rag-cutting rooms; one such woman and her two daughters, aged 13 and 17, working at South Darenth Mill, Kent, earned over 27s. per week between them in the 1860's; the joint earnings of a family at another mill were 75s. weekly.[2]

When John Dickinson's daughter commented in a letter on the gloom and distress of that grim year 1848, she wrote in revealing terms of workers in general and of her father's paper-mill workers in particular:[3]

Every year seems to accumulate luxury on the one hand and distress and misery on the other. Who can wonder if even a false hope of bettering their conditions should tempt the famishing multitude from their duty? On the whole we do not

[1] Ibid. (1843), p. k 4.
[2] Ibid., pp. G 24, r 10; ibid. (1865), pp. 150, 154 and *passim*; *The Endless Web*, p. 95 and apps. A, B, and C.
[3] Quoted in *Time and Chance*, p. 74.

have to witness much distress here. Papa's Mills give employment to so many, and the people in this village having both better and more regular pay than the agricultural labourers, get many little comforts about them and are not reduced to starvation on the first disaster. You see books on their tables and muslin blinds in their windows, very often, and altogether a degree of civilization about the place which is very comforting to witness. I should be miserable if the wealth that built this house had been made by 'grinding the faces of the poor'. As it is we know the very prosperity of this part of the country is bound up in the prosperity of our Mills. . . .

Amongst the workers of this industry it was not poverty, by the standards of the time at least, that fashioned family life or determined the conditions of work.

(iii)

The paper industry emerges from the inquiries of 1843 and 1865[1] with an extremely good record. Its buildings were, in general, airy and commodious; they were situated 'in the most beautiful and healthy situations through nearly the whole kingdom'.[2] Many of its employers were 'men of superior intelligence and education'.[3] Boys and girls in the industry were generally better fed, better clothed, and healthier than in other industries. There is no evidence of the brutality of adult workers to children which is so readily encountered in the reports on other trades. 'I have not,' wrote W. H. Lord, reporting on the paper industry to the Commis-

---

[1] The two reports, with their accompanying minutes of evidence, of the Commissioners on the Employment of Children and Young Persons, provide the main source of information on the lives and labours of paper-mill workers in this period. Supplemented by other sorts of evidence they can tell much that goes beyond the relatively narrow limits of the Commission's main subject.

[2] *Children's Employment* (1843), p. 5.   [3] Ibid. (1865), p. 148.

sioners in 1865, 'speaking generally, in any manufactories, seen a happier looking lot of children.'[1] Their
average state of education—low as it was and only too
often a bare literacy—was higher than in other trades;
their parents, who so often also worked in the industry,
were relatively well paid; at a few mills both housing and
schooling were provided by employers for their workers
and their children.

This rosy glow of diffused virtue needs some light and
shade. If we fill in some of the details and try to see
some of the changes wrought, we may get a more balanced
picture.

Of working conditions in the many tiny mills of the
earlier centuries, or indeed of the early nineteenth century, little is known. But it is not unreasonable to assume
that some of the adverse comments on the older mills,
made in the two reports, are relevant here. In all mills,
small or large, old or new, the most unattractive and
unhealthy places were the rooms where the rags were
sorted and cut. Amongst the Kentish mills, some new
but many of them old in 1843, 'the rag houses differ very
much, many of them being lofty, large and, where the
finer sorts of paper are made, very clean, as the rags are
much less foul; others low and narrow'. Though ventilation of sorts was provided, in those mills where very dirty
rags were used 'a hurricane blowing through them would
fail in clearing the abominably dense atmosphere of
heavy dust'. In general, ventilation was tolerable, if
hardly very efficient, though some exceptions to this were
noted in Northumberland and Durham.[2] Twenty years
later, in spite of improvements in the techniques of
dusting rags, the same broad picture was painted: some
mills were clean, spacious, and well-ventilated, but 'others,

[1] Ibid. (1865), p. 147.   [2] Ibid. (1843), p. 41.

especially those of older date are very much the reverse; close, crowded, dirty and hot'.[1]

Many parts of paper-mills were, and still are, hot and steamy. No great harm seems to have arisen from this, in spite of temperatures of 90° F. or more,[2] though rheumatism was not uncommon among those working in these conditions. The dust and dirt of the rag rooms seems to have had varying effects upon the workers. In some it probably gave rise to, or aggravated, respiratory troubles, such as asthma, bronchitis, or tuberculosis; in others it caused merely temporary irritations. There were also those who seemed quite unaffected, like the women rag-cutters of a mill near Wigan who said they preferred the work to that in cotton-mills, in hay-making, and even to 'charing and doing house-work'.[3] The work of the paper-makers themselves in vat mills was heavy and tiring, involving as it did continual bending and lifting over warm, steamy pulp. It was here that, as might be expected, rheumatism was complained of, as well as dyspepsia and bronchitis. Yet both these workers and their successors in the machine mills were generally regarded as a healthy and long-lived section of the artisan class. Though not especially robust, they were, as a Fife-shire surgeon put it in 1841, 'usually tolerably healthy . . . generally respectable and rather temperate'. By contrast he spoke of most cotton spinners and printers as being prematurely decayed by 45 years of age, of iron-smelters, moulders, and smiths as short-lived and intemperate, of glass-blowers dying of asthma and debility at an early

[1] *Children's Employment* (1865), pp. 142–3.
[2] It is interesting, perhaps, to speculate how much these conditions were responsible for the important part earlier played in the workers' arrangements by wine-drinking in France and beer-drinking in England (see *supra*, pp. 261, n. 1, 297–8.).
[3] *Children's Employment* (1865), p. 174.

age, and the poverty-stricken and numerous hand-loom weavers as worst afflicted of all in health.[1]

Perhaps the most unpleasant feature of working conditions in paper-mills during this period of early mechanization was the prevalence of accidents arising from unfenced or inadequately fenced machinery and from tiredness or carelessness by employees. The numbers of accidents varied from mill to mill. They were said to have decreased between 1843 and 1865, but no statistics were quoted to support this. The author of the 1865 report told of many accidents and confessed himself incredulous of some of the assurances which he received when he observed the amount of unprotected shafting and gearing about some mills.[2] In the mills of the Home Counties and of Lancashire accidents were reported as not uncommon in the 1840's; children employed at cutting or glazing had their fingers cut off, hands crushed or jammed between cog-wheels or caught in moving belts; in the West of England such accidents were described as 'extremely frequent'. Accidents of this sort sometimes, though less frequently, happened to adults; some ended in amputations, some were fatal. Here the record is not very good, though by comparison with the frequency and seriousness of accidents in collieries it was good indeed.[3]

The hours, long by modern standards, which were worked in paper-making as in other industries, were followed by children and young persons as well as by adults. The hours varied from area to area, from mill to mill, even from department to department in the mill: vat crews in hand-made mills worked a shorter day than those tending machines; rag-cutters than those at the

[1] Ibid. (1843), pp. b 59–60, k 5–7, m 73.
[2] Ibid. (1865), p. 147.
[3] Ibid. (1843), pp. 93, D 4, M 73–74.

beating-engines. But, as we have already noted, overtime was common in all mills, vat and machine, and the effective working day probably averaged about 12 hours for most people. In this was included a time for meals which varied from a 1½-hour break to merely eating whilst still at work. The use of machinery brought continuous production and the development of various sorts of shifts arrangements for workers tending that machinery. Broadly speaking, three sorts of shift schemes came to be worked: 12 hours on and 12 hours off, usually from 6 a.m. to 6 p.m. and vice versa; 24 hours on and 24 hours off; and an intermediate arrangement by which those at the beaters did their 12- or 24-hour shifts and those on the machines worked a day of 15 or 16 hours' duration.

As a result of the frequent overtime children and young persons were at work at the cutting-machines or glazing-rolls from 12 to 16 hours at a time. Such arrangements were true of mills in the 1840's and in the 1860's.[1] At Annandale's Polton Mill, Lasswade, near Edinburgh, in 1842, girls of 10 and 12 years, taking paper out of the machine or from the cutter, normally worked short shifts of 12 hours from 6 a.m. to 6 p.m. and two long shifts per week of 18 hours from 6 a.m. to 12 p.m.; twenty-five years later a girl of 12 working in the glazing-room at Joynson's mill remarked that she periodically worked from 7 a.m. to 9 p.m. and the last time she did so was for a fortnight.[2] Examples could be multiplied from all over the country for all ages and both sexes.

Those who reported for the Children's Employment Commission commented adversely on these hours. But as was pointed out by Major J. G. Burns, reporting on

---

[1] On hours of work generally see *Children's Employment* (1843), pp. 63–64 and *passim* and ibid. (1865), pp. 144–6 and *passim*.
[2] Ibid. (1843), pp. k 4–5; ibid. (1865), p. 152.

paper-mills in 1843, 'as the greater part of it is over-work, and paid for as such, it is doubtful how far they or their parents would relish any legislative restriction, as the consequence would of necessity entail a diminution of profit'.[1] Many employers also found this a good reason for thinking likewise. 'The prohibition of our night work would stop our works and prevent the boys from their trade', complained Mr. Ladell of Ladell & Ibotson of Wraysbury Mill; or there was the authentic note of thunder from Mr. Venables of Taplow Mill: '. . . the present Government, having done all that can be done to injure and ruin the papermaking trade in the United Kingdom by the protection and assistance given to the foreign manufacturer, any further interference would be unjust and arbitrary in the extreme, and uncalled for'.[2]

But other manufacturers thought otherwise and some-times acted otherwise. It was, significantly enough, often the bigger employers who curtailed the hours of their younger workers, built schools, provided houses for their employees, and encouraged them in more humane and civilizing ways. Cowans in Scotland restricted the hours worked by children in their mills to 10 and, in the 1840's, refused to employ children under 13 years of age; they insisted on certain standards of education, maintained an infant school for the children of their workmen and an evening school at which all boys had to attend from 13 years until they were 21; ran a benefit society for the women; and did not normally employ women who had young children. Thomas Wrigley expressed the view that night work could be avoided: it was 'a mere question of capital, of extra hands and additional machinery'; he saw no reason why paper-mills should be exempt from factory legislation. Balstons in the 1860's required that no girls

[1] Ibid. (1843), p. A 7.   [2] Ibid. (1865), p. 164.

under 18 years should work more than 12 hours per day. In Hertfordshire, Dickinson, his wife, and later his partner John Evans, founded schools in the villages adjoining their mills; William Joynson built Sunday and day-schools at St. Mary Cray. In Devon C. R. Collins's Hele Mills had a system of compulsory schooling for the younger hands.[1]

Such were some of the enterprising and enlightened employers. Their example might perhaps have come earlier or gone farther; it was hardly enough. Factory legislation came to paper-mills and compulsory education gradually arrived on the English scene. Ignorance was not simply a product of poverty. Sometimes, especially where comparatively extravagant habits formed amongst the better-off artisans, it was in inverse relationship to poverty. The proprietor of Scotswood Mill, Northumberland, commented in 1842, for instance, that it was often the lower paid men who send most children to school whilst a worker with nine children, himself making 30s. and with family earnings of £3–4 per week, did not send any of them to school.[2] This was probably not so very exceptional in the industry,[3] and it will serve to emphasize the point that it was not simply a class of avid capitalists eager to exploit the cheap labour of children who were responsible for sustaining long hours of industrial labour at tender ages, and all that that implied. In the long run it needed the intervention of the State, moved by the activities of enlightened men, to change things which, long sanctioned in the past, were intolerable in the changed conditions of industrialized life.

---

[1] *Children's Employment* (1843), pp. k 1–2; ibid. (1865), pp. 150, 152, 159, 173, 178, 179; *The Endless Web*, pp. 60, 89.
[2] *Children's Employment* (1843), pp. l 32–33.
[3] Cf. the similar example given in ibid. (1865), p. 150.

PART III

THE END OF A PERIOD

XII

Free Trade and the End of the Paper Duties

(i)

THE bare skeleton of change in the rates of taxation, both Customs and Excise, during the first sixty years of the nineteenth century, is exhibited in Tables XXV and XXVI.[1]

TABLE XXV

*Import Duties (net) on Paper, Board, and Rags, 1802–61**

Date	Paper Class I per lb.	Paper Class II per lb.	Board per cwt.	Rags per ton	Act
1802	1s. 0½d.	6¼d.	£2. 2s.		42 Geo. III, c. 94
1803	1s.	6d.	£2. 2s.	15s. 9d.	43 Geo. III, c. 68
1803			all, + 12½%		43 Geo. III, c. 70
1804			all, + further 12½%		44 Geo. III, c. 53
1809	1s. 4d.	8d.	£2. 17s. 4d.	{ In Brit. ships £1. 1s. 8d. / in for. ships £1. 3s.	49 Geo. III, c. 98
1813			all, + 25% or 66 2/3%†		53 Geo. III, c. 33
1819	1s. 7d.	10d.	£3. 8s. 2d.	{ in Brit. ships £1. 6s. / in for. ships £1. 10s.	59 Geo. III, c. 52
1825	9d.	3d.	£3. 8s. 2d.	5s.	6 Geo. IV, c. 111
1840			all + 5%		3 & 4 Vic., c. 17
1842	4¼d. + 5%	3d. + 5%	£1. 10s. + 5%	6d. + 5% (pulp of rags 5s. + 5%)	5 & 6 Vic., c. 47
1845				FREE (rags and pulp of rags)	8 & 9 Vic., c. 90
1853	2½d.	2½d.			16 & 17 Vic., c. 106
1860	16s. per cwt.		15s. & 16s.		23 & 24 Vic., c. 110
1861	FREE				24 Vic., c. 20

* Applies to U.K. from 1826; Irish tariff separate before that date.

† 66 2/3% if product of France or of territory under French control.

The forces which bore upon these bastions of long-established taxation and finally, in the name of Free Trade, brought about their downfall, were broadly three in number. First, there was the agitation of the paper

[1] For details of the difference between class I and class II paper see *infra*, p. 322.

manufacturers themselves. They did not always speak with a single voice; they were not convinced Free Traders; they naturally wanted that amount of freedom which was most agreeable to themselves and they formed to this end a moderately powerful lobby. Second, there was the body of agitation aimed against what came to be called the

TABLE XXVI

Excise on Paper and Board, 1802–61 *

Date	Paper		Board† per cwt.	Act
	Class I per lb.	Class II per lb.		
1802 .	3d.	1½d.	£1. 1s.	42 Geo. III, c. 94
1803 .	3d.	1½d.	£1. 1s.	43 Geo. III, c. 69
1836 .		1½d.		6 & 7 Wm. IV, c. 52
1840 .		1½d.+5%		3 & 4 Vic., c. 17
1861 .		Free		24 Vic., c. 20

* Applies to U.K. from 1826. Irish Excise charged on different basis before then.
† Slight changes in rates for boards of different types, 1816–36 not shown.

'Taxes on Knowledge', being mainly the newspaper tax but also including the paper duties. This was a force in which the troops were mixed: amongst the ranks were Radical agitators, economists, publishers, and printers, and a miscellaneous collection of persons to whom the exactions of the State were odious in principle and unprofitable in practice. Finally, there was the government or, to be more precise, the various governments in power during these years. In those governments were men who brought to bear upon the particular problems of revenue and taxation, as upon financial and commercial policy in general, the tenets of Adam Smith and his successors. It was ultimately the legislation initiated by Huskisson, Peel, and Gladstone which banished the paper duties.

To examine the course of change it will be convenient

to split the period into roughly two parts: before the 1825 tariff Act and the 1836 Excise reduction; and thereafter.

(ii)

The level of the import duties on paper, as on most goods during the early decades of the century, had been dictated almost entirely by the needs of war finance. The duties remained at the same level and in the same form as they had been put in 1794[1] until 1802, when, like the Excise, they were cast in the simplified form shown in Table XXV. In the following year the import duty on rags which had been repealed in 1725 was brought back under the stress of the revenue needs of the day. Then both rag and paper import duties were subject to a series of increases: in 1803 and 1804 amounting to 25 per cent.; in 1809 a consolidation at the old or permanent duty plus a flat rate increase known as the War or Temporary duty, amounting in practice to a net increase of $33\frac{1}{3}$ per cent. on the old rate; in 1813 a further supposedly temporary increase of 25 per cent. (or $66\frac{2}{3}$ if from French territory). After the war the temporary expedients were made permanent; and three years later the then existing duties were repealed and the war-time increases incorporated in new flat rates, representing a total increase of about 58 per cent. in seventeen years.

It was not until Huskisson went to the Board of Trade that the work of thinning out the tariff jungle, started under Pitt, was resumed. It was as a part of his reforms that the import duties on paper and rags were substantially reduced in 1825. At the same time the separate Irish tariff system was swept away and all duties assimilated to a single United Kingdom tariff.

This first step in the lowering of the protective wall

[1] For details see *supra*, p. 136.

around the industry did not, so far as I have been able
to ascertain, call forth any noteworthy protests from the
manufacturers. Nor indeed is it very likely that it would.
The new machinery was putting them well ahead of
their overseas rivals; the volume of their export trade
being slight compared with the growing home market,
they were not particularly interested in the possibility of
reciprocal tariff reductions; and, moreover, they were
still left with a very substantial protective differential
between Customs and Excise.

Reference has already been made[1] to the doubling of
the Excise rates in 1801 and the ensuing battle which was
concluded by their reduction. In 1802 they assumed the
form and the rates as set out in Table XXVI, and with
minor alterations thus remained until 1836. Meanwhile
the Irish duty had been brought into line in 1824.[2] Since
its first imposition in 1798 the Irish Excise on paper had
been payable either on the same lines as in England or
by means of an assessment on the capacity of the beating-
engine. The latter, however, had been based on the time
and capacity relevant to making good writing-paper; a
far larger quantity of the pulp needed to make coarse
papers could be turned out in a much shorter time.
Accordingly the second method had virtually superseded the former, with the result both that the effective
rate of duty and the revenues were very low and, moreover, that the tax was reinforcing other factors tending to
a concentration on lower-grade papers.[3] Reform not only
brought uniformity with the mainland but also a substantial increase in revenue from Ireland.[4]

---

[1] *Supra*, pp. 275–6.   [2] 5 Geo. IV, c. 55.
[3] The charge was at the rate of 12s. 6d. per month per cubic foot. The
effects of the old system are analysed and examined in *Eighth Report* (1824).
See also *supra*, pp. 224–5.
[4] For details of revenue see *First Inland Revenue Report* (1857), app. 22c. The

Throughout these early decades of the century agitation against the Excise continued. Political protest during these years was aimed primarily at the stamp duty on newspaper, the advertisement and pamphlet duties, and the whole body of legislation designed to control the Press.[1] The agitation drew its strength mainly from the Radicals and it impinged upon the paper duties in so far as they were seen as contributing to the high cost of publication and thus militating against the education of the poorer classes. It was associated with such men as Lord Brougham, Joseph Hume, Dr. Birkbeck, Charles Knight, and Francis Place; with such bodies as the Society for the Diffusion of Useful Knowledge; and with such publications as Knight's *Penny Magazine* or Henry Hetherington's *Poor Man's Guardian*. So far as the paper duty was concerned the force of agitation of this type was to be of greater importance in the mid-century. Meanwhile the simultaneous reduction of the paper Excise and of the newspaper duty in 1836 as well as the modification of the control of the Press brought a lull on this front and also stimulated an expansion in publishing.[2]

An attack from the exponents of political economy came from J. H. McCulloch in 1832.[3] Pointing out that the industry gave employment to more people than was immediately apparent because of the various ancillary trades affected by paper-making, he then accused the

other side of the medal may also have been that the application of this more effective duty to the backward Irish industry tended to restrict or depress it still further.

[1] It was calculated that in the 1830's $5\frac{1}{2}d$. out of each $7d$. charged for a London morning newspaper was attributable to the combined paper, stamp, and advertisement duties (*The History of the Times*, vol. i, p. 318).

[2] See in general on this, C. D. Collet, *History of the Taxes on Knowledge* (London, 1899), esp. vol. i *passim*; A. Aspinall, *Politics and the Press* (London, 1949), especially pp. 16–23; and R. K. Webb, op. cit., chap. iii.

[3] *Dictionary of Commerce* (London, 1832).

government of having 'loaded it with an Excise duty amounting to more than three times as much as the total wages of the workpeople'. Whatever the accuracy or even the precise meaning of this statement, at least McCulloch was on surer ground when he attacked the Excise for its weight, for the complexity of the regulations controlling its collection, and for the frauds arising from the nature of the distinction between class I and class II paper.[1]

These were the main targets upon which the papermakers themselves trained their guns. The basis of the distinction between the two classes was simply that class II should comprise 'brown paper made from old ropes or cordage only, without separating or extracting the pitch or tar therefrom, and without any mixture of other materials therewith'. Class I comprised all other paper, board being considered separately. Now this may have been appropriate in 1802 when it was formulated[2] and when most brown wrappings were probably still thus made from the then cheapest raw materials. But the spread of chlorine-bleaching and other advances in the techniques of pulp-preparation permitting the use of a wider range of rags, waste, mill sweepings, and so forth, had led to the anomalous position that, by the 1830's, whilst old ropes cost £11 per ton, the materials from which brown wrappings could now be made cost only £3. 10s. per ton.[3] The Excise officers could originally detect the class II paper by smelling the tar therein, but now new methods enabled the smell to be removed. Given this situation, the frauds and the anomalies are not difficult to imagine. On the one hand, low-priced wrap-

---

[1] These points were all quoted in an extract from McCulloch in *Fourteenth Report* (1835), app. 2, pp. 43–50.

[2] In 42 Geo. III, c. 94.   [3] *Fourteenth Report* (1835), p. 114.

pings or 'whited-browns' went into class I and paid as
high a duty per lb. as the best-quality and most expensive
writing-papers; on the other hand, as it was not difficult
to add some appropriate smelling and colouring matters,
or indeed other raw materials, to low-priced rags or
waste, brown paper or millboard could be made in such
a way as to secure classification by the Excise officers in
class II and thus pay a lower rate of duty though not in
the least related in origin to old tarred ropes.[1]

When to this source of confusion there is added the
falling prices of paper, it is evident that a flat rate duty
by weight was producing a capricious and often very
heavy incidence of taxation. It varied from 22 per cent.
on the finest sorts to about 200 per cent. on the coarsest.[2]
This state of affairs in turn gave rise not merely to fraud
as between the two classes but to efforts to evade the
duty altogether, especially by the smaller makers in the
remoter areas. It did not perhaps surprise the Commissioners of Excise Inquiry to learn that Ireland was the
main scene of this smuggling.[3]

The formidable regulations governing the collection of
the paper Excise gained alike in complexity and in
irrelevance to the changing circumstances of the new
machine industry during the early decades of the nineteenth century.[4] A pleasingly ironic example of the conflict
of commerce, regulation, and Irish ingenuity is provided
by the following example. In 1814 a firm of Belfast
merchants shipped sixteen bales of paper to Liverpool

[1] Ibid., pp. 10–19.   [2] Ibid., p. 114.

[3] In 1833 prosecutions against paper-makers under the Excise laws
numbered only thirteen in England and two in Scotland, nearly all for minor
offences; in Ireland, with a very much smaller number of mills, the comparable number was thirty-one, and most of these were for the major offence
of concealing paper in order to evade duty (ibid., app. 30 b, p. 82).

[4] See ibid., pp. 6–10, for extracts from the regulations, which give some
idea of their intricacy.

whence the paper was to be exported to a Spanish South American market. As, however, the paper was packed in sheaves and in reams of 400 sheets in the Spanish manner, and not in quires of 24 sheets and reams of 20 quires according to the Act of Parliament, it was seized by the Excise officers. Duty had been paid in Ireland whilst the paper was packed in the orthodox fashion; it was then repacked in the Spanish manner and duly seized in Liverpool. In petitioning the Treasury the Belfast merchants pointed out the peculiar dilemma in which they found themselves:

... the said Paper having been designed for an Imitation of real Spanish Paper and being destined for a Spanish market it was absolutely necessary for the success of the Speculation that it should be packed and put up according to the Spanish Mode. . . . Had not your Memorialists complied with the Spanish Mode of packing and putting up the Papers and taking off every Mark which might betray it to be British Manufacture, the great expence and trouble which they have incurred to produce a perfect imitation of the Spanish Manufacture would have been of no avail.[1]

The channels through which paper manufacturers might make known their views on the duty did not include direct access to the Board of Excise.[2] They petitioned the Treasury which reported to the Excise which advised the Treasury; and so, with due delay, an answer went back to the petitioning manufacturers. And petition they did, singly and in groups, about anomalies and about grievances, some real, some imaginary. They also made their views known in the course of legal activities arising out of Excise cases; they arranged meetings such as that of 1831 when a committee was set up to organize

[1] C. & E.: Excise-Treasury Letters, 1809–15, ff. 219–24.
[2] *Fourteenth Report* (1835), pp. 24–25.

lobbying to secure the repeal of the duty; and they were able to give evidence to the Commissioners of Excise Inquiry.[1] For much of the eighteenth century the Board of Excise had tended to treat the regulations governing the collection of duties as immutable; petitions for change battered against them in vain.[2] But the transformations of the Industrial Revolution brought some change in the attitude of the Excise authorities. A more liberal outlook saw the need of exceptions and the possibilities of error. In the example mentioned above, for instance, the petitioners' case was allowed. But it needed more substantial reform to secure the needed adjustment to changing conditions. Its first instalment came, for this industry, by way of the recommendations of the *Fourteenth Report of the Commissioners of Excise Inquiry* and the Acts which put the more important of these into law. Under the guidance of the financial reformer, Sir Henry Parnell, the Commissioners' report stressed the desirability of lowering and consolidating the duties and of simplifying the apparatus of collection. It was made clear, moreover, that the reduction of the duty was regarded as only an interim measure, 'until circumstances shall admit of realizing the still more beneficial effects which would result from a total abolition of the duty'.[3]

(iii)

In the seventeenth and eighteenth centuries it had been the demands of war upon a none too wealthy State

[1] Evidence of these petitions, &c., will be found in C. & E.: Excise-Treasury Letters and Excise Trials; also in *Fourteenth Report* (1835), *passim*.

[2] See *supra*, pp. 129–38.

[3] *Fourteenth Report* (1835), p. 28. The recommendations of the report were largely put into effect in 1836 and 1839 by 6 & 7 Wm. IV, c. 52, and by the consolidating Act 2 & 3 Vic., c. 23, which brought together all the various Excise regulations.

which successively laid the bricks of a tariff wall; during the nineteenth century it was the great and growing wealth of a community substantially untroubled by war which allowed them to be knocked down by statesmen acting in the name of Free Trade. The reduction of the paper import duty in 1842 and the freeing of rags from duty in 1845 were both effected as part of general tariff changes carried by Peel. The further lowering of the paper import duty by Gladstone in 1853 was a part of his first great budget, the whole of which was 'stamped with the hall-mark of Peelite finance'.[1] The final Acts of 1860 and 1861 were also part and parcel of Free Trade policy, entwined as they were both with the Cobden Treaty with France and with Gladstone's sweeping away of the Excise on paper.

The early moves in this campaign met with little opposition from the paper interests. In 1840 one of the secretaries to the Board of Trade had stated categorically that 'in regard to common paper the principal paper manufacturers require scarcely any protection at all'; as for writing-paper he had been informed by Alderman Venables that this country did not fear any competition.[2] Some idea of the trifling amount of paper imports at that time and of the utter insignificance of the duties may be gathered from the fact that in 1839 out of a total net produce from Customs duties on imports into Great Britain and Ireland of nearly £23 million, duties on paper and paper hangings together only accounted for £1,573.[3]

When, however, the next dose of Free Trade medicine was about to be administered in 1853, the patient pro-tested in the vigorous tones of John Dickinson. Hearing

---

[1] K. Feiling, *A History of England* (London, 1950), p. 906.
[2] *Report from the Select Committee on Import Duties* (B.P.P. 1840, vol. v), evidence of John McGregor, p. 14.   [3] Ibid., pp. 5–6.

of the mooted further reductions, he called a meeting of
the leading paper manufacturers, drew up a petition,
and saw the Secretary to the Treasury.[1] The argument
which was then used to prevent too great a reduction
was one which was to play an important part in com-
plicating all further negotiations in connexion with the
repeal of both Excise and Customs on paper. It was
based on the imposition by foreign governments, notably
of France, Germany, and Belgium, of duties or even
prohibitions on the export of rags.[2] This it was claimed
gave the foreign maker an advantage over the British.
As a result of these representations the Custom was
fixed at $2\frac{1}{2}d$. per lb., the differential $1d$. between it and
the Excise of $1\frac{1}{2}d$. being designed, or so it was then
alleged, to compensate for this disadvantage.[3]

Seven years later, when the problem of paper duties
arose in connexion with the trade treaty with France, the
differential $1d$. was apparently assumed by those concerned with the negotiations for the treaty to owe its
existence to quite another principle. It was then said that
the discriminating duty was retained to compensate the
British makers for the restrictions imposed by the Excise.[4]
And it was in accordance with the principles of Free
Trade embodied in the treaty, which had been agreed to
in January and was to come into force in August 1860,
that in February of that year Gladstone proposed, as a
part of his budget, to abolish both Customs and Excise on
paper. The intention to repeal the Excise was embodied
in the Paper Duty Repeal Bill. This passed its second
reading with a majority of 53 in March 1860, got through
its third reading by a bare 9 votes on 8 May, and was

---

[1] *Select Committee* (1861), p. 58.
[2] For some details of these duties see *infra*, p. 331, n. 2.
[3] *Select Committee* (1861), p. 58.   [4] Ibid., p. 74.

rejected by the House of Lords on the 21st of the same month.[1] This precipitated something of a constitutional crisis, involving as it did the question of the right of the Lords to control taxation. Perhaps for the first time in its history the paper industry found itself an object of general public discussion. For the constitutional issue provided a glow of publicity in which was illuminated the paper-makers' indignation at losing what they regarded as protection against the foreign duties or prohibitions on rag exports. They saw themselves as being sacrificed to the dogma of Free Trade and in order to protect themselves from this, they were forced into the ironic position of having to oppose the removal of the Excise against which they had been campaigning for the preceding one hundred and fifty years.

Meanwhile, however, the industry was already getting into the public eye by reason of the agitation against the Excise, considered wholly apart from the Customs, which had been going on in the previous decade. The leading roles in this were played by the assorted Radicals and various printers and publishers who were fighting to secure the destruction of the Taxes on Knowledge. In 1849 the Newspaper Stamp Abolition Committee was formed with the ageing Francis Place as Treasurer. It managed to attract the favourable attention of a number of M.P.s, notably Richard Cobden, John Bright, and Thomas Milner-Gibson who was to play a leading part in finally securing the repeal of the taxes. Out of this committee was developed two years later the Association for the Repeal of the Taxes on Knowledge.[2]

[1] *Hansard*, series 3, vol. clvii, p. 436; vol. clviii, pp. 967, 1545.

[2] C. D. Collet, op. cit., vol. i, chaps. vi and viii. It was established in London in Feb. 1851, with Milner-Gibson as President and with a number of prominent and influential persons on its committee. See Collet, vol. i, p. 137.

Meanwhile other bodies had been formed for these purposes, and amongst them the industry was represented. A committee of newspaper proprietors, founded in 1849 to agitate against the advertisement duty, had one of the Spicers as its Treasurer. Another, aiming specifically at the paper duty, was composed of publishers and papermakers; the latter were Messrs. Baldwin of Birmingham, John Crompton and Thomas Wrigley from Lancashire, and Charles Cowan, M.P., from Edinburgh.[1] In 1851 a meeting was held in London which was attended by paper-makers active against the paper duty and by Radicals active against all the taxes on knowledge. The mixture proved to be uncongenial and both Crompton and Wrigley withdrew, partly because they did not like the colour of the political movement in which they found themselves involved.[2]

The first objectives in the Radical campaign were reached in 1853 and 1855 with the repeal of the advertisement and newspaper stamp duties respectively.[3] The paper duty, which in 1850 had produced almost twice as much in revenue as the combined yield of the other two,[4] stood alone. The *Economist* had meanwhile joined in the attack upon it. In May 1852 it damned the Excise comprehensively on a dozen counts and in the best Free Trade manner.[5] Only a small part of this blast was accurately aimed, but no doubt it served its purpose by making a great deal of noise. The *Economist* later published several articles on the subject, especially between 1858 and 1861, advocating repeal and supporting the

---

[1] Ibid., vol. i, p. 105.
[2] Ibid., vol. i, pp. 126–31, 143. Some other paper manufacturers did join the Radical committee.
[3] Ibid., vol. i, chap. xi, and vol. ii, chap. xiii.
[4] Ibid., vol. i, p. 104.
[5] *Economist*, 1 May, 1852. See *infra*, pp. 332–3.

use of the income tax to replace the revenue which the paper Excise raised.[1]

When Gladstone introduced his measure of repeal in 1860, it was accordingly attacked by those who disliked the income tax, by those who spoke for the paper-makers who wanted to retain the Customs duty in order to compensate for the foreign duty on rags, as well as by those whose dislike was based on general political grounds. The paper manufacturers lobbied Parliament vigorously and repeatedly. The Paper Makers Association, with John Evans as chairman, met in February.[2] Evans met Gladstone in March but reported him as being 'determined to have his own way and . . . positive some new material will be discovered'.[3] A deputation of forty or fifty paper-makers waited on Palmerston, and Evans and Wrigley saw him again in July. *The Times*, connected as it was with influential paper-making families,[4] attacked Gladstone's policy. But the conservative tone of the industry generally may well have echoed the sentiments which the wife of one of the partners in the Dickinson concern wrote in her diary on the House of Lords' rejection of the Bill in May 1860: '. . . Lord Derby gave one of his most eloquent and powerful speeches, perfectly smashing Gladstone and his policy, and his Budget and his Treaty.'[5]

[1] See, e.g., *Economist*, 26 June 1858, 10 Mar. 1860, 12 May 1860, 2 June 1860, 28 July 1860, and 4 Aug. 1860.

[2] *The Endless Web*, pp. 103 et seq.; Collet, op. cit., vol. ii, pp. 89–91.

[3] *The Endless Web*, p. 104.

[4] Ibid.; the Delanes of *The Times* were personal friends of the families concerned in the Dickinson business; and Frederick Delane was a partner in Delane, Magnay & Co., which firm supplied *The Times* with paper (*supra*, p. 242).

[5] Ibid., p. 105. It should perhaps be mentioned that the conservatism of the paper manufacturers of the time seems to have been mysteriously carried forward into Dr. Joan Evans's book which between pp. 103 and 106 has a number of wholly incorrect statements about Gladstone and the duties. They culminate in the curious remark on p. 108 that 'only when the Conservatives were in, in 1860, was the import duty on rags removed'. The

But they were all far from being smashed. The constitutional crisis was patched up and Gladstone introduced a compromise plan to reduce the Customs duty by so much as to make it equal to the Excise. This was carried and came into effect in August 1860.[1] The paper-makers' position could well evoke sympathy. Rag prices had been rising throughout the 1850's and were still rising; imports of foreign paper were rising, though still very small; the availability of substitutes for rags was far from proven. Meanwhile the foreign export duties on rags were unquestionably very stiff.[2] The paper-makers' protests continued and were directed mainly to the likely sympathy of Palmerston. A large deputation saw him in March 1861; in the following month Frederick Pratt Barlow tackled Gladstone.[3] Both availed little. In April 1861 Gladstone produced his budget, incorporated in which was again the repeal of the duties. After lengthy debate the Financial Bill was passed in June, the repeal of both the Customs and Excise to take effect from October.[4] All that the paper-makers got was the appointment of a Select Committee which reported in July of the same year. It gave a number of manufacturers a chance to air their grievances and recommended in its report that 'the British Government should continue strenuous exertions to effect the removal of all restrictions abroad upon the export of

Conservatives were not in power in 1860, the import duty on rags had been removed in 1845; if, alternatively, Dr. Evans means the foreign export duties on rags, these were not removed in 1860 and Conservatism had little or nothing to do with their final fate.

[1] 23 & 24 Vic., c. 110.
[2] They were £4. 17s. 2d. per ton in France, which country had until then prohibited their export as Belgium still did, £6. 4s. 7d. in Russia, £7. 5s. in Austria and Austrian Italy, £8. 8s., in Holland, and £9. 3s. in Prussia (*B.P.P.* 1861, vol. lviii).
[3] Collett, op. cit., vol. ii, p. 117; *The Endless Web*, p. 107.
[4] Collett, op. cit., vol. ii, chap. xx; *Hansard*, series 3, vol. clxiii, *passim*.

all paper making materials'.[1] Its deliberations and evidence are interesting, but probably more useful in retrospect to the historian than they were consoling to the indignant paper-makers of the day.

In fact, as will be shown in the final chapter, the paper industry was not ruined by the removal of an Excise which had lasted for a century and a half and a protective Customs wall which had been built up over two centuries, any more than the farmers had been ruined by the repeal of the Corn Laws in 1846.

(iv)

What were the effects of the paper duties in the last sixty years of their existence? Of the Customs duties little need be said. For most of the time they were more prohibitive than protective. And once machinery had put the British industry ahead of its rivals, as it had by the 1820's, they were also pointless. But the lowering of this barrier, the high price of rags in Britain, and the development of machine manufacture abroad were tending by the last years of the period towards a reversal of that situation. It was no more than a pointer. The British industry was still well ahead of its foreign rivals and had little need to shrink at the wind of competition, particularly when the wind was scarcely more than a faint breeze.[2] But long years of protection often make such draughts seem like howling gales.

About the evil effects of the Excise there was much talk, some of it nonsense, some merely contradictory, and some certainly or probably true. The comprehensive indictment of *The Economist* in 1852 may serve as an example of all categories. The article lamented that the

---

[1] *Select Committee* (1861), p. v.
[2] Cf. Spicer, pp. 121–2.

industry had not grown to be a major national industry like that of cotton manufacture and also observed that former small mills were disappearing and that paper-making was being concentrated into larger hands. This and far more besides was laid at the door of the Excise. Not only does the Excise frustrate enterprise but it 'checks the diffusion of knowledge, cherishes ignorance, keeps up the price of articles indispensable to civilization, and forces business into putrifying heaps, instead of allowing it to be equably and healthily diffused throughout the land'. The Excise officer was said to be constantly at the manufacturer's elbow, so that it was chiefly by continually evading Excise regulations 'that the paper manufacturer has improved his art and extended his business'.[1]

It did not grow like the cotton industry for the good reason that the demand for paper was quite unlike the demand for textiles. It was neither so large nor so elastic. Absence of the Excise would certainly have permitted the price of paper to have been lower and it is possible that more would have been used for wrapping and other industrial purposes and perhaps some more for writing and printing; but in an age when limited literacy still closely confined the latter demands for paper, it seems unlikely that it could have grown in the same manner as did the cotton industry. What is noticeable, on the other hand, is the comparatively slow development of the export trade. As drawbacks of the Excise were given on export, however, the reason for this is more likely to lie in the presence of a good protected home market, together with perhaps a certain lack of enterprise by the stationers who handled much of the export trade.

The notion that the Excise was responsible for the dis-

[1] *Economist*, 1 May 1952, pp. 476–7.

appearance of small mills was taken up by Gladstone. The duty, he said, 'has controlled the trade in a few great hands. Village mills are hardly to be found. I want to see, and I do not despair of seeing, those village mills spring up again and flourish.'[1] So far from believing that the Excise caused this, the paper-makers themselves suggested in 1835 that the collection of the Excise so operated as to provide the small maker with credit and thus enabled him precariously to survive; and in 1861 they blamed the *reduction* of the Excise and the curtailing of the period of credit in 1836 for the disappearance of these mills.[2] There can hardly be any doubt that, quite irrespective of any effect which the Excise may have had either way, this change was mainly being wrought by the advent of mechanization and all that it implied. Had the mills remained 'equally . . . diffused through the land' there would have been even less likelihood that the industry would have grown as rapidly as cotton manufacture.

Objection to the paper Excise as a tax on knowledge was a good rallying cry and was in part a matter of the general objection to any indirect taxation. Its specific application varied greatly. As we have seen, before 1836 the tax was undoubtedly growing more onerous as paper prices fell. Thereafter, although the weight was less great, it did bear much more heavily on cheap publications using the poorer quality printing-paper, than on the more expensive books. What mattered little to the publishers of Macaulay's *History of England* or *The Cornhill* was more pressing to those interested in tracts, pamphlets, cheap newspapers, and popular education.[3] On the other hand,

---

[1] *Hansard*, series 3, vol. clvi, p. 862.

[2] *Fourteenth Report* (1835), pp. 26–27, and *Select Committee* (1861), pp. 25 and 96. See also *supra*, p. 253.

[3] See Commons debate on the second reading of the Paper Duty Repeal Bill, Mar. 1860 (*Hansard*, series 3, vol. clvii, pp. 354–435).

the agitators who were so fond of quoting the total Excise revenue—about £1½ million gross in 1859—invariably omitted to mention that some unknown but certainly substantial portion of that was derived from taxing paper which played no part whatsoever in disseminating knowledge—wrappings, wallpaper, and board.

The Excise regulations were undoubtedly tiresome, time-absorbing, and, before 1836, conducive to evasion. But even so there is little to prove that the duty acted as a brake upon technical initiative, though it often became necessary to secure some amendment in the strict letter of the regulations in order that they should be adapted to changed methods.[1] In their report of 1857 the Commissioners of Inland Revenue stated that since the consolidation of the regulation in 1839, many concessions had been made to the manufacturers by the authorities, to such an extent that 'the duty is now charged and collected without any appreciable restriction upon their Trade, and that their complaints, at one time frequent, have entirely ceased'.[2] The requirements of the Excise officers did not interfere with the carrying out of experiments in manufacture.[3] Nevertheless as the uses of paper became more diverse the claims for drawbacks and exemptions grew in number, so that the duty was becoming more and more difficult to administer with any sort of fairness or accuracy. And it was on these grounds that this tax was finally condemned by the Board of Inland Revenue itself.[4]

There is, in short, much to suggest that although the

---

[1] *Fourteenth Report* (1835), p. 127; Collet, op. cit., vol. ii, pp. 78–79.

[2] *First Inland Revenue Report* (1857), p. 13.

[3] *Select Committee* (1861), p. 14.

[4] *Report of the Commissioners of Inland Revenue to the Treasury upon the Repeal of the Duty upon Paper*, Mar. 1860 (*B.P.P.* 1860, vol. xl); see also Collett, op. cit., vol. ii, chap. xvi; Spicer, pp. 117–18.

Excise may have been obnoxious it was not nearly so obnoxious as it was made out to be; that although during the period of its greatest weight, i.e. from 1787 to 1836, it certainly raised the price of paper appreciably, it is very doubtful whether it stifled enterprise and advance in the industry. There is no reason at all to suppose that it was responsible for frustrating attempts to find a workable substitute for rags. And this, by the 1860's, was a far more important problem than either the Customs or the Excise. The repeal of the Excise made little or no difference to the industry, in output or in organization. In Spicer's words, 'the probable effect of the repeal was that after the excitement was over, the British papermaking industry went on in the same way as in earlier days'.[1] The changes that did come within the next few decades sprang from other sources.

[1] Spicer, p. 123.

XIII

The Continuing Problem and the Future

THE depression which paper manufacturers bewailed in the years around 1860, and for which they naturally blamed the government of the day, had at least part of its origin in that recurrent problem of the industry—raw materials. The troubles were not dissimilar to those of the late eighteenth century, though operating in changed circumstances. Foreign competition was increasing, and the policy of 1861 had admittedly left an unfavourable balance of foreign duties and domestic free trade. But it was the impact of these on the problems of rag supply that seemed to form the real threat.

Machinery was finding its way into paper-mills both on the Continent and in the U.S.A. and thus creating a marked increase in the demand for raw materials. The U.S.A. also became a substantial importer of European rags.[1] Although the total supply of cotton and linen fabrics was also increasing on a big scale, there is reason to suppose that the supply of rags, mainly from these fabrics, was not increasing proportionately. The growing supply of and demand for cheaper woollen fabrics meant some replacement of the earlier use of cheap cottons or mixtures of cotton and linen. Thomas Wrigley recalled, in 1861, the time when the term 'fustian jackets' had been descriptive of a large class of persons, but that now many

[1] Imports of foreign rags, mainly from Italy, into New York, for example, rose by some three-and-a-half times between 1845 and 1859 (L. T. Stevenson, *The Background and Economics of American Paper Making* (New York, 1940), pp. 17–22).

men and women are dressed with cheap woollen fabrics or mixtures of wool, cotton, or silk—all useless for the paper-maker.[1] Furthermore, methods of rag-collection remained much the same as they had long been: the itinerant rag-and-bone man and the wholesale rag merchant continued to be the two main pillars of these arrangements. An increase in rag prices would not readily call forth an appreciably greater quantity of a waste product thus collected. The rag merchant, sitting astride this inelastic supply line, was not likely, nor indeed would he have found it easy, so to reorganize methods of collection as to produce a substantially larger flow of rags.[2]

The consequence of all this was the usual rise in prices and, with rags still accounting for 50 per cent. of the cost of paper,[3] the usual lamentations and the usual flurry to find substitutes. Prices rose to a peak in about 1854, fell a little, then rose again in the last years. The price of rags used in the making of ordinary printing-paper rose by 28 per cent. from an average of 12s. 6d. per cwt. in 1848–52, to 16s. per cwt. in 1853–6; some other grades showed similar increases varying from 20 per cent. to 30 per cent. between 1852 and 1860; others rose less than this, others more.[4] The price increase was by no means catastrophic, nor was the industry as a whole nearly so dependent on foreign rags as some manufacturers tried to make out.[5] Moreover this was to be the last serious upswing in rag prices for many years. The gloom of 1860–1 was not so murky as the paper-makers thought it was. It was in fact a turning-point in the industry's

[1] *Select Committee* (1861), p. 35.
[2] Ibid., p. 35; Spicer, pp. 27–29.
[3] *Select Committee* (1861), p. 34.
[4] Ibid., p. 61; *First Inland Revenue Report* (1857), app. 6, pp. x–xi.
[5] *Select Committee* (1861), pp. 65, 71, 88 et seq., and 110.

growth. Rag prices had reached their peak and were on the down-turn; they were to fall steadily for the next twenty years and more.[1] But the crisis of rising raw material prices, however real or however exaggerated, left its mark in so far as it helped to stimulate the search for substitutes.

John Evans told the Select Committee of 1861 that there were 'upwards of 100 patents taken out for different materials for the manufacture of paper'.[2] There were indeed; and the timing of these is a mirror of the paper-makers' worries, for out of 120 such patents taken out from 1800 to 1859, 92 were taken out from 1850 on-wards.[3] (See Fig. 6, *supra*, p. 196.) In 1854 *The Times* had offered a prize of £1,000 for a substitute for rags, and this perhaps helped to swell the flood of patents, although the reward was not in fact given.[4] The patents covered the usual fantastic range of suggestions: paper from rope or from turf, from coconuts or cork, leather or rhubarb. There were a few patents that were important, a few experiments which worked in practice. It was all very well for the indefatigable reformer of the Taxes on Knowledge, C. D. Collet, to tell the Committee of 1861 that rhubarb made 'capital paper' and to press the merits of thistles, nettles, and willow peelings, but even he boggled at the notion of extensive crops of thistles being planted in the English countryside to supply the paper industry and had to admit that the trade was hardly likely to be much relieved by either thistles or nettles.[5]

In practice, two main sorts of raw materials, other

[1] Spicer, p. 32.   [2] *Select Committee* (1861), p. 10.
[3] See *Abridgements of the Specifications relating to the Manufacture of Paper*, &c. These figures are not precise. I have included any patent apparently concerned with finding a substitute for rags.
[4] *Select Committee* (1861), pp. 10, 12.
[5] Ibid., pp. 94–101.

than the traditional rags and old ropes had come into use in the production of certain sorts of paper: mill sweepings and straw. Their use was limited but they had passed from experiment to effective commercial work.

A number of the Lancashire firms making the medium grades of printing-paper exploited as much as they could the local supplies of cotton waste from the mills which loomed large around them. C. E. and J. G. Potter of Darwen and Wrigleys of Bury were amongst the paper firms extensively using this material, as well as ropes and rags. Dickinsons had set up a plant at Manchester specifically to prepare cotton waste. Flax refuse was also used by these and other makers for similar grades of paper; Irish as well as Lancashire manufacturers drew on the waste of flax-spinning mills. But these raw materials were also subject to the peculiar disadvantages attendant upon their being waste products, for although the paper manufacturers wanted as much of them as possible, the textile manufacturers wanted as little of them as possible. And in the course of time the latter managed to lessen the amount of waste produced.[1] So, quite apart from the influence upon the price of mill sweepings exerted by the price of rags, other forces were tending to push up the price of this waste product. According to Frederick Magnay in 1861, 'Cotton waste was first of all given away; it was then £2 or £3 a ton, and now something like £8 a ton'. Wrigley said at the same time that his mill where he bought waste on yearly contracts from the neighbouring cotton-spinners was not then getting so much waste as seven years earlier, although the cotton-mills themselves had increased in size and consumed more raw cotton. There were other and rapidly growing demands, too, for this elusive substance: the railways

---

[1] *Select Committee* (1861), pp. 11, 35, 59, 61.

wanted it as cleaning waste; thereafter it was either too much saturated with oil and grease to be of any use to the paper-makers or it was simply never collected.[1] But if this sort of raw material was proving to have drawbacks in the gloomy days of 1860, it had certainly acted as an important rag substitute. There can be little doubt that the growth of the industry in Lancashire during the early nineteenth century owed much to the supply of cotton and flax waste from the local spinning-mills.

Straw presented stiffer and also rather different problems. It was used by a small number of mills, though not much by the bigger makers, in the production of cheap, low-grade printing-papers. Some newspapers were printed on straw paper but it was generally looked down upon because of the poor colour and quality. It was used both alone and in conjunction with rags but even then was not suitable for making the better qualities of printing- or writing-papers. The main problems in its use arose from the large quantities of chemicals and coal required in its preparation; rather different equipment was employed and this in turn meant an initial capital outlay which made it no simple matter to switch to the use of straw. Furthermore, there was a high wastage, some 3 tons of straw being needed to make 1 ton of paper. The quality of straw varied and prices rose as paper-makers started buying it up; in Kent, for instance, it was said that two neighbouring mills used straw at the rate of about 100 tons per week and that the price had doubled since it started to be used for paper-making. All these factors combined to make it a marginally economical material: at £2 to £2. 15s. per ton it was thought to be worth while, but if it rose to £4 it would be just as

[1] Ibid., pp. 15, 35, 43.

dear as rags, and would be making a paper which was patently not as good as rag paper and was not regarded as a substitute for it.[1]

Of these potential substitutes which were still the subject of experiment rather than practice, only one had attracted the attention of the British paper industry: esparto grass.[2] The success it had achieved by 1860 was limited and not much publicized. But it had a future. It was substantially through the medium of a rapid advance in its use that rag prices were soon to fall and a new contentment to gladden the hearts of paper manufacturers.

A number of makers, including the Potters of Darwen in 1856, experimented in vain with esparto.[3] After some early patents[4] had been taken out covering its use, the successful development of it was pioneered by Thomas Routledge who took out patents in 1856 and 1860.[5] He himself operated a mill at Eynsham, Oxfordshire. By 1861 some others in the industry had apparently purchased the right to work his process though it seems not to have been in at all widespread use at that time.[6] Routledge conducted some experiments with esparto at Wrigley's mill in 1860 and again in 1861; in the second of these, as Wrigley admitted, a very satisfactory pulp was made though the amounts of alkali and chlorine needed in the process seemed to him to be so great as to make the use of esparto excessively costly.[7] Other makers

---

[1] *Select Committee* (1861), pp. 9, 12–15, 21, 23, 46, 47–50, 52, 62–63.

[2] A wild grass (*Stipa tenacissima*) growing mainly in the lands bordering the western Mediterranean, especially Algeria and Spain (Spicer, pp. 14–15, 33–34; Labarre, op. cit., p. 91).

[3] *Select Committee* (1861), p. 60.

[4] By Miles Berry in 1839 (Patent No. 8273), Jules Dehau in 1853 (Patent No. 1452), and James Murdoch in 1854 (Patent No. 294).

[5] Nos. 1816 (July 1856) and 274 (Feb. 1860).

[6] *Select Committee* (1861), pp. 95 et seq.   [7] Ibid., pp. 102–3.

thought otherwise. Dickinson, at the same time, joined with Routledge in setting up a works near Sunderland which came to be used for the preparation of half-stuff from esparto for use at Dickinson's Hertfordshire mills.[1] The growth of the esparto using industry lies outside the scope of this book. Suffice it to say that within the following twenty years esparto imports had soared from under 1,000 tons annually to over 200,000 tons.[2] On this basis the esparto industry became a flourishing section of the trade, especially in Scotland.

The extensive use of esparto became, and remains, largely a British specialization in paper-making. Quite unmentioned in the deliberations of the 1861 Committee was another raw material, already being experimented with on the Continent, but apparently unheeded by the majority of British manufacturers: wood-pulp. A small number of patents had been taken out in this country in the 1840's and 50's; they came to nothing, though those of H. Burgess and C. Watt in 1851 and Israel Swindells in 1854 are perhaps of some importance in anticipating later and more successful methods of preparing pulp from wood.[3] In Germany F. G. Keller had patented a method of making pulp from mechanically ground wood in 1840, and paper made from a mixture of rags and ground wood was being commercially produced there in the 1850's.[4] Most of the subsequent development of the chemical methods of preparing wood-pulp also originated on the Continent and were rapidly extended in America, which is perhaps not surprising in view of the great reserves of soft-wood timber there waiting for exploitation. Although

---

[1] *The Endless Web*, pp. 111–12. [2] Spicer, app. I.
[3] Burgess & Watt's patent was No. 1942 of Aug. 1853 and Swindell's No. 1511 of July 1854. See also Hunter, p. 390, and J. Strachan, 'The Invention of Wood Pulp Processes in Britain during the 19th Century', *The Paper Maker* (Annual No., 1949). [4] Hunter, p. 376.

some pioneering work was proceeding in the late 1850's, all the effective steps forward were taken after the period with which we are here concerned. They culminate in the successful development of the sulphite process by the Swedish chemist, C. D. Ekman, and his introduction of it into this country in the 1880's and the roughly contemporaneous invention of the sulphate process by C. F. Dahl.[1] It is on the basis of these processes and of this raw material that the modern paper industry has grown up. To the woeful British makers of 1861 wood-pulp and the future it represented were unknown. Many of them said, as did John Evans, 'I think there is no probability of any substitute for rags being discovered.'[2] Forty years later, we were importing 16,000 tons of rags, 194,000 tons of esparto, and 448,000 tons of wood-pulp.[3] Today we import about 2,000,000 tons of wood-pulp annually. The decades of the 1860's and 1880's are a true dividing line in the history of paper-making. They mark the creation of what is in some senses, though only in some senses, a new industry. After eighteen centuries of existence as a manufacture based on rags and nearly four hundred years of existence in Britain, it found a major new raw material. It has continued to use the old in relatively small quantities; but it is wood pulp that has made possible the many and diverse guises in which paper appears in modern life and which has formed the rationale of the modern international pulp and paper industry. But that is another story.

---

[1] See Hunter, pp. 376–81 and 389–93; Strachan, loc. cit.; 'Wood Pulp Fifty Years Ago', *World's Paper Trade Review*, 2 Nov. 1934; Spicer, pp. 20–24; Labarre, op. cit., p. 298. The two processes are so named because the latter involves the treatment of wood with sulphate of soda, the former the use of bisulphate of lime or magnesia.

[2] *Select Committee* (1861), p. 9.   [3] Spicer, app. I.

APPENDIX I

Statistics, Sources, and Maps

Tables and Graphs of Output and Trade

Tables I and II. These statistics were drawn from the following sources: 1560: *S.P. Dom. Eliz.* 8/31; 1565: B.M. Lansdowne MSS. 8/17 (these give values of paper imports as £3,304 and £3,000 respectively; they have been converted at a rate of 2*s*. 6*d*. per ream); 1567–8 and 1587–8: P.R.O. K.R. Exchq. Port Books, E. 190/4/2, 7/8, 8/1. For the figures from 1609 to 1640 inclusive, also derived from the Port Books, I am indebted to Mrs. A. M. Millard who kindly provided me with the quantities from which are calculated the valuations for these and other imports as given in her thesis, *The Import Trade of London, 1600–40* (unpublished Ph.D. thesis, London 1956). 1662–3 and 1668–9: B.M. Add. MSS. 36785; 1667–79: P.R.O. E.190/51/4, 51/8, 53/9, 58/1, 63/7, 64/1, 66/1, 68/1, 75/1, 73/2, 81/1, 85/1; 1697–1720: P.R.O. Customs 3/1–22. The white paper imports from France in 1685–6, given in Table II only, are from *The British Merchant*, vol. i, p. 285.

Fig. 2. The curves showing the imports of paper and rags were derived from P.R.O. Customs 3/4–80, and Customs 17/6–22. For the years 1781–1800 only the values of paper imports are given in the ledgers; amounts have been calculated from the average value per ream for the imports in the preceding period 1770–80.

The main sources for the production curve were the printed Excise returns in *First Inland Revenue Report* (*B.P.P.* 1857, vol. iv), appendix 22a, supplemented by the MS. returns in C. & E.: Quantities, Rates and Amounts of Excise Duties, 1684–1798. For reasons which are examined in Chapter V it was evident that the printed returns for the period before 1781 were unacceptable. This was mainly because, until the reform in the method of assessment at that time, an increasing proportion of the

output was being charged *ad valorem*, instead of at certain specified flat rates. This in turn was partly because of the widening
range of types of paper made and partly because it was advan-
tageous, except for some of the lower quality paper, to persuade
the Excise officials to rate paper for the *ad valorem* duty, and at the
same time to ensure that it was undervalued. It is clear that much
paper was being thus undervalued. As the MS. records (but not
the printed returns) contain annual figures for the total value
of paper rated *ad valorem*, the problem resolved itself into one of
finding some factor with which to turn values into physical
quantities and thus to obtain estimates of total production.

The evidence in the nineteenth-century reports of the Commissioners of Excise Inquiry suggests that, except in Ireland,
the extent of evasion of duty was not then so great as seriously
to impair the value of the returns as estimates of output. It was
accordingly assumed that the printed returns for the period
1785–1855 were reasonably reliable, or at any rate consistent
throughout. It was observed that the curve of the annual values
of paper rated *ad valorem* showed, from 1740 onwards (before
1740 it was virtually stationary), the same rate of growth as
that of the 1785–1855 curve. By fitting exponential curves to
these latter figures and also to the *ad valorem* figures, and obtaining the closest fit for the period 1740–85, a factor was obtained which worked out at rather over 2s. per ream, a low but
plausible figure considering the general undervaluation. The
resulting curve of estimated total production shows a course of
development conforming to that suggested by other, non-
quantitative evidence. Final figures in tons were thus obtained
from the following formula:

[Amount of paper charged in reams+2 (amount of paper
    charged in bundles) × 9·712 (value of paper charged *ad
    valorem* in £s)] × 20/2240
1 bundle = 2 reams (10 Anne, c. 19)
1 ream   = 20 lb. (an average figure calculated from various
                sources, e.g. B.M. Add. MSS. 15054;
                B.P.P. 1801–2, vol. ii; *Eighth Report*,
                &c.).

Fig. 7. The output curves for paper and pasteboard were derived from figures given in *B.P.P.* 1857, vol. iv, app. 22a and 1860, vol. xl; Spicer, app. ix. As board is not given separately after 1837, it has been included throughout. Those for the trade in paper are from P.R.O. Customs 5/5–22; *B.P.P.* 1860, vol. xl; 1861, vol. xi. For that in rags from P.R.O. Customs 17/22–30, 4/5–7, 5/2–19; *B.P.P.* 1861, vol. xi, app. 3.

Paper exports continued to be lumped together with those of stationery generally in the early years of the nineteenth century, so no attempt has been made to give any figures until the printed returns for the U.K. starting in 1834.

Figures for paper imports are missing from 1800–15 because during that time the Customs ledgers give only total values in which are included imports of stained paper. Thereafter it is possible to separate out the paper figures.

In this graph, as in the text, the term U.K. includes the whole of Ireland. In giving trade statistics before 1800, however, trade with Ireland has been included in the English figures (e.g. as in Table VI). After 1800 they have been excluded. Accordingly for the years 1816–25 paper imports from Ireland have been deducted from the Customs ledger totals. The imports from Ireland disappeared from these records in 1826 on the assimilation of the Irish tariff system to the British. Separate figures for imports into Ireland have not been obtained. The coverage of paper imports is thus of G.B. only for 1816–33. The same is true for the rag import figures for 1800–29.

During the years 1816–25 the figures for the imports of Irish paper show that although the total amounts examined were very small the trade expanded from 29 tons in 1816 to 290 tons in 1823. The trade in Irish rags was similarly rising. For 1800–4 the annual average was about 70 tons; in 1810–15 (1813 is missing) it had risen to 318; and in the last two years before the tariff changes, 1824 and 1825, it was 571 tons annually, representing about 5 per cent. of total British rag imports.

General observations on paper import statistics. The figures derived both from the Port Books and from the Customs ledgers are open to the normal charges of inadequacy to which these records are subject. It seems likely, however, that paper, even during the later seventeenth and the eighteenth centuries when price differentials and protective barriers were probably both at their highest, was less attractive to smugglers than were other goods in a similar economic situation. It was bulky and not of very high value relative to its bulk; demand for it was comparatively limited; and its extreme liability to damage, especially by water, further jeopardized its attractiveness for illegal trade. The impression gathered from various sorts of records of accounts is that paper was never smuggled on anything like the same scale as such commodities as brandy, wool, or tea.

Fig. 8. This curve traces the median of the prices of printing demy bought by the London publishing firm of Messrs. Longman during the period 1794–1860. The data are contained in the firm's Impression Books which record both sizes and prices of paper purchased. In the first three years the number of purchases of demy recorded was small, but thereafter a sample of some thirty to fifty quotations per year has been used as the basis of calculation. The very few purchases of special types of demy, e.g. fine or plate paper, at prices obviously higher than the ordinary level, have been omitted.

Maps

Fig. 1. The identification of early mill sites is a lengthy and tricky business. Some sites shown on the map are of dubious authenticity, being based on the mere mention of a papermaker here or a paper-mill there. The existence of others is reasonably certain, in that it rests on contemporary eyewitness accounts of a mill at work, though the precise location of that mill is another matter. I have no doubt that future research will discover sites not shown here or correct the location of those that are.

Fig. 11. This is based entirely on the 1816 Excise List (C. & E.: General Letter (1816)).

Fig. 12. The source of this is the return of paper-mills in the U.K. given in *B.P.P.* 1852, vol. li.

In identifying, even only approximately, the sites of the mills in each of these maps, a wide variety of sources has been used which it would be tedious to enumerate. They include local maps, modern and contemporary; many volumes of the *V.C.H.*; commercial directories; contemporary topographical works; evidences of names and trades mentioned in various sorts of documents; as well as many of the specific sources mentioned earlier in the text. Above all I have drawn extensively and inevitably on the work of Dr. A. H. Shorter, both as laid out in his unpublished Ph.D. thesis (*The Historical Geography of the Paper-Making Industry in England*) and as it had previously appeared in the many articles which Dr. Shorter has published mainly in the transactions of local historical and archaeological societies.

For none of these maps, and least of all for Fig. 1, would I wish to claim any high degree of accuracy. They may serve, however, to give a general and not, I hope, misleading impression of the distribution of the industry across the country.

APPENDIX II

Paper Production and Excise Tables, 1782, 1788, and 1793[1]

(reams)

TABLE I. *Writing*

Type	Size (inches)	Value (1781)	Quantity 1782	1788	1793
		s. d.			
Imperial	22 × 30¼	51. 0	570	1,061	1,868
Super Royal . .	19¼ × 27½	38. 0	496	1,017	987
Royal	19¼ × 24	29. 0	1,843	2,914	3,857
Medium	17½ × 22½	22. 6	2,122	3,299	5,348
Demy	15½ × 20	16. 0	8,519	10,979	13,807
Thick Post . .	15¼ × 19½	13. 0	11,290	17,981	21,431
Thin Post . .	15¼ × 19½	10. 0	21,938	20,493	22,624
Small Post . .	13½ × 16½	7. 6	1,786	1,435	1,506
Large Thick Post . .	—	—	—	1,744	4,730
Large Thin Post . .	—	—	—	3,802	6,229
Foolscap	13½ × 16¾	9. 0	46,026	77,576	71,887
Pot	12½ × 15½	6. 0	17,964	30,191	26,387
TOTAL . . .	—	—	112,554	172,492	180,661

TABLE 2. *Writing or Copper-Plate Printing*

Type	Size	Value	1782	1788	1793
Double Atlas (or Antiquarian) . . .	55 × 33½	300. 0	16	1	22
Demy . . .	15½ × 20	12. 0	3,917	2,043	3,937
Copy or Bastard . .	16 × 20¼	7. 6	11,325	18,419	22,601
Foolscap . .	13½ × 16¾	6. 0	73,059	51,295	76,048
Littris Foolscap . .	13½ × 17½	6. 0	13,648	14,471	11,724
Pot	12½ × 15½	4. 0	38,215	40,196	44,431
Grand Eagle or Double Eagle	20¾ × 40	80. 0	78	125	163
Colombier . . .	23½ × 34½	50. 0	12	141	224
Atlas . . .	26¼ × 34	60. 0	31	123	138
Atlas . . .	26¼ × 34	40. 0	2	3	69
Small Atlas . . .	25 × 31	30. 0	24	25	66
Imperial	22 × 30¼	30. 0	163	639	971
Super Royal . .	19¼ × 27½	25. 0	27	120	726
Long Royal . .	27½ × 18	20. 0	278	58	98
Royal	19¼ × 24	18. 0	77	498	2,319
Demy	17 × 22	13. 0	157	1,047	632
Short Demy or Crowns .	{ 14 × 20¼ or 15 × 20 }	9. 0	1,083	3,568	2,904
Large Fan . . .	23½ × 20	14. 0	497	75	46
Small Fan . . .	22¼ × 13¼	11. 0	662	618	477
Elephant . . .	23 × 28	15. 0	992	4,045	2,774
Paper for Bank or Bankers' Bills or Notes allowing 2 Bills or Notes in each sheet	—	—	426	3,145	2,610
TOTAL . . .	—	—	144,689	140,654	172,980

[1] C. & E.: Quantities, Rates and Amounts of Excise Duties, 1684–1798.

TABLE 3. *Printing*

Type	Size (inches)	Value (1781)	Quantity 1782	1788	1793
		s. d.			
*Double Demy	26¼ × 38½	19. 0	12,510	16,856	15,888
*Royal	19½ × 24¼ or 20 × 26	12. 0	2,362	4,428	6,332
*Royal Inferior	19½ × 24¼	7. 0	2,956	7,984	7,098
*Medium	18 × 23	10. 0	3,346	13,740	14,464
*Demy Single	17½ × 22 or 19¼ × 21¼	8. 6	28,214	46,632	40,544
*Demy Inferior	17½ × 22	5. 0	31,958	30,816	41,212
*Double Crown	20 × 30	8. 6	3,510	8,132	5,008
*Double Crown Inferior	20 × 30	6. 0	13,264	17,922	24,964
*Single Crown	15 × 20	6. 6	6,040	6,268	3,410
*Single Crown Inferior	15 × 20	4. 0	12,670	8,938	9,104
*Demy Tissue	17½ × 22	4. 0	7,254	6,158	7,728
*Crown Tissue	15 × 20	2. 6	7,532	13,508	8,864
Double Pot	17 × 25½	4. 6	2,384	7,080	8,192
TOTAL		—	134,000	188,462	192,808

TABLE 4. *Ordinary and Coloured*

Cartridge	21 × 26		5,085	4,694	6,535
Cartridge Square	24½ × 27½		89	322	159
Cartridge Small	19¼ × 24		480	240	452
Elephant Common	23 × 28		13,703	15,931	12,338
Sugar Blue	21½ × 33		3,486	4,365	2,929
Sugar Blue Smaller	18¾ × 27		1,840	4,570	3,491
Sugar Blue Demy	17½ × 22		783	1,621	1,171
Sugar Blue Crown	15 × 20		146	38	265
Purple Royal	19½ × 20¼		1,741	3,202	3,259
Blue Elephant	23 × 28		836	709	2,502
*Blue Royal	19½ × 24¼		2,050	3,690	3,876
*Blue Demy and Blossom	17 × 22		15,818	22,742	22,288
*Blue Crown Single	15 × 20		6,460	21,006	21,674
TOTAL		—	52,517	83,130	80,939

TABLE 5. *Whited Brown and Brown*

Type	Size (inches)	Quantity 1782	1788	1793
Royal Hand Thick . .	24 × 19¼	1,286	1,674	1,732
*Royal Hand . . .	24 × 19¼	16,116	28,062	32,964
*Lumber Hand . . .	23 × 18	15,724	9,730	12,518
*Double Two Pound . .	24 × 16	26,972	18,892	22,812
*Single Two Pound . .	16 × 11	44,778	28,766	38,450
*Middle Hand Double .	33 × 21	2,512	3,192	4,172
*Middle Hand . . .	22 × 16	32,946	26,524	23,220
*Small Hand Double . .	32 × 20	12,780	21,404	23,302
*Small Hand . . .	19¾ × 16	126,498	222,176	216,952
*Couples Pound and Half Pound	⎰ 12 × 10 ⎱ or ⎰ 9 × 7½ ⎱	78,930	81,200	68,244
Imperial Cap . . .	29 × 22	13,230	17,328	21,689
Havon Cap . . .	24 × 22	9,977	8,373	7,319
Bag Cap	23½ × 19	32,277	37,766	44,702
Kentish Cap . . .	21 × 18	15,292	13,596	12,477
Four Pounds . . .	20 × 16	7,032	4,535	5,089
Small Cap . . .	20 × 15	11,953	19,654	17,762
Double Four Pounds . .	33 × 20	4,894	6,256	7,902
*Single Two Pounds . .	16 × 11	10,330	9,866	6,300
TOTAL	—	463,527	558,994	567,606

Grand Totals

	1782	1788	1793
Table 1	112,554	172,492	180,661
Table 2	144,689	140,654	172,980
Table 3	134,000	188,462	192,808
Table 4	52,517	83,130	80,939
Table 5	463,527	558,994	567,606
	907,287	1,143,732	1,194,994

* Those marked * are given in the original in bundles. These have been converted into reams at the stated rate of 2 reams = 1 bundle and the values where given adjusted accordingly. No values are given for Tables 4 and 5. Excluded from the above are some very small amounts of paper rated *ad valorem*.

APPENDIX III

Prices before 1800

THE heterogeneous nature of paper presents great difficulties in making comparisons in values or in obtaining accurate price series over any length of time. In addition to the familiar difficulties which arise from changes in quality over a period, there are others arising from the variations in size, weight, and quality which at any one time helped to determine the value of a type of paper. Moreover, the final users of paper rarely distinguish between the various types or sizes: to them paper tends to be simply printing-, writing-, wrapping-, or the like; alternatively, the sizes are given unaccompanied by further definition. As the number of different types multiplied over the years so were these difficulties aggravated. Indeed, it is possible that paper price series in England from the period before about 1650, with a comparatively narrow range of types, are more reliable than those from later years when a wider range became available. Without numerous quotations of sorts and sizes known to be comparable, reliable price comparisons cannot be made for the later period; only for the years after 1800 have I found such figures.[1]

It is hardly surprising, then, that paper is often absent from historical price indices. Figures are given in Thorold Rogers and in Beveridge, but their coverage is usually limited and their value sometimes dubious. They may, however, be used to give some idea of the general course of prices in the long run, and it is for this reason that Fig. 13 has been constructed.[2] Up to about the middle of the seventeenth century the picture it offers is probably reliable; that for 1700–81 is also plausible enough.[3]

[1] See Fig. 8, p. 203.
[2] Rogers, op. cit., vol. iv, p. 605; vol. v, p. 607; Beveridge, op. cit., pp. 455–8.
[3] The earlier figures are mainly based on long series of purchases by colleges, e.g. New College and Eton; the later figures rely on purchases by the Lord Chamberlain's department.

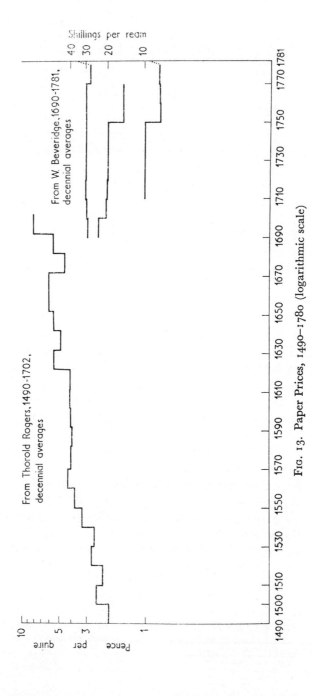

FIG. 13. Paper Prices, 1490–1780 (logarithmic scale)

But for the crucial intervening half-century—when a reliable price series would be particularly valuable—the scattered figures from which Thorold Rogers derived his decennial averages are quite inadequate; they are so inadequate in the 1650's, 60's, and 90's as to make the averages themselves virtually meaningless and they are of no value as a measure of the relations between supply and demand. They are certainly no basis for the observation that 'the average retail price went up from 5s. 3d. per ream in 1677 to 11s. in 1696'.[1] Contemporaries commented that paper became dearer, and with the cutting of the French supply line this is scarcely surprising. It is likely that these rising prices may have been a force encouraging capital to flow into the industry. But the amount, the duration, and the power of these price changes are not revealed in this evidence.

[1] Jenkins, p. 178.

INDEX